Mutuality Matters

Mutuality Matters

Family, Faith, and Just Love

EDITED BY HERBERT ANDERSON, EDWARD FOLEY,
BONNIE MILLER-MCLEMORE, AND ROBERT SCHREITER

A SHEED & WARD BOOK

ROWMAN & LITTLEFIELD PUBLISHERS, INC.
Lanham • Boulder • New York • Toronto • Oxford

A SHEED & WARD BOOK

ROWMAN & LITTLEFIELD PUBLISHERS, INC.

Published in the United States of America
by Rowman & Littlefield Publishers, Inc.
A wholly owned subsidiary of The Rowman & Littlefield Publishing Group, Inc.
4501 Forbes Boulevard, Suite 200, Lanham, Maryland 20706
www.rowmanlittlefield.com

PO Box 317
Oxford
OX2 9RU, UK

British Library Cataloguing in Publication Information Available

Library of Congress Cataloging-in-Publication Data

Mutuality matters : family, faith, and just love / edited by Edward Foley ... [et al.].
    p. cm.
Includes bibliographical references and index.
ISBN 0-7425-3154-6 (alk. paper) — ISBN 0-7425-3155-4 (pbk. : alk. paper)
    1. Family—Religious aspects—Catholic Church. 2. Marriage—Religious aspects—
Catholic Church. I. Foley, Edward. II. Title.

BX2351.M88 2003
261.8'358—dc21   2003013742

Printed in the United States of America

♾™ The paper used in this publication meets the minimum requirements of American
National Standard for Information Sciences—Permanence of Paper for Printed Library
Materials, ANSI/NISO Z39.48-1992.

Contents

Introduction

Herbert Anderson, Edward Foley,
Bonnie Miller-McLemore, and Robert Schreiter

The radical democratization of intimacy that has occurred over the last several decades marks a major revolution not just in the United States but around the world. Prior to the twentieth century, principles of hierarchy, inequality, and duty defined family relationships. In the last century, more fluid bonds of equality, intimacy, emotional self-disclosure, communication, and mutual trust gradually replaced the fixed roles and obligations of headship and submission. Women and children, previously considered property without rights of their own, are increasingly considered equal partners in marriage and family. This change is neither universal nor without controversy. Nonetheless, the assumption that women should submit to their husbands or sacrifice themselves for their children has come under increasing suspicion. And the idea that parents must respect children's rights to have basic needs met has become more common.

PROMISE AND PERIL

Democratic families, however, bring both promise and peril. When each individual within the family is regarded as unique and worthy of respect, family members flourish. Rich relationships between partners, parents, and children evolve as family responsibilities are more genuinely shared. Persons develop intimate connections with others and yet have the freedom to carve out satisfying work of their own. Just families attempt to sustain authentic mutuality and encourage their members to imagine the rich potential of wider public democracy.

1

Yet achieving democracy in families is never easy. Old hierarchical assumptions change more slowly in families than in the political arena because such change cannot be legislated. Misleading rhetoric about equality ignores the complicated nitty-gritty realities of daily family life that often require accommodation and sacrifice. To negotiate life's daily decisions and sustain higher levels of economic, educational, and political equality between spouses and partners requires a new and more demanding level of communicative competence. Considering a new job offer or dividing the long list of chores can all too easily devolve into conflicts over who is doing more work to sustain the family or who should give way to whom.

Families are also pushed and pulled by many external forces and values that undermine efforts at democratization. The demands of a free market economy still presume workers who are unencumbered by the unpredictable claims of children or aging parents. Cultural patterns that support expressive individualism conflict with a family's need for accommodation and compromise of personal desires in order to maintain mutuality. A key problem has arisen around the struggle over how to sustain both gender equality and strong families. In other words, the promise and perils of family democracy leave people with a troubling question: How exactly do families sustain genuine mutuality and democracy in the face of these and other related challenges?

WHY MUTUALITY MATTERS

Figuring out good answers to this question is the major theme of this book and the origin of the title *Mutuality Matters*. Three common strategies for creating just relationships have arisen: political and legal reform, smarter negotiating by women, and new cultural perceptions. While the authors in this book attend to all three strategies to different degrees, the primary focus is the third strategy: changing our cultural understanding of committed relationships. Moreover, to effect genuine cultural change, the authors recognize the need to enlist the help of religion as a key culture-forming element.

Although the book aims primarily to foster just marriage, this does not rule out its importance for same sex relationships. It simply confirms that heterosexual couples face a long historical legacy of lingering sexism and patriarchy that continues to make mutuality difficult. Homosexual couples face other biases. However, since sexism and heterosexism are inextricably linked, changing heterosexual partnerships bears directly upon fostering justice and benevolence for and within gay and lesbian relationships. Establishing Mutuality is equally significant in same-sex families. Hence, many claims throughout the book about just love pertain to all families, regardless of sexual orientation.

Christianity continues to shape prominent cultural assumptions and ideals about love and family life more than most people realize. Love is at the heart of the Christian message. It is, as Paul argues in his letter to the Corinthians, the greatest spiritual gift. It is patient, kind, respectful, never jealous, boastful, arrogant, rude, irritable, resentful, or insistent on its own way. Despite this lyrical catalogue of love's qualities, theologians over history have quarreled about its meaning, especially as it takes shape within families. Some scholars believe that the early Christian movement promoted more egalitarian families and mutual service without domination modeled after the love of Christ. Yet other scriptural passages clearly reestablish the hierarchical patterns of the surrounding Greco-Roman and Jewish culture that expected greater submission and compliance on the part of women, slaves, and children. Even when marriage later became an official sacrament within the Roman Catholic Church, the aim was holiness and fidelity in love more than equality.

The debate about the nature of familial love received a new twist several centuries ago with Martin Luther. The heart of Luther's social ethics opposes self-love to love of others. As theologian William H. Lazareth describes Luther's position, "the Christian lives not for himself but for the benefit of others. And nowhere is this more apparent and important than in the God-ordained fortress of our common life, the Christian household."[1] Theologians in the last several decades, such as Anders Nygren, Gene Outka, Valerie Saiving, and Judith Plaskow, have especially sparred over the place of self-sacrifice.[2] Is unconditional sacrifice, often equated with love as agape, the highest Christian ideal? Or is *caritas*, often associated with a equal regard that includes but does not idealize sacrifice, more fundamental to the Christian message? Major changes in families in the last several decades have both sparked and exacerbated this debate. Moreover, equality, freedom from oppression, and resistance to injustice and violence became major themes in Christian theology in general and these ideals have had a significant impact on the family in particular.

Conventional cultural norms of marriage tend to suspend ordinary principles of justice that apply everywhere else and portray marriage as exclusively a relationship of unconditional love. However, many Christian theologians and secular scholars question this dichotomized view of justice as only applicable in the public sphere and make a case for just love and equal regard at the heart of intimate relationships. It is possible to legislate equality in the public sphere but not in the sanctity of the home. Families may create clear guidelines to regulate household responsibilities, but just love will not come about through asserting policy or developing rules and regulations. Its actualization requires transformation of cultural ideals, changes in personal disposition, careful and empathic communication, negotiation, and persuasion.

Mutuality has become a common way for theologians from a variety of perspectives to talk about a more just love, a love that combines affection and justice. But many questions have been left unanswered.

- What exactly do people believe they have promised when they align themselves with Christian claims about love in their rituals of marriage and partnership?
- Because accommodation or sacrifice is inevitable in any intimate human community, how can families ensure that it will be mutual and just?
- How are relationships strengthened if justice is added to love at the core of mutuality?
- What does mutuality mean across time and distance, when participants are parents and children, when fathers are absent, when parents should be honored, or within a violent context?
- Is it possible to have democratic families without mutual sacrifice? Can submission be mutual?

On these and other questions, the authors of this volume claim distinctive responsibility for rethinking Christian convictions about love and family life around the theme of mutuality and for strengthening the ministry of religious communities as those communities seek to empower and support families in their practice of mutuality.

THE ORIGIN OF THE BOOK

This book began as a *Festschrift* on the family as a place for theology, organized by Edward Foley and Robert Schreiter, to honor Herbert Anderson on his sixty-fifth birthday. The essays were written by friends and colleagues of Anderson representing several disciplines, a wide ecumenical perspective, and a desire to wed two of his passions—pastoral theology and the family. Herbert Anderson is a Lutheran pastor who did his graduate study at a United Methodist theological seminary and then taught at Presbyterian, Lutheran, and Roman Catholic institutions during his thirty-one-year teaching career. He wrote many, many seminal articles and books on the family (see the bibliography in the appendix), taught and employed family systems theory in his counseling and pastoral ministry, and bravely faced the challenges of living out the contradictions and joys of mutuality in his family and professional relationships. Since retirement, he has served as an adjunct faculty member at the Seattle campus of Fuller Theological Seminary, an evangelical Protestant institution, at Seattle University School of Theology and Ministry, and on the staff of an Episcopal

Cathedral in Seattle, continuing his reflection on and ministry with families. This ecumenical and family odyssey has positioned him in a special way to understand the contributions of American Christianity toward a cultural transformation of perceptions of marriage and family living.

An odd twist of fate has turned a general book on the family into a more intentional, richer exploration of a specific issue and normative ideal at the heart of family life—mutuality.

The organization and, in some cases, the content of the book has undergone revision to make the topic of mutuality more explicit. Two essays from the initial collection are not included because they were personal reflections on the life and work of Anderson. Some essays have been reworked to lift up their relevance for mutuality. Other essays already openly debated the subject. Four new essays have been added, including Anderson's especially fine chapter on the rhetoric and realities of mutuality. Two authors who address the complexities of realizing mutuality in families are, not coincidentally, Anderson's son and daughter-in-law, Joel Anderson and Pauline Kleingeld. The authors and editors of this volume are grateful to Sheed & Ward and editor Jeremy Langford for their willingness to publish this refashioned collection on a timely subject.

The contributions to this volume reflect seven recurring and interweaving themes in Anderson's work:

- The family is a human system that has a life of its own that must be understood in terms of ever expanding contexts of mutual influence.
- The family has a history that is best understood as a life cycle with predictable transitions and unpredictable crises.
- Paradox is not only a central theological concept; it is an unavoidable family dynamic that necessitates holding in tension multiple sides and contradictory truths.
- Enactment is a term that points to the actualization of internal states in human interaction between thought and action, feeling and behavior, myth and ritual.
- Justice, especially in gender and spousal relations, challenges us to rethink traditional patterns of family.
- Empathy is a vital necessity for all forms of human community and particularly in the family. It is a virtue in short supply in modern societies and one that needs to be more consciously employed in a pluralistic world.
- Being separate together is the paradoxical connection between autonomy and community that is at the core of every vital human system.

Anderson's theology is about how we all stand before God as broken, but grace-filled human beings and how God stands before us as the font of mercy and justice. Careful reflection on these themes provides a creative framework for conversation with the culture ideals and assumptions surrounding marriage and family living. Despite the ups and downs of moving this book toward publication, we believe that this volume is a rich and more focused text and perhaps an even more appropriate honoring of Anderson's life and work.

THE CONTENTS OF THE BOOK

This book begins by examining several theoretical perspectives on mutuality in family life. Paul Wadell insists that love is mutual, and that the aim of all genuine love "is to bring others more fully to life" by closely attending to one another. Kleingeld, writing from a Kantian perspective, proposes that we reconceive the ideal of marriage as essentially not only a matter of love but also of justice. This commitment to justice at the core of marriage deepens mutuality between wives and husbands by forging a common vision of their life together. Don Browning argues that hermeneutic reason reveals and grounds mutuality and equal regard more richly than modern teleological ethics or liberal Kantian deontology. Carolyn Osiek examines Pauline injunctions about family relations, especially in regard to gender relations. She proposes, in the midst of recent rhetoric about wives submitting to husbands, a reclaiming of mutuality, of being "servants to one another in love"(Gal. 5:13).

The second section of the book looks at "mutuality matters in marriage." Herbert Anderson proposes that marriages will endure and flourish when husbands and wives have achieved a kind of mutual recognition in which each honors the others as subjects worthy of respect and equal regard. Christie Neuger looks at redefining the family in the light of the endemic violence embedded in some gender narratives. She asks what role the Church might play in the transition to new understandings. Joel Anderson examines the relationship between career and marriage. Even if couples were to choose more traditional role patterns, Anderson argues that marriage in modern industrial societies inevitably presents couples with unexpected conflicts and unseen rocky shoals that require a wide array of skills and virtues best sustained by mutual regard. Sam Lee asks whether Western notions of love as *agape* and *caritas* formed in a monocultural context can be applied to a multicultural context. He answers by looking at the dynamics of the Korean American bicultural family and argues for a mutual respect for the sometimes diverging cultural ideals of Confucianism and Christianity. The question in many contexts is not whether hierarchy and egalitarianism can coexist but how they might do so in the healthiest and appropriate fashion.

In the third section, the authors contextualize mutuality in family living. Bonnie Miller-McLemore contends that most theological explorations of mutuality ignore children and focus almost solely on adult-to-adult relationships. Taking children into consideration requires significant nuances in conceptualizations of mutuality. Pamela Couture looks at the complex pressures placed on family relationships by geographic distance and professional commitments and how adult children and parents communicate when geographically separate. Dianne Bergant finds wisdom in the Book of Sirach for one of the most fundamental aspects of mutuality in the family: the injunction to honor one's father and one's mother. Anthropologist Anthony Gittins, aware of the variety of kinship patterns that constitute families around the world, examines forms more congenial to survival and flourishing in the United States around the image of a "good enough" family.

The final four essays explore ways in which mutuality is fostered through congregational life and ministry. Homer Ashby provides an in-depth study of the issues of the absence of the father in the African-American family, and the work and advocacy that the Black church might undertake to address this issue. Gilbert Ostdiek picks up one thread of this discussion around the question of baptizing children, and considers what this means for living in the family and the larger human community. Thomas Groome revisits a discussion from nineteenth-century Protestant circles that has become salient for Roman Catholics today: Where should the energies of religious education and formation be concentrated? James Poling uses a systems view to set out the potential dynamics of the congregation as a healing community, especially as it pertains to the agency of congregational leadership. While not directly addressing mutuality in families, each of these essays underscore the critical role congregations play in supporting families and creating the possibility for mutuality.

CONCLUDING THOUGHTS

The essays reflect the development of practical theology as one method for exploring the religious meanings of family and enhancing the practice of family living. Practical theology focuses on the intersection of theory and practice. It assumes that all theory has implications for practice and all practices are theory laden. The result is an ongoing conversation between theory and practice, a conversation that is itself good theology. Practical theology also works best when it draws into dialogue the knowledge and interpretations of a variety of perspectives across traditional disciplinary boundaries. Remarkably, in this book the fields of philosophy, biblical criticism, anthropology, liturgical studies, pastoral care, ethics, cross-cultural studies, and religious education are all well represented. This collection of essays is noteworthy for both this interdisciplinary scope and its richly ecumenical representation.

In this book, matters of mutuality are addressed primarily in the context of heterosexual marriage. But many of the same issues of mutuality and just love arise for unmarried couples and partners in same-sex unions. Heterosexual couples do face the added challenge of lingering sexism as they strive for mutuality. Regardless of sexual orientation, however, establishing mutuality is of fundamental significance for all families.

The process and exercise of fashioning this book also reflects the enactment of mutuality itself. The internal debate between disciplines and among perspectives demonstrates the power of mutuality in human relationships and discourse when contending values are given equal weight even in the midst of conflict. Mutuality is only possible when people can empathetically imagine the world of another without fear of losing their own voice and when they are able to change their mind or be changed by another as a result. While one person may work harder on this idea or that task, in the end mutuality demands reciprocity. At some level, mutuality requires, presumes, and, in the best of all possible worlds, fosters a shared vision. What began as a tribute to a friend, therefore, has become a common vision regarding mutuality as the fundamental image of full humanity and as essential for vital marriage and family living. The authors hope that this book might move the world one small step closer to the best of all possible worlds that God would have us usher in.

NOTES

1. William H. Lazareth, *Luther on the Christian Home: An Application of the Social Ethics of the Reformation* (Philadelphia: Muhlenberg Press, 1960), viii, 131.

2. Anders Nygren, *Agape and Eros* (Philadelphia: Westminster, 1953); Gene Outka, *Agape: An Ethical Analysis* (New Haven: Yale, 1972); Louis Janssens, "Norms and Priorities in a Love Ethic," *Louvain Studies* 6 (1977): 207–38; Valerie Saiving, "The Human Situation: A Feminine Viewpoint," *Journal of Religion* (April 1960): 100–112; Judith Plaskow, *Sex, Sin and Grace: Women's Experience and the Theologies of Reinhold Niebuhr and Paul Tillich* (Lanham, MD: University Press of America, 1980); Susan Nelson Dunfee, *Beyond Servanthood: Christianity and the Liberation of Women* (Lanham, MD: University Press of America, 1989); Gene Outka, "Universal Love and Impartiality," in *The Love Commandments: Essays in Christian Ethics and Moral Philosophy*, ed. Edmund N. Santurri and William Werpehowski (Washington, DC: Georgetown University Press, 1992), 1–103; Don S. Browning, "Altruism and Christian Love," *Zygon* 27 (1992): 421–36; Stephen J. Pope, "'Equal Regard' versus 'Special Relations'? Reaffirming the Inclusiveness of Agape," *The Journal of Religion* 77, no. 3 (July 1997): 353–79.

I

PERSPECTIVES ON LOVE AND MUTUALITY

1

The Family as a Crucible of Grace: Finding God in the Mutuality of Love

Paul J. Wadell

Several years ago, when teaching a course on the theology of marriage, I asked my parents if they would be willing to make a tape on which they shared their reflections and insights about their then forty years of married life together. Although initially reluctant, they promised to do whatever they could if I thought it would be helpful for the class. What they shared was more than helpful; indeed, it was an exquisite, moving reflection on marriage and family life as a graced and gracious vocation through which people, brought together by love, help each other learn lessons in love.

One story stands out. My father spoke of their first Christmas together in 1946 and how beautiful Mom and he thought their first Christmas tree was. But both agreed what made the tree precious was all my father had to go through to get it. They did not have a car in 1946, so Dad walked two miles in search of the perfect tree. Dad told of how carefully he looked for this tree and how proud he was when he picked it out. He was able to get it for a dollar, a paltry sum today but not in 1946 for a young couple struggling financially. Proud of his purchase and anxious to show it to Mom, Dad still had to walk the two miles home. It started to snow and the wind was so blustery Dad said he wasn't sure if he was carrying the tree or the tree was carrying him. That story is a metaphor for the kind of mutuality present in their marriage. One never knew who was carrying whom.

Whether in bringing home Christmas trees, caring for children, consoling and comforting each another, being patient and forgiving to one another, or building one another up through kindness, challenge, teasing or

11

an affectionate hug, marriage and family life can be a graced context for encountering God and growing in authentic mutual love. Like any true vocation, redemptive possibilities abound in marriage and family life because God is at work everywhere, especially in the details of our everyday lives. For Christians, marriage and family life ought to be a true "crucible of grace," a setting in which individuals who have been given one another by God can discover, experience, and grow in mutual love. Indeed, it is through mutual, just love that persons are transformed by the attentiveness, care, and devotion of others and, therefore, come to image God more fully.

In this essay I want to focus on marriage and family life as a setting for growing together in mutual love by reflecting on three points: (1) why the human vocation is eminently the vocation to learn and to grow in mutual, reciprocal love; (2) why marriage and family life is a particularly apt context for learning the discipline and art of love, and for growing together in the transformative power of love; and (3) why for Christians marriage and family life is full of redemptive possibilities.

THE HUMAN VOCATION TO LOVE

In his 1981 pastoral letter on marriage and family life, *Familiaris Consortio*, Pope John Paul II wrote that "God inscribed in the humanity of man and woman the vocation, and thus the capacity and responsibility, of love and communion. Love," he said, "is therefore the fundamental and innate vocation of every human being."[1] John Paul II suggests that the one call every human being receives is the call to live in mutual love, because the very possibility of growing and developing as human beings hinges on our capacity to imitate the love of God by which we were created. We have life through love. We flourish as God's creatures only insofar as we, God's inimitable images, learn to give and receive love. In this way, love is always mutual. Learning what it means to love and living in communities of love is the absolute and inescapable vocation of every human being. Becoming accomplished in the mutuality of love is the indispensable key to becoming human, and it is a skill that ought to be learned, practiced, and fulfilled in marriage and family life.

The vocation of love is not an option because, first of all, we are images of a Trinitarian God who has been revealed to us as a flourishing community of mutual, reciprocal love in which each person's love gives life and identity to the other. Christians have steadfastly believed that God is not the loneliness of three utterly separate and disconnected persons, but an intimate *family of persons* characterized by mutual, generous, life-giving love. Indeed, we can speak of God in exactly the same way the Second

Vatican Council spoke of marriage and family life: an "intimate community of life and love." What we see in God, and are called to imitate in our marriages and families, is a community of persons in which the uniquely personal love of one sustains, enlivens, and brings joy to another. Thus, the Trinity reveals God as the most excellent and exquisite manifestation of what authentic intimacy and mutuality involve.

Second, the call to love is everyone's vocation because if we are living, breathing images of a God *who is love*, then we have life as God has life. We are authentically human and know happiness when we do what God does and live as God lives, namely in relationships and communities characterized by mutual, generous, life-giving love. The intimacy and mutuality experienced in these relationships—as every marriage and family attests—will always be partial, fragile, and frustratingly incomplete; however, we cannot avoid the summons to intimacy and mutuality because the love from which they flow and the love they continue to shape is oxygen for our spirits and food for our souls. As David Thomas comments, "Being created in the image of God means, at its deepest level, being made to love. No one is exempt from this calling. Perhaps the greatest tragedy of a human life is not to have experienced being loved, or not to have taken the risk of loving another."[2] We are born to love and to be loved. We are born to know, grow in, and be transformed by relationships of mutual love. Mutuality matters because it is only in relationships where love is given and received, where persons are affirmed, challenged, and respected, that we mirror the divine love that completes us. It is this absolute and unavoidable necessity of loving and being loved in a way that models the love of God that makes marriage and family life highly significant for humanization and happiness.

What a Trinitarian God teaches us about the importance of marriage and family life is that if the image of God in us is both our *capacity* to love and our *absolute need* to love, then we need settings in life where God's love can be learned, modeled, and experienced. Either we love and are loved or we perish. Mutual, generous, life-giving love keeps us alive. We are not to love simply because God loves, but because love is the deepest need of our nature and because, like God, love is our most perfecting activity. It is what we are created to do. Genuine mutual love, whether in friendship, marriage, or community life, develops us most fully and properly as humans. Such love is, as Vincent Genovesi suggests, "the most fundamental law of our human nature." Ignore the law of love, Genovesi says, and "we are engaged in a process of serious self-frustration that runs its course finally in self-destruction."[3] A great gift of marriage and family life is to teach us that it is only in mutual, generous love that true fulfillment can be found, to show us what such life-giving love involves, and to give us a setting for growing in it.

If the quintessential challenge of every human life is to become skilled in the habits and practices of mutual love, then it is crucial that we are able to distinguish genuine love from counterfeit love. Marriage and family life should be a place where we learn and experience the difference. Love may be the most powerful word in any language, but it is also true that no word is so frequently manipulated and misused. Much harm has been done in love's name, which is why there may be more "impersonations of love" than real instances of love.[4] All of us have known and suffered from counterfeit love, behavior that at first glance looks like love but is only manipulation and deceit masked as love. And all of us have likely contributed to counterfeit love, bringing hurt to another where we ought to have given life.

Furthermore, true mutual love is a *habitus*, a well-developed virtue and way of being, not a natural aptitude. We may have a natural need for love, but we do not naturally know how to love. As any spouse or parent can attest, love is a skill and an art we need to learn and develop, a discipline into which we must be continually initiated.

MARKS OF AUTHENTIC MUTUAL LOVE

How can we distinguish genuine mutual love from its imposters? First, as Vincent Genovesi suggests, "love expresses our desire and our willingness to live creatively in the service of others' fulfillment,"[5] just as they live in service of our own, something spouses, parents, and children do in their life together. Love is the thoughtful and deliberate practice of attending to the needs, concerns, and well-being of others. A loving person is one who seeks the good of another for his or her sake; indeed, we know a person truly loves us when she not only wants what is best for us but also is actively devoted to helping us achieve it. With its focus on the flourishing of another, love is the antithesis of self-centeredness. Love turns us outward so that we commit our time, energies, and abilities to fostering the happiness and prosperity of others. Still, precisely because all love is relational, the aim of love is to have the affection and attentiveness we extend to another returned to us. The essential quality of authentic love is not sacrifice and selflessness, but mutuality and equal regard. Love prospers, and is most delightful, when the faithful devotion we extend to another is met by their care and concern for us.

Second, the power and aim of all mutual love is to bring one another more fully to life and to help each other flourish. Genuine love is creative and liberating. Freedom and life are always gifts of real love, whether it is parents patiently drawing their children more fully to life through everyday acts of affection, affirmation, or challenge, or spouses helping one another grow through support, compassion, truthfulness, forgiveness, or humor. The love of those who are devoted to us helps us grow and flourish because such attentive, affirming love works to free us from whatever hinders our proper development as human beings. One sure proof of genuine love is when another guides us to attitudes, behavior, convictions, and even feelings that are liberating precisely because they help us become more authentically human.

We are agents of one another's creation, channels to one another's ever deepening freedom and peace. This is the beauty and the power of authentic mutual love. In mutual love each person shapes the ongoing creation and liberation of the other because through love each makes the other persons they could never have become on their own. Spouses do this for one another, parents do it for children and children for parents, and sisters and brothers do it for one another, often in amazing ways. Love is an art and a skilled lover is like an artist. Someone who loves us well not only sees who we are and loves us, but also sees who we are called by God to be and helps us bring that graced promise to life. Most importantly, a true lover sees the unique image of God that has been specially entrusted to us, and knows how to draw that image out of us and help us embody it more completely. Helping one another grow in the distinctive identity given them by God is the gracious work of genuine mutual love.

Rough Strife, a novel by Lynne Sharon Schwartz, captures this. It is the story of Ivan and Caroline, spouses who grow through the care, attentiveness, and affection they receive from each other. Early in the novel Caroline reminisces about the unfinished sculptures of Michelangelo she and Ivan had seen in Florence. She recalls those "figures hidden in the block of stone, uncovered only by the artist's chipping away the excess, the superficial blur, till smooth and spare, the true shape is revealed," and then realizes that "she and Ivan were hammer and chisel to each other."[6]

It is a captivating image of the creative power of mutual love, whether that love is exercised in marriage and family life, in communities, or in friendships. There is a graced promise hidden away in each of us and it is the work of love not only to unveil that promise, but also to bring it more fully to life. Love works to chisel and polish that grace, faithfully and patiently shaping it into something beautiful and good. We can glimpse the power of such love when we ask, "What is the cumulative effect of being loved faithfully and creatively by another?" Reflecting on that question reveals that the liberating transformation wrought by love is largely the work of another, whether that other be a spouse, a friend, a parent, a brother or sister, or God.

A third quality of mutual love is that such love must be insightful. Love is not an anonymous, undifferentiated regard for others; rather, love is the capacity to seek the good of another precisely because we have taken time to know her *as other*. As a spouse or as a parent, we cannot work for another's good and contribute to her well-being without some understanding of who she is and who she hopes to be. Love is a matter of vision, of seeing another as fully and truthfully and compassionately as possible. Love requires the seasoned knowledge that allows us to see one's goodness and promise, her special interests, needs, cares and concerns, but also her limitations, shortcomings, and struggles. Indeed, there can be no true mutual love unless we learn to see the world through the eyes of the other.

Love must be insightful because we cannot love persons graciously and creatively unless we first learn who they really are and have some knowledge of their distinctive desires, concerns, hopes, and fears. Thus, we gain the insight necessary for love by being attentive to those we have promised to love. Love is illuminating because through love we acquire the vision and perceptiveness that allows us to recognize what is unique and distinctive about another—what it is that makes him different from anybody else. For instance, parents may seek to love all their children equally, but they also love each of them uniquely because their love is informed by insight into what makes each of their children different.

This third quality of love reminds us that real love, despite the popular claim, cannot afford to be blind. Love is rooted in the recognition of what makes the other a unique expression of God's infinite creativity. Therefore, beyond careful listening, insight into the world of another (spouse, parent, child) presumes the capacity to imagine their world. Understanding is increased and judgment is diminished when we are able to live through an experience from the standpoint of the other. Ordinarily, empathy is the word used to describe this capacity to understand the world of another *as they understand it*. For example, partners in marriage are more likely to be receptive to one another's experience if each is confident their story will be heard and validated. When empathy is mutual, both sides are respectfully heard and love is deepened.

LEARNING THE DISCIPLINE AND ART OF MUTUAL LOVE

Even though all of us naturally need love and naturally want love, none of us naturally knows how to love. One of the things that makes marriage and family life a "crucible of grace" is that it is a prime setting for learning the discipline and art of love. Love is not a natural aptitude, it is an acquired skill, a virtue or *habitus* that characterizes persons who consistently are able to attend to the needs, well-being, and concerns of others, and find joy in doing so. Nothing kills marriage or family life faster than stinginess of spirit, whether it is expressed by ignoring one's spouse, withdrawing into oneself, an unwillingness to share, or lack of presence to one another. If marriage is to be a mutual communion of life and love—a partnership of intimacy—and if families are to be real communities of grace, selfishness must be overcome as husbands, wives, and children learn lessons in mutual, just love.

Marriage and family life are graced settings in which persons learn how to love in three ways: spouses help each other to love, raising children deepens spouses' skills in love, and parents teach children to love.

Married couples learn lessons in love by reorienting and restructuring their lives so that each can regularly attend to the needs and well-being of the other. Precisely because by getting married one spouse declares that the other irrevocably *matters* and must always be taken into account, marriage involves nothing less than allowing another to influence one's thinking, attitudes, behavior, and everyday actions. Marital commitment demands including the good of another in all of one's decisions. Most importantly, it means allowing the beloved to have an abiding claim on one's time, energy, and talents. In the friendship of marriage, love means rearranging one's life and priorities so that one's partner is never overlooked or neglected. This is a matter of justice and faithfulness. "When we truly love another," David Thomas observes, "this whole process of me-first is changed as the needs of another person are allowed to influence personal choice. Someone else counts in personal reckoning. In the personal decision-making process, where interest, time and resources are allocated, I include my beloved in my calculations."[7] Thomas is not suggesting that a spouse must be so completely attentive to the needs of his partner that his own needs no longer matter; rather, the very mutuality of love means that each one's life must be enlarged in order to receive and be influenced by the other.

Practicing such love is not easy, not only because all of us wrestle with tendencies toward selfishness, apathy, and resentment, but also because the persons we are called to love in marriage and family life are as flawed and imperfect as ourselves. The aim of a skillful lover is to draw to life the special image of God in the beloved, but that image can be obscured by pettiness, fear, envy, and all the amazingly ordinary ways human beings can be sinful. There are rough edges to all of us, unflattering dimensions that tarnish the image of God in us and make it downright difficult for us to be loved. This is why in *Rough Strife* Lynne Sharon Schwartz says so much of marriage comes down to "love of a flawed object,"[8] and why Elizabeth Achtemeier suggests the real test of love is not in loving when it is easy to love, but in "learning to love and value the other for the imperfect person he or she is."[9]

Loving well in marriage is hard work, a rigorous, demanding discipline that is not always immediately rewarding. There is an unavoidable asceticism to real love because it insists on loving when there is scant gratification in doing so. Learning to love a "flawed object" deepens and refines love. It makes love resilient. None of us is given perfect spouses and children to love; rather, the persons entrusted to our love are so maddeningly like ourselves, creatures full of unredeemed dimensions and hobbled by imperfections a lifetime of love may never erase. This is why the virtue of fidelity is necessary for sustaining and steadying love, especially in those moments when we are not sure we have the patience steadfast love requires.

The beauty of true mutual love is precisely its power to see and to still love, to know and yet to embrace. Sustaining such love amidst disappointments, setbacks, hurts, and all the assaults wrought by human frailty, demands patience, commitment, compassion, lots of humility, and a good sense of humor. To be skilled in such faithful, mutual love is a precious grace not only for the person who receives it, but also for the person who discovers in herself resilience and ingenuity in loving she did not have before. This, too, is part of the life of grace unveiled in a marriage.

Nowhere is the discipline and art of love more challengingly learned than in raising and caring for children. If we think of love as an expenditure of energy on behalf of another, nothing demands more energy, extraordinary generosity, seemingly endless amounts of patience and sacrifice, and absolute availability than parenting. Once a child is born parents know their time is no longer their own because now they are accountable to another who depends on them completely. As the theologian Roger Mehl observed, "parenthood brings with it 'manifold servitudes'"[10] because raising children ensures countless limitations on one's time and choices, seemingly endless interruptions, and no shortage of occasions to leave one feeling defeated.

But lessons in love are equally learned as children grow and become more independent. How is love tested when children make choices with which parents deeply disagree? How is it tested when the child one lives to love seems bitter and ungrateful, more skilled in resentment than gratitude? Children bring great joy to parents' lives, but they can also bring great pain and terrible disappointment. In such moments love is challenged as it is asked to forgive rather than to resent, and to move beyond hurt instead of settling into it. Hopefully, children will one day return the love they received, but in parenting love is given with no guarantee of return. Such love is an act of faith, a commitment to minister God's love and mercy and goodness to another without the assurance that the gift of love will be received and reciprocated. When it isn't, love can seem more a barren duty than a gracious joy, but in that respect it mirrors the steadfast, sacrificial love of God whose love is proffered much more than returned.

Finally, a third way marriage and family life can be a setting for learning lessons of love is through parents who teach children what it means to love. The purpose of Christian family life is forming people who know how to love. How then are children initiated into the skills and practices of love?

In *Familiaris Consortio* Pope John Paul II wrote, "The family is the first and irreplaceable school of social life, an example and stimulus for the broader community of relationships marked by respect, justice, dialogue and love."[11] He envisioned the family as the setting in which parents help children develop the attitudes, values, and virtues necessary for entering and contributing to the larger society. Parents should form children in the qualities of character essential for a healthy and just society, especially the virtues of sharing and cooperation, the virtues of tolerance and truthfulness, and the virtues of generosity and justice. If this does not occur, society becomes little more than a chaotic conglomeration of individuals, each pursuing his or her private ends.

Children have to be socialized somewhere. They need to learn what it means to live cooperatively with others. They need some place where they learn to restrain their worst inclinations and cultivate their best ones. This kind of moral and spiritual education should take place in the family. True, it cannot be achieved by parents alone. Parents must be aided and supported by the larger community, by schools, the government, and especially by the churches. Nonetheless, the family is the indispensable and central locus for initiating children into the lifelong transformation from selfishness to love. Put differently, if children do not learn how to live well with others in the family, they will not know how to live well with others in society. The crucial social virtues of sharing, dialogue, kindness, justice, solidarity, love, and respect must be honed in the crucible of family life if overly gratified children are not to develop into boorish and irresponsible adults. Educating their children in lessons of justice and love is the most enduring gift parents can give their offspring.

CHRISTIAN MARRIAGE AND FAMILY LIFE:
A REDEMPTIVE ENCOUNTER WITH CHRIST

Christian marriage and family life is a graced and hopeful encounter with Christ and a setting for faithful discipleship. In Catholic theology, each of the sacraments celebrates the gracious availability of God in the ordinary affairs of human life. We find God where we live and God, through grace, Christ, and the Spirit, is always actively involved in our lives. Sacramental theology is deeply incarnational, testifying to God's steadfast desire to participate in our lives in a loving and redemptive manner.

Nowhere are the splendors of grace more routinely experienced than within the fabric of everyday married and family life. This is not to idealize or romanticize family life by denying the frustrations, disappointments, hurts, and simple boredom that are often part of it, but to insist that God can be found even amidst those thistles and thorns. It is how redemption occurs. We are sanctified by responding to God in the ordinariness of everyday life. We imitate Christ and grow in holiness not by stepping outside the commitments and loyalties of our lives, but by growing more deeply in them.

This is what Theodore Mackin meant when he described Christian marriage and family life as "susceptible . . . to God's transforming intention."[12] When marriage and family life are embraced in faith, they become settings in which persons love God, imitate Christ, and *together* grow in holiness each day. To say that marriage and family life is "susceptible to God's transforming intention" means there is no better place to encounter God, experience God's love, and respond to it in gracious imitation. Put differently, God's grace and love are mediated through ordinary human realities such as friendships, marriages, and family life. Each of these can constitute a "community of graced life" because God is present there in sanctifying and redemptive ways.

In their book *Promises to Keep*, Kathleen Fischer and Thomas Hart speak of the "sacredness of the ordinary."[13] Christian marriage and family life are made up of lots of ordinary things, but if God is present there, truly an active participant in the family, then every aspect of a family's life together has the potential of leading them closer to God. What from one perspective can seem sheer routine or hopeless drudgery, seen through the optic of faith can be a saving encounter with Christ and an everyday opportunity to practice Christ like love. This is why marriage and family life has the power to restore people to God.

Marriage and family life is a true crucible of salvation because Christ's redemptive love grasps everything in Christian family life and sanctifies it. Nothing is profane, nothing is void of redemptive possibility because Christ works creatively and graciously through every element of a family's life together. We glimpse the "sacredness of the ordinary" when spouses and family members care for one another, when they are patient and forgiving with one another, when they look for the best in one another, when they face hardships together, and when they refuse to give up on one another. We see it when families work together, when they ease the tension by making one another laugh, when they pray and worship together, and when they call one another to what is most hopeful. In all the simple everyday things that constitute married and family life, spouses, parents, and children are "instruments of salvation" through whom God continues to bless and to sanctify. Such a life may not be easy, but it is immensely graced and full of hope.

In this chapter I have tried to show why marriage and family life can be a "crucible of grace," a particularly apt context for learning, growing in, and modeling the mutual, affirming love that lives at the heart of God. Such love may be rigorous and demanding, but it is the indispensable path to our humanization and happiness, and, hopefully, key to our sanctification. If the quintessential human vocation is the vocation to give and receive love, there is no better setting for living out this call than in marriage and family life because both tutor us in the qualities and characteristics of authentic love. Most importantly, for Christians the truly redemptive dimension to genuine mutual love is knowing that God is a partner to our love, sharing in our lives, accompanying us on our way, continually looking for ways to bless us and do good for us. Knowing that God shares in our lives down to the most intimate and ordinary details is what makes marriage and family life such compelling and hopeful vocations. In an age that is often cynically dismissive of the possibility of faithful, mutual love, much less the gracious goodness of marriage and family, there may be no more urgent task for Christians than to show why marriage and family life are among God's sweetest mercies.

NOTES

1. John Paul II, *Familiaris Consortio*, n. 11.

2. David Thomas, *Christian Marriage: A Journey Together* (Wilmington, Del.: Michael Glazier, Inc., 1983), 49.

3. Vincent J. Genovesi, *In Pursuit of Love: Catholic Morality and Human Sexuality* (Collegeville, Minn.: The Liturgical Press, 1996), 22.

4. Genovesi, 25.

5. Genovesi, 25–26.

6. Lynne Sharon Schwartz, *Rough Strife* (New York: Harper & Row, 1980), 17–18.

7. Thomas, 33.

8. Schwartz, 8.

9. Elizabeth Achtemeier, *The Committed Marriage* (Philadelphia: The Westminster Press, 1976), 43.

10. Achtemeier, 192.

11. John Paul II, *Familiaris Consortio*, n. 41.

12. Theodore Mackin, "How To Understand the Sacrament of Marriage," in *Commitment to Partnership: Explorations of the Theology of Marriage*, ed. William P. Roberts (New York: Paulist Press, 1987), 43.

13. Kathleen R. Fischer and Thomas N. Hart, *Promises to Keep: Developing the Skills of Marriage* (New York: Paulist Press, 1991), 6.

2

Just Love? Marriage
and the Question of Justice

Pauline Kleingeld

From Hallmark cards to wedding vows, marriage is viewed as a matter of love and affection, of romance and physical attraction, and of sensitivity and care.[1] The legal aspects of marriage are generally viewed as a bureaucratically imposed appendage to an essentially emotional commitment. Few people get married with the explicit intention to distribute burdens and benefits justly, to respect each other's bodily integrity, to establish fair procedures for conflict resolution. In this essay, I argue that this widespread view of the meaning of marriage is a hindrance to the realization of justice within marriage.

I start with a brief sketch of the legal and cultural background of the current situation, pointing out the patriarchal context in which the modern view of marriage emerged and the continuing presence of injustice within relationships of love and affection. I then discuss two important strategies for promoting justice within marriage. The first focuses on social reform through laws and policies, the second on what individual women can accomplish through smart planning and bargaining. I argue that while both strategies are indispensable, they do not go far enough, because the full realization of justice within marriage requires a cultural reconceptualization of marriage itself as not merely a relationship of love, but as *also* a commitment to interpersonal justice. In the third section, I discuss what such a reconceptualization would mean in practice and address several possible objections to the view defended here. In two final, short sections I show why it is important to change the legal institution of marriage (instead of abolishing it), and how such change might be brought about.

1. INJUSTICE IN MARRIAGE

For centuries, the common law doctrine of coverture codified male dominance over women.[2] Under coverture, the married couple was regarded as a unity, the "head and master" of which was the husband. Among other things, coverture denied the wife civil existence, bodily integrity, and control over her own property. Coverture included sexual subordination, leaving the concept of marital rape a legal contradiction in terms.[3] The law required a wife to obey her husband, giving her little choice as to whether to perform reproductive and domestic labor. Although there were a few men, like John Stuart Mill and Henry B. Blackwell,[4] who wanted to rid themselves of their marital prerogatives, the system of coverture made it impossible for them to do so.[5]

Beginning in the early modern period, a view came to dominate according to which the family was considered a private realm entirely distinct from the outside political, economic, and public spheres.[6] This notion of the family played an important role in legitimating women's legally, economically, politically, sexually, and personally inferior status. The family was conceived of as a special sphere of life depending on the total dedication of women, who were said to be suited for the special tasks of domestic life because of their refined sensibilities and their emotional attachment to husband and children—the very qualities that made them unsuited for the harsh world of economics, learning, and politics. This family was said to operate purely on the basis of love, and to form a harmonious, complementary unity of interests. As a result, according to the dominant view of the time, it was enough for one person to represent this unity in the public sphere. And the husband, with his greater rational powers and control of his feelings, was thought to be the only one suited for this task.

As a result of the women's movement, this gender ideology has been undermined, the legal institution of marriage has become less unjust, and coverture has gradually disappeared. Married women's property rights, labor rights, domicile liberties, and so on, have been brought more on a par with those of married men. As of 1981, a husband is no longer legally regarded as the "head and master" of the household.[7] In the few U.S. states that have a community property regime, the male managerial rules have been replaced with joint control, equal control, or separate property systems.[8]

But these legal and cultural changes have by no means eradicated injustice from marriage. First, not all elements of injustice and sexism have been taken out of the legal construction of marriage. For example, there still are states that fail to regard the rape of a wife by a husband as a crime.[9] Second, marriage continues to make many women vulnerable, limit their exit options, and keep them in practice locked into an unjust situation.[10] Marriage as a social institution is still largely determined by gender ideology as well as by laws, policies, and institutions that reinforce the traditional patriarchal form of marriage. As household labor studies have consistently shown, women continue to perform more housework than men.[11] Even women with full-time paid jobs often work a "second shift," putting in significantly more hours per week than their male counterparts. This makes it easier for men and harder for women to improve their position in the labor market (by working overtime, taking evening courses, and so on).[12] Moreover, women stand to suffer a sharp drop in their standard of living after divorce.[13] The fact that women assume most of the responsibilities for child care—in part as a result of their weaker position economically, educationally, and in the marriage[14]—further affects their potential to be independent through paid jobs, and thus perpetuates this situation of inequality.[15] Clearly, then, elements of gender injustice persist in both the legal and the social reality of marriage.

The current culturally dominant normative ideal of marriage, however, hinders attempts to address these injustices by making it difficult to conceive of justice as a central component of marriage. According to this ideal, spouses interact purely on the basis of love. Bringing in considerations of justice means changing the mode of interaction within a good marriage. As expressed (and defended) by Jeremy Waldron, the standard view is that bringing explicit claims of justice into the context of a "normal loving marriage" indicates "that something has already gone wrong with the interplay of desire and affection between the partners." He continues: "Such behavior would be seen as a way of blocking and preventing warmth and intimacy, replacing relatively unbounded and immediate care and sensitivity with rigid and abstract formulas of justice."[16] According to the current normative ideal of marriage, principles of justice that we generally recognize as holding between individuals are actually *suspended* within marriage, because "normal" marriage partners are thought to interact exclusively on the basis of care and affection.

In the next section, I show why this view is a hindrance to achieving justice within marriage. I do this by discussing two strategies for eliminating injustice in marriage and showing the problems that remain as long as they do not include a focus on changing public opinion regarding the essence of marriage. The first strategy, exemplified here by the work of Susan Moller Okin, emphasizes legal reform and the adoption of policies conducive to justice in the family. The second, illustrated here by the work of Rhona Mahony, promotes sophisticated and conscious strategizing on the part of women as a way to bring about positive change.

2. TWO SOLUTIONS AND THE PROBLEMS THAT REMAIN

a. Social and legal reform

In *Justice, Gender, and the Family*, Susan Moller Okin directs well-argued criticisms at political theorists for regarding the family as a domain in which the category of justice does not apply. She argues that major contemporary political philosophers—be they libertarians, communitarians, or liberal egalitarians—assume the existence of a gender-structured family, but fail to examine the family in light of their own proposed standard of justice. Okin also shows convincingly that their reasoning for not applying their standards of justice to the family, if made explicit at all, is deeply incoherent and often rests on a view of the family as "beyond justice." Once one does apply standards of justice to the family in its currently dominant form, it fails to meet them.

In her proposals for making families more just, however, Okin fails to extend her criticism of philosophers into the broader cultural realm. Although she does argue that principles of justice ought to guide family life, she does not address the culturally prevalent view of marriage, choosing to focus instead on legal and political change as the path to more just families.[17] I will argue that although such reforms are very important, their implementation will be hampered if there is not also a change in the cultural perception of what marriage involves. My argument is not intended as a critique of Okin's proposals, but rather as an extension of her own criticism of political theorists to the cultural realm, so as to complement the reforms she proposes.

Okin argues that public policies and laws generally should assume no social differentiation of the sexes. Her proposals are much more detailed than I can indicate here, but a few examples should suffice for making clear the sorts of laws and policies she proposes. She argues that it should be made easier for parents to share the responsibility for child care[18] and to access high-quality day care, and that policies relating to pregnancy and birth should be disconnected from those relating to parenting. She suggests that employers should make it easier for all workers to attend to the needs of family members by greater flexibility of hours, and that schools should actively de-emphasize gender and teach both boys and girls how to combine working and parenting. And, as far as marital arrangements are concerned, in cases where partners do not contribute equally to the household income but one is a part-time or full-time home-maker, both should have equal legal entitlement to household income. This economic equality should also extend into post-divorce situations. Okin stresses that the legal system of a society that allows people to choose a traditional division of labor *must* take responsibility for the vulnerable position in which marital breakdown places the partner who has completely or partially lost the capacity to be economically self-supporting as a result of this private arrangement.[19]

However necessary such changes are, there are three reasons for thinking that they are not sufficient. First, laws and policies of the sort proposed by Okin can make it *easier* for spouses to be just to each other, but they do not bring about that they actually are. For example, the availability of good parental leave options makes it easier for a couple to share child care responsibilities. But for fathers actually to *take* parental leaves and share in caretaking—especially if they wished their wives would assume full responsibility for it—more is required than the mere existence of the option. For such fathers voluntarily to start doing their share, they must be committed to a just division of child care responsibilities. In short, they must start to care about their marriages being just.

A second reason that laws and policies do not suffice is that many cases of injustice within marriage are beyond the reach of policies and laws. One can make laws that guarantee an equal legal entitlement of both spouses to all household earnings, but one cannot legislate—and Okin does not suggest one should—how couples work out the division of labor among themselves: who cooks dinner how often, who takes care of the kids, and so on. Such issues have to be dealt with by couples themselves. The weight of tradition, power, or social pressure, however, is likely to decide the outcome in favor of the husband. To avoid this, his wife would have to put up a fight. Neither scenario is ideal. A conscious commitment to justice on the part of both spouses would seem necessary to bring about more just arrangements by nonadversarial means.

There is a third problem that can be addressed only by explicitly including justice in the ideal of marriage. Given the prevalent view of marriage as operating purely in terms of love and affection, a couple may be less likely to perceive issues of justice as such. Failing to perceive an issue as an issue of justice makes one less likely to deal with it adequately.

Take a familiar example. A husband retires from his paid job. For all his working life, his wife had taken care of the domestic labor. He now spends his days at home but fails to increase his participation in household tasks.[20] Rather than suggesting that they rethink the division of labor in light of this new situation, his wife says: "I'd really appreciate it if you helped me in the kitchen." She appeals to his willingness to do something for her that she will appreciate. She figures that if he loves her, he will do it. He too understands the request in terms of love and affection, and, disliking kitchen work, he decides to show his love in some other way, for example, by buying chocolates. He does not (or does not want to) perceive the situation as a problem of justice. Nor does she, and even if she does, she feels she cannot bring up the issue without giving him the impression that she thinks he does not really love her. She is afraid that if she asks him to sit down at the table and talk about their division of labor, she would create a tense atmosphere that both regard as antithetical to what a good marriage should be like. She is afraid that he would think, in Waldron's words, that "something has already gone wrong" in their marriage. Yet the real problem in this example is not a lack of love, but of a just distribution of tasks. As long as raising the issue of justice is seen as something antithetical to what marriage is really about, raising it is going to be hard, and solving it even harder. An understanding of marriage purely in terms of love and affection here hinders the achievement of justice by making it harder to perceive injustice as such, and by creating an atmosphere in which raising the issue may be regarded as an accusation of lovelessness or as "blocking and preventing warmth and intimacy."

In sum, reconceiving the ideal of marriage so as to include a concern with justice would be conducive to implementing justice-oriented laws and policies, to realizing justice beyond the scope of the law, and to recognizing issues of justice as such in the first place. In addition, it would open up a space in which women's concerns can be fully addressed.

Of course, laws and policies of the sort proposed by Okin are likely to bring about some change in the view of marriage. Good and widely publicized policies supporting paternal leave, for instance, do carry a message. But if such policies all by themselves bring about change in the ideal of marriage, they do so indirectly. It would be better *also* to address the dominant cultural view of marriage head-on.

b. Game theory for women

Whereas Okin addresses social policies and laws that impact marriages from the outside, so to speak, Rhona Mahony concentrates on intramarital negotiation.[21] In *Kidding Ourselves: Breadwinning, Babies, and Bargaining Power*, she offers a game-theoretical explanation of how women end up assuming primary care responsibilities for children, often against their wishes. More importantly, she offers strategies for women to change this pattern, focusing on how they can strengthen their bargaining positions and make it more likely that men will do half of the child raising. As Mahony puts it: "The good news is that the dream of real, practical equality between women and men isn't a dream anymore. Women can make it happen. The bad news is that it is up to women themselves."[22]

Mahony analyzes both socioeconomic and psychological factors. An example of the first is that women usually "marry up," earn less than men, and prepare themselves less well for higher-paying jobs. Thus, when couples have to answer the question of who is to assume primary child care responsibilities, it often makes economic sense for the wife (and not the husband) to work fewer hours or take a less demanding job. Moreover, her bargaining position is much weaker than his, since she stands to lose more from a divorce. Thus, she may find herself forced to go along with an arrangement that is unjust to her by going against her wishes and locking her into a vulnerable position. An example of psychological factors is found in Mahony's discussion of the impact of breastfeeding on women's role in taking care of babies. Women tend to spend more intimate time with infants early on and become the "experts." As a result, they find it difficult to let go and let the father gain hands-on experience. While this situation does not itself constitute injustice, women who keep control of child care set themselves up for a situation in which they have no choice but to do most of the child care, which means they have less time for their jobs, further diminish their ability to be independent, lose more bargaining power, and enter a situation in which injustice can more easily occur.

Mahony's strategic suggestions as to what women can do to break through these patterns range from well-known strategies, such as getting the right education, to novel proposals, such as "marrying down" (marrying men with less prospective income, or of younger age)[23] or "affirmative action for fathers" (leaving a father alone with the child for long stretches of time so that he too acquires the knowledge and dispositions of an "expert"). As Mahony shows in her book, it takes far more than this to fully address the psychological effects of prior socialization that make women feel (and hold them to be) more responsible than men do for the daily condition of a child. I have mentioned merely two examples here that are representative of her general approach.

It is clearly important to emphasize, as Mahony does, what individual women can do to promote justice through goal-oriented planning and negotiating. Awareness of inequalities and injustice, and, even more, awareness of the ways to prevent them, are crucial to their elimination.

Even in combination with social reform of the type proposed by Okin, however, Mahony's approach faces two problems. First, it has the disadvantage that unless the ideal of marriage itself changes, women will have to live—as many already do—with a schizophrenic view of marriage. On the one hand, they grow up with the idea that spouses ideally interact on the basis of mutual love and affection. On the other hand, they know they have to fend for themselves if they do not want to end up seriously shortchanged. There is little reason to think this schizophrenia can be cured unless the ideal of marriage itself changes. Were the ideal of marriage itself to include justice, the struggle for justice and equality would no longer have to rest on the shoulders of women alone, and it would no longer be seen as antithetical to the marriage ideal.

Mahony discusses justice as a norm within marriage in a brief section entitled "Moral Language."[24] There, she praises language of fairness and equality because of its useful role in bargaining, and because it can serve as a "commitment mechanism": the more people can be led to talk about the importance of fairness, the harder they make it for themselves to be unfair, because of the social expectations they raise on the part of their audience. By commending the ideal of justice in this way, however, Mahony instrumentalizes it in the service of personal aims. Her perspective is that of the individual self-centered spouse concerned with her own bargaining position.

This leads to a second problem, namely, that any intimate relationship is in trouble if one has to regard one's partner as a permanent potential threat. Permanently living in negotiating mode and having to keep track of one's bargaining position is likely to strain a relationship by creating an atmosphere of competition and mutual threat that one or both spouses will feel is not what a marriage should be like.

I do not mean to say that it is always unwarranted for a spouse to look out for her or his own self-interest. It may be necessary to do so if this is the only way to avoid or end a situation of injustice, and the great value of Mahony's approach consists precisely in developing strategies for such cases and in increasing women's knowledge of the mechanisms that create unjust situations. Nor do I mean to say that fairly negotiated bargains are unjust. Instead, my point is that a view *of marriage* that instrumentalizes justice and expects equality to arise from egocentric and antagonistic negotiation conflicts with a view of marriage as based on love and trust.

If justice is to be an important aspect of marriage, it needs to be able to *unite* spouses instead of structurally pitting them against each other. Fortunately, it is not difficult to conceive of justice in exactly this way. The only thing necessary is that married couples recognize justice itself and for its own sake (not as mere rhetorical tool) as an important aim. Once couples regard "a just marriage" as a shared goal, they move beyond the model of two competitively bargaining individuals and replace it with a model of two spouses committed to a shared effort to achieve justice.

c. Two aims in marriage

This leads to the central claim of this paper. In order to promote justice in marriage, the social perception of the essence of marriage must be changed in such a way that the ideal of marriage is conceived of as not only a matter of love, but also of justice. It is necessary to move beyond the ideology—historically rooted in an era of male dominance—according to which marriage is a matter of love only, at the exclusion of justice. On the view I am proposing, married couples ideally would think of themselves as sharing at least two overarching aims: a loving marriage and a just marriage. If the cultural understanding of marriage changed in this way, this would mean, first, that couples would understand them-selves not only as communities of love, but also as communities of free and interdependent equals who treat each other in accordance with prin-ciples of justice. They would pursue fairness and reciprocity in the recog-nition of each other's interests, and they would pursue a just distribution of benefits and burdens as well as a just resolution of conflicts. Thus, spouses would regard it as their ideal not only to foster the emotional bond between them, but also to promote justice in their relationship. In addition, the concern with intramarital justice on the part of individuals would become embedded in a broader social and cultural context. Once justice becomes a part of the way the ideal marriage is conceived, this will support and reinforce the efforts of individual couples.

Such a change in the cultural ideal of marriage would help solve the problems noted in the first two parts of this section. First, it would pro-vide the cultural context for the implementation of policies and laws aimed at marital justice. Second, it would further the realization of justice in private domains beyond the scope of the law. Third, it would diminish the fear that raising an issue of justice with one's spouse is going to be perceived as an accusation of a lack of love, because justice would be re-garded as an important marital value in its own right. Fourth, it would transform negotiations with egocentric premises into joint deliberations aiming at a shared ideal of justice. This would overcome the schizo-phrenic view of marriage on the part of women and provide a shared goal that is in principle able to unite spouses instead of separating them.

The thesis defended in this paper does not depend on any particular theoretical conception of justice. It applies to all those conceptions of jus-tice according to which the state of affairs described in the first section of this paper constitutes injustice in marriage. Regardless of one's theory of justice, if one thinks there exists a situation of structural marital injustice that should be abolished, this social goal will be achieved more easily if marriage itself is not culturally regarded as an institution within which considerations of justice have no natural place.

In emphasizing the importance of a cultural change in the dominant view of marriage, I do not wish to deny that many people already work hard to make their marriages not only emotionally strong and stable, but also just. Perhaps they do so out of a generally good sense of justice that overrules the predominant view of marriage, perhaps they have already changed their view of marriage to incorporate a concern with justice. I am not arguing that no one thinks marriage includes a commitment to justice. But the discussion here shows that, given the predominant view of mar-riage, proposals that aim at promoting justice within marriage through social reform or through enhancing women's strategic skills need to also include a change in the culturally dominant conception of marriage.

3. HOW TO COMBINE JUSTICE AND LOVE

The view I have outlined does not call for the flat-out rejection of the currently dominant conception of marriage as a matter of love and affection. The problem with this conception does not lie in its focus on love per se, but in the exclusivity of this focus. It should be changed by *adding* an explicit concern with justice to it,[25] not by replacing affection with justice. But this proposal raises a number of questions, to which I now turn. It might be thought that matters are not really so simple, and that there are various reasons for thinking that love and justice cannot be combined so easily.

Acts of Love

First, someone might ask: Doesn't love sometimes call for sacrifices, for attending to the particular needs of the loved other in a way that would require one person to go against her or his self-interest for the benefit of the other? Or put differently, does a concern with justice leave any room for spontaneous acts of love?

These questions can be answered by pointing out that there is nothing inherently unjust about a selfless act of love that stems from a genuine voluntary choice, a decision made while the spouse was free to decide otherwise had she wanted to.[26] Given the social expectations regarding selfless acts of women, and given that women may be forced in practice to give in to arrangements that put them at a disadvantage, it may sometimes be hard to decide whether particular acts are really done freely and voluntarily. But even if the line between free and coerced decisions may in some instances be hard to draw, this does not invalidate the general point that a concern with marital justice is compatible with acts that go beyond what justice requires.

A Breakdown of Marriage?

More fundamentally, it might be objected that emphasizing justice within marriage is a structural threat to the strength of marriages. Some conservative critics have assumed that current cultural trends—the decline of tradition and the increasing pressures to choose one's own form of life autonomously—lead straightforwardly to a "breakdown of the family," and that we had better brace ourselves for a time dominated by cold egoism. They charge that marriage is increasingly reduced to a contract between calculating individuals who are merely pursuing their own interests and who are ready to divorce as soon as they do not personally benefit enough from it.[27] For these critics, the conception of marriage I have outlined here, with its post-traditionalist premise of equality and justice between spouses, might seem to exemplify or even exacerbate the slide into egoism.

This objection, however, rests on a false understanding of how justice can be implemented in marriage. According to the view I have outlined above, good marriages are *not* thought of as operating purely through self-interested, profit-oriented negotiation. Whoever thinks that *all* mutually binding agreements between equals take the form of egoistically premised contracts is a captive of that very market way of thinking that is alleged to be a threat. The model suitable for marriages is one of cooperation between individuals who recognize each other as equals in a shared pursuit, not a model of negotiation between rational economic agents maximizing their individual profit. Such a cooperative model stands in sharp contrast to profit-oriented market contracts.

Claiming Rights

Nevertheless, a critic may still have misgivings about what introducing justice into the ideal of marriage would mean in practice. In "When Justice Replaces Affection: The Need for Rights,"[28] Jeremy Waldron defends the view that "normal" spouses interact on the basis of affection, not considerations of justice, and that appeals to justice create an atmosphere of hostility and separation. In this article, Waldron develops two compelling arguments for the need for legal rights. First, he argues that "the strength and security of the marriage commitment in the modern world depend in part on there being an array of legalistic rights and duties that the partners know they can fall back on, if ever their mutual affection fades."[29] Second, Waldron stresses that legal rights are necessary to make marriage possible in the first place, and to make it possible even in a situation in which a couple is alienated from the "affective bonds of existing attachments and community."[30] In both cases, Waldron convincingly shows that legal rights are necessary because one cannot always count on affection.

But Waldron also defends a broader claim, namely, that appealing to one's rights can be taken as a sign that "something has gone wrong" with marital affection, and that this is true not merely for the appeal to contractual and other legal rights, but also for the "general idea" of a right.[31] Given the examples he mentions, this notion seems to include moral rights. Ideally, according to Waldron, spouses interact on the basis of love and intimacy. When one spouse claims his or her "*right* to be relieved of child care or domestic chores once in a while," or a "*right* to pursue a career" this means the "opening of hostilities; and it is to acknowledge that other warmer bonds of kinship, affection, and intimacy can no longer hold." According to Waldron, equality and equity should instead be the "natural outcome" of the intimate and mutual concern and respect of the partners.[32]

One can subscribe to Waldron's view on the importance of legal rights without sharing his broader claim concerning the "unpleasantness" of any rights claims within marriage. The relationship between justice and affection within marriage can be much more harmonious than Waldron's discussion suggests. Objecting to one's spouse—"It's my turn" (to be relieved of child care, to pursue a career opportunity, and so on)—constitutes a claim of a right, but it does not necessarily constitute an "opening of hostilities" or an announcement that the bonds of affection and intimacy "can no longer hold." For one thing, if one's spouse finds it important to arrange matters justly, she or he may grant the claim and be happy to have this pointed out, or, if she or he doubts the validity of the claim, ask for further discussion. Even if it were true, as Waldron suggests, that equality is the "natural outcome" of the affection-guided interaction of spouses, one cannot always count on affection. Involuntary oversight, lapses of attention, or temporary insensitivity may call for correction by a claim of justice. What matters here, however, is that if spouses care about achieving a just marriage, claims of justice can even be *welcomed* ("I'm glad you mentioned it"), instead of having to be interpreted as the opening of hostilities and the end of affection.[33]

Thus, the response to Waldron can be the same as the response to the conservative critics. Although the two objections come from different directions, they are both premised on the same false dilemma between a purely sentimental model of marital interaction and an egocentric and atomistic model of fairness. If, instead, one conceives of marital justice as a shared pursuit on the part of both spouses, justice and love are very well compatible. Thus, there is no reason to assume that a concern with justice leads to a breakdown of marriage, and no reason to assume that such a concern has to "replace" (instead of add to) love and affection.

Motivation

John Hardwig has voiced a similar objection. But whereas Waldron focuses on the act of claiming a right, Hardwig examines the character of agents' motivations. Hardwig claims that doing something for a loved one out of a sense of obligation "taints" the act and makes it "perhaps even unacceptable." He says: "In fact, my responsibilities in personal relationships cannot be fulfilled out of a sense of obligation without seriously undermining the whole relationship or revealing thereby that it is not what we had hoped and wanted it to be."[34] Insofar as a commitment to a just marriage entails that spouses sometimes act out of a sense of obligation, Hardwig's claim is also directed against the thesis I am defending.

Hardwig does not substantiate his claim with the kind of empirical evidence from psychology that it would seem to call for, to show that acting out of obligation really does undermine relationships. But there is also a philosophical reason to doubt the truth of Hardwig's claims. While it seems plausible that if *all* the good things one does for one's spouse are done only from a sense of obligation, it is unlikely that one loves him or her, this does not imply that if *some* acts are done from duty this shows the absence of love. Few if any of us are saints, and many of us are pulled by our own interests at times. If a good sense of justice can straighten us out at such times, this is far preferable—both from the perspective of the health of the relationship and from a moral perspective—to following one's egoistic inclinations. As long as there is enough evidence of genuine love, it is unclear why this would seriously undermine a relationship. The extent to which it does, and the point at which the proportion of acts done from duty alone becomes a problem, are empirical issues. Here it suffices to say that while Hardwig's worry may be justified when *all* behavior is motivated by general obligation, he has not shown that *some* cases of such behavior in a given marriage context are problematic.

Of course, the fact that a sense of obligation sometimes needs to set us straight does not imply that doing what is just is always doing something one does not desire to do. What is just may very well coincide with one's spontaneous and loving inclinations. Doing the right thing need not be a burden, and being just toward someone one loves may often be easy.

Particularity

A second worry brought up by Hardwig is that doing something for a loved one out of a sense of duty or out of an obligation to respect her rights violates her particularity. If one could say to one's spouse: "And I would have done the same for anyone in your situation," says Hardwig, "that would only make matters worse." "Rights are general or universal in the sense that anyone in a similar situation can claim the same rights, whereas my relationship to those I am close to is not general or universal, and it cannot be impersonally defined."[35]

Yet, here too, the argument is unconvincing. For one thing, not everyone is "in your situation," since this means in the situation of being my spouse. And being my spouse means sharing with me a sphere of decision making and responsibility that we do not share with others. How far this sphere extends can vary, but if a couple decides to live in one household, for instance, they will have to find a just way to keep it clean. If they decide to split domestic chores evenly, that does not mean that they have to do the same with everyone else in the neighborhood. Nor does it mean that if they divorce they will necessarily have to divide up domestic labor in the same way with their spouse in a second marriage, since their new partners may have relevantly different needs and interests that have to be taken into consideration. Thus, saying "I would have done the same for everyone in your situation" does not mean that I would have done the same for everyone or that I would treat everyone else the same as you.

This leads to a further point, namely, Hardwig's claim that in trying to be just toward my spouse I have to disregard the unique particularity of his or her person. The situation is quite the opposite. Unless one defends a notion of justice as a mathematically even distribution of goods regardless of the needs and desires of the individuals in question, the very specific personality traits, desires, needs, and values of both spouses are crucial in their attempt to find out what is just. Suppose the company my spouse works for requires him to relocate to a big city or quit, and I only thrive in vast, uninhabited spaces. If financial survival and the existence of other options leave us some choice, it is relevant to know how important this job is to him and mine to me, what each of us finds important for a happy, fulfilling life (a career, more time with the children, life in a city, life in the mountains, proximity of family members, and so on), for us to work out a just solution. Thus, it is of the utmost importance to be sensitive to the uniqueness of one's spouse and to the details of the relationship.

Tensions

It is now possible to address a final issue. This is the worry that love and justice can and should coexist within marriage, but that there is an unavoidable tension between these two principles. This is the view defended by Axel Honneth in "Between Justice and Affection: The Family as a Field of Moral Disputes." Although he draws on Waldron's paper, Honneth indicates in the title of his article that he is more positive about the role of appeals to justice within the family. On his view, the ideal of the family as a sphere governed purely by affection is no longer tenable in the modern era: While the affective bond is certainly essential, legal and moral principles of justice are also necessary to protect vulnerable family members. But Honneth conceives the two orientations of the modern marriage (love and justice) as being in *tension*, or even in *conflict* with each other. The family is a "social sphere in which both moral orientations collide permanently."[36] In order for this tragic predicament not to become destructive, family members must themselves set a "limit" to the scope and validity of principles of justice.[37]

It may be hard to justify setting such limits, but I will not pursue that criticism here, since the problem can be dealt with at a more fundamental level. Honneth's view is more tragic than necessary. The reason he has to conceive of the principles of justice and affection as colliding is that he does not conceive of principles of justice as operating *within* the marriage, but as *external* courts of appeal. On his view, general moral rules are brought into the sphere of marriage to arbitrate in the case of conflicts. But if, according to the view defended in this article, spouses commit to striving for a just marriage (in addition to a loving marriage), they make the justice orientation their own in a way that makes it no longer appear as a rival, foreign principle that collides with their affection-based interaction.

I have argued that there is no necessary tension between justice and affection, and that a genuine commitment to a just marriage is compatible with genuine love of one's spouse. That does not imply, of course, that there are no tensions between spouses when it comes to realizing a just and loving marriage: misunderstanding may hamper their communication, occasional egoism may seduce them to present their needs in a distorted way, their love or their commitment to justice may turn out not to go very deep, after all. Such problems and the tensions resulting from them, however, are not caused by an in-principle incompatibility of justice and affection. Rather, they result from a lack of love, weakness of will, an incapacity to engage in deliberation, and so on. The fact that some (or even many) people who wish for a loving and just marriage are not able fully to realize it does not mean that the ideal is inconsistent or worthless. (After all, the same is true for the marriage ideal as we know it.) And as long as justice is regarded as a category that is not applicable to marriage, chances that marriages will be just are even slimmer. A just marriage can become a positive ideal. It can (and should) become part of the cultural view of what an ideal marriage is like, without negatively affecting the character of marriage as a relationship based on love.

4. WHY MARRY?

So far I have talked about "married couples" and not "couples" in general. The main reason for doing so is that it is precisely *marriage*—and not cohabitation or other forms of living as a couple—that is the powerful legal and cultural institution seen as ideally operating in terms of affection and love, not justice.

One could of course ask why, if the cultural and legal institution of marriage is problematic, we should not simply do away with the institution. The answer is that the legal institution of marriage can potentially fulfill a very useful role for achieving justice within marriage. Waldron is correct in pointing out that the strength and the security of marriage depend on a good legal framework. For people who wish to commit themselves to forming a stable relationship with one another, the fact that there are background guarantees that state the terms of exit may put them in a position in which they can afford to make this commitment in the first place.

Moreover, the marriage contract, in its optimal form, can function as a small-scale "constitution" for couples, stating broadly formulated ground rules of mutual support, including just marital property arrangements, rules about the integrity of the body, rules about the dissolution of the marriage in case love fails, and so on. To a large extent these ground rules can also be achieved through private contracts, establishing the functional equivalent of marriage. But as yet there is an important domain of rules a couple cannot possibly legally contract into, except through marriage as legally defined—for instance, the commitment to stay together.

I wish to add that in addition to eradicating all traces of sexism, it is necessary to do away with the heterosexism in marriage law. Lesbian and gay couples are currently excluded from the possibility of making a legal commitment to stay together, and hence from establishing such a basis for a stable long-term relationship. As William Hohengarten has convincingly shown, the legal grounds given in defense of this exclusion are inconsistent, ad hoc, and indicate an underlying extralegal preconception about the unwantedness of homosexual relationships.[38]

5. CHANGING THE IDEAL OF MARRIAGE

Changing the culturally dominant conception of marriage is no small matter, of course, but given the enormous changes in gender ideology that have taken place during this century there is no reason to think that this further step is impossible to take.

Insofar as states have just marriage laws, a shift in the public understanding of marriage could be furthered by making explicit to couples what marriage already implies. If and insofar as it is nonsexist, legal marriage already is a commitment of equals to mutual support and aid, one that embodies minimal standards of justice. In such instances, increasing the awareness among married persons of the legal content of their marriage contract can serve to promote the larger goal of changing the dominant cultural understanding of marriage to include a commitment to justice. Where marriage law is still sexist, of course, this strategy does not work. Telling marrying couples that marital rape is not a crime is not going to make them think that justice is important within marriage. To the extent that a legal system is still sexist, a shift can only be brought about by influence through the public and political spheres—that is to say, in much the same way as many of the feminist reforms so far have been achieved.

In this essay, I have argued that promoting justice within marriage requires—in addition to changes in laws and policies, and in addition to a heightened awareness of the mechanisms that produce unjust gendered patterns—a cultural reconceptualization of marriage. It requires coming to view marriage as not merely a relationship of love, but as *also* a commitment to justice.[39]

This essay first appeared in *Social Theory and Practice* 24:2 (Summer 1998): 261–81 and is used with permission of the copyright holder.

NOTES

1. See, for instance, The Roper Organization, *The 1990 Virginia Slims Opinion Poll: A 20-Year Perspective on Women's Issues* (Storrs, Conn.: The Roper Center, n.d.), 47, on the question of what people regard as "very important" in marriage. The list of possible answers the respondents could choose from is as significant as the ranking they produced. See also Rushworth Kidder, "Marriage in America," *Christian Science Monitor*, November 25, 26, 27, 29, and December 2, 1985. Especially the last part of the series, "Why Marry?" December 2, 1985, 34–35.

2. See the famous formulation in William Blackstone's *Commentaries*: "By marriage, the husband and wife are one person in law: that is, the very being or legal existence of the woman is suspended during the marriage, or at least is incorporated and consolidated into that of the husband: under whose wing, protection, and cover, she performs everything; and is therefore called in our law-french a feme-covert; is said to be covert-baron, or under the protection and influence of her husband, her baron, or lord; and her condition during her marriage is called her coverture." Sir William Blackstone, *Commentaries on the Laws of England* (Philadelphia: Welsh & Co, 1902), vol. I, 442.

3. Carole Pateman has shown the many ways in which the marriage contract was sexist and sex-centered, requiring women to give up bodily integrity. See *The Sexual Contract* (Stanford: Stanford University Press, 1988).

4. See Mill's personal declaration and protest against the existing marital law, reprinted in John Stuart Mill and Harriet Taylor Mill, *Essays on Sex Equality*, ed. Alice S. Rossi (Chicago: University of Chicago Press, 1970), 45–46. The personal marriage contract of Lucy Stone and Henry B. Blackwell is printed in *Feminism: The Essential Historical Writings*, ed. Miriam Schneir (New York: Vintage Books/Random House, 1972), 104–5.

5. One of the reasons why the marriage contract is an anomalous type of legal contract is that the parties cannot set the terms. See *Maynard v. Hill*, 125 US 190 (1887): "Other contracts may be modified, restricted, or enlarged, or entirely released upon the consent of the parties. Not so with marriage. The relation once formed, the law steps in and holds the parties to various obligations and liabilities." In essence this is still the case. Many states have adopted laws to allow prenuptial agreements in which spouses determine some of the details of their marriage agreement. But the state still determines the bounds within which this freedom exists.

6. On the development of this view of marriage (and on the contradictions philosophers defending it involved themselves in), see Susan Moller Okin, "Women and the Making of the Sentimental Family," *Philosophy and Public Affairs* 11 (1981): 65–88.

7. The US Supreme Court's decision in *Kirchberg v. Feenstra*, 450 US 455 (1981).

8. D. Kelly Weisberg and Susan Frelich Appleton, *Modern Family Law: Cases and Materials* (New York: Aspen, 1998), ch. 3.

9. Lalenya Weintraub Siegel, "The Marital Rape Exemption: Evolution to Extinction," *Cleveland State Law Review* 43 (1995): 351–78. See also Rebecca M. Ryan, "The Sex Right: A Legal History of the Marital Rape Exemption," *Law and Social Inquiry* 20 (1995): 941–1001.

10. Susan Moller Okin, *Justice, Gender, and the Family* (New York: Basic Books, 1989), 134–69.

11. For literature, see Laura Sanchez and Emily W. Kane, "Women's and Men's Constructions of Perceptions of Housework Fairness," *Journal of Family Issues* 17 (1996): 358–87, here 359.

12. See, for instance, Arlie Hochschild, *The Second Shift: Working Parents and the Revolution at Home* (New York: Viking, 1989).

13. See Lenore Weitzman's influential study, *The Divorce Revolution: The Unexpected Social and Economic Consequences for Women and Children in America* (New York: Free Press, 1985). See also Okin, *Justice, Gender, and the Family*, 160–67, who also discusses the fact that although Weitzman's study has been challenged and women's and men's economic situations after divorce do not diverge as much as she has suggested, the general tendency noted by Weitzman certainly exists.

14. This is only a partial explanation. The full explanation also needs to take into account the fact that women are socialized more than men to *want* to engage in the nurture and care of children and to be competent to do so.

15. Sociological evidence shows that the more women are dependent within marriage, the less they can afford to perceive an unequal division of labor as unfair. Sanchez and Kane (op. cit.) show that "men's power may, to some extent, encourage women to accept men's preferences and to view the gendered division of labor as fair" (363), and that conversely, "[t]he more women feel that they would be better off without their current union the more likely they are to perceive the division of labor as unfair to themselves" (379).

16. Jeremy Waldron, "When Justice Replaces Affection: The Need for Rights," in *Liberal Rights: Collected Papers 1981–1991* (Cambridge: Cambridge University Press, 1993), 370–91, here 372–73. Examples from child care and domestic chores indicate that Waldron is not merely speaking of legal claims, but also of moral claims of justice.

17. Okin suggests "social reforms, including changes in public policies and reforms of family law" as the mechanisms to help work toward a solution to the injustices of gender: *Justice, Gender, and the Family*, 172.

18. Ibid., 100, 107, 171, 176. Will Kymlicka and J. S. Russell each have pointed out that Okin's justification of equal sharing on the grounds that it leads to "a more complete *human* personality than has hitherto been possible" (107) presupposes a notion of the good that stands in tension with the Rawlsian elements in her work: Will Kymlicka, "Rethinking the Family," *Philosophy and Public Affairs* 20 (1991): 77–97; J.S. Russell, "Okin's Rawlsian Feminism? Justice in the Family and Another Liberalism," *Social Theory and Practice* 21 (1995): 397–426.

19. Okin, *Justice, Gender, and the Family*, 134–169, 183.

20. Scott M. Myers and Alan Booth show that a retiring husband's expecting his wife's continued household services, even if she is still working, is an important

factor in a decline of marital satisfaction after men's retirement: "Men's Retirement and Marital Quality," *Journal of Family Issues* 17 (1996): 336–57. For a comprehensive discussion of the factors influencing women's contentment with the division of labor in their families, see Brenda Major, "Gender, Entitlement, and the Distribution of Family Labor," *Journal of Social Issues* 49 (1993): 141–59, esp. 149–54.

21. This is a matter of emphasis. Mahony supports reform-oriented laws and policies: cf. 190–214.

22. Rhona Mahony, *Kidding Ourselves: Breadwinning, Babies, and Bargaining Power* (New York: Basic Books, 1995), 6.

23. This strategy is only open to women who have reason to think they have qualifications that will make them economically secure. Mahony's book speaks here most directly to the well-educated. Working poor women in minimum-wage jobs cannot afford this decision.

24. Mahony, *Kidding Ourselves*, 57–59.

25. For an excellent discussion of the integration of considerations of care and justice, see Marilyn Friedman, *What Are Friends For? Feminist Perspectives on Personal Relationships and Moral Theory* (Ithaca, N.Y.: Cornell University Press, 1993).

26. A similar point has been hinted at by Martha Nussbaum: "Real generosity and real love, we would insist, should at least be just; and it seems right to demand of the family that it meet the basic requirements of fairness, no matter what higher ends it pursues." Martha Nussbaum, "Justice For Women!" *The New York Review of Books*, October 8 (1992): 43–48, here 43.

27. See, for instance, David Blankenhorn, "American Family Dilemmas," in *Rebuilding the Nest: A New Commitment to the American Family*, ed. David Blankenhorn, Steven Bayne, and Jean Bethke Elshtain (Milwaukee Wisc.: Family Service America, 1990), 3–25; and Robert N. Bellah, "The Invasion of the Money World," in *Rebuilding the Nest*, 227–36.

28. See above, n. 16.

29. Waldron, "When Justice Replaces Affection," 373–74.

30. Ibid., 376.

31. Ibid., 372.

32. Ibid., 373.

33. This is also the point of the written agreements used by some couples to make the domestic division of tasks explicit. These texts are usually intended as a standard to which the spouses want to be held.

34. John Hardwig, "Should Women Think in Terms of Rights?" in *Feminism & Political Theory*, ed. Cass R. Sunstein (Chicago: University of Chicago Press, 1990), 53–67, here 55 (orig. publ. *Ethics* 94 (1984): 441–55).

35. Ibid., 55–56.

36. Axel Henneth, "Zwischen Gerechtigkeit und affektiver Bindung: Die Familie im Brennpunkt moralischer Kontroversen," *Deutsche Zeitschrift für Philosophie* 43 (1995): 989–1004, here 999.

37. Ibid., 998–1004.

38. William M. Hohengarten, "Same-Sex Marriage and the Right of Privacy," *The Yale Law Journal* 103 (1994): 1495–531.

39. I wish to thank Joel, Herbert, and Phyllis Anderson for valuable comments on an earlier draft of this paper, and for the many other ways in which they have helped me develop my thoughts on the topics here discussed.

3

✛

Mutuality, Reason, and Family Policy

Don Browning

Many Americans believe that an ethic of mutuality or equal regard should characterize marriage and family relations. But some people on the political and religious right do not hold to this ethic. Furthermore, the various models of reason that we apply to marriage and family policy are not equally capable of justifying the importance of the mutual or equal-regard marriage and family. This is true for the family policy of society as a whole; it is also true for the church's approach to families and what it promotes for families both within its own inner life *and* in its public witness to the wider society.

To ask about the role of reason in family policy requires a discussion of a particular form of reason, i.e., the nature of practical reason. But there are competing models of practical reason. They are not equally capable of defending mutuality in marriage and family while also determining what is good for both families and the wider society. In fact, some of the most popular modern models of reason either sacrifice mutuality or give inadequate accounts of the goods that families should achieve and that public policy should promote.

I will review three models of practical reason—teleological, deontological, and hermeneutic views. I grant that these unfamiliar terms for the three forms of practical reason are intimidating. But their meaning can be, and will be, defined in this article. And the effort to understand them is worthwhile. Before attempting this, I will state my argument. I maintain that in spite of the popularity, both in society and in the church, of teleological and deontological forms of practical reason, hermeneutical practical reason is more consistent with the traditions of the church and better able to ground mutuality in families for both the church and public policy.

43

TELEOLOGICAL VIEWS OF MORAL REASON

To understand the moral discourse of the contemporary family debate, it pays to attend to what distinguishes these three models of practical reason. Two of the most popular modern teleological views are utilitarianism and ethical egoism. These two modes of reason are used increasingly by modern law, the health sciences, sociology, and psychology in their thinking about family and marriage. They both see moral reason as calculative; moral action is a matter of calculating whether our actions produce more nonmoral (or premoral) good over nonmoral evil for either self, other, or community.[1]

By nonmoral or premoral, I do not mean immoral. Rather, these concepts signal ways we use the word good to refer to things and qualities that are pleasant, fulfilling, or essential for survival, but not moral in the full sense of the word. Food, wealth, health, transportation, shelter and the exercise of our capabilities are goods in the premoral sense.[2] But they are not moral goods as such; it would not be intelligible to speak of a moral steak, a moral automobile, or even moral health. These things can be either moral or immoral depending on the intentions we bring to our use of them, but they are not morally good in themselves.

Teleologists tell us that what makes an act moral is not only the goods being promoted, but the orientation of our wills in pursuing such goods. According to modern teleologists, there are two basic ways to orient our wills morally while pursuing the nonmoral goods of life. One way is to will the greatest amount of nonmoral good possible, primarily for oneself. The second is to act as to bring about the greatest good for the largest number of people. The first approach is called ethical egoism; the second is known as some form of utilitarianism.[3]

Increasingly, either ethical egoism or utilitarianism is used by government, business, the health professions, and think tanks to guide thinking about the functions of marriage and family. No longer are these leadership domains informed by the great marriage and family passages of the Bible—Genesis 1 and 2, Matthew 19, I Corinthians 7, or Ephesians 5—as they once were. It must be acknowledged, however, that increasingly one hears these two modes of practical reason used in the churches as well.

Take utilitarianism: most contemporary theological and philosophical critiques of utilitarianism have judged it as morally defective. If a policy produces the most good for the greatest number—for instance, the majority of families—utilitarians must deem it as morally justifiable even if large numbers of people suffer and many are treated unequally (without mutuality and equal regard). Nor does ethical egoism pass the test. The ethical egoist may always tell the truth, appear to treat others with respect, and fulfill promises, but he does so always because he believes such behaviors pay off for his own well-being. When his or her good conflicts with that of another, the ethical egoist must hope that the other will yield in his or her favor. Many marriage and family advice manuals and much of the field of family health and marriage education are mainly predicated on appeals to what is good for the individuals involved. Mutuality and teleological thinking in the form of ethical egoism are finally in conflict with one another.

Much of present public discussion about marriage and families is proceeding in terms of these two teleological approaches. For instance, ethical egoism was behind the casual acceptance by the social sciences of marriage and family disruption in the 1970s and 1980s. Sociologist Jessie Bernard contended that divorce and out-of-wedlock births would not be damaging but instead would provide more freedom and self-actualization, especially for women, for whom marriage, she held, was not a particularly good deal anyway.[4] Her evaluations unwittingly came from an ethical-egoist view of moral reason.

On the other hand, when in the 1990s social scientists began showing the on-average negative consequences to society of divorce, nonmarital births, and single parenthood, the logic of evaluation shifted to a kind of utilitarianism. The overall good of the community became the framework for judgment; particular individuals might be better off, but on the whole family disruption was contributing to the growing impoverishment of mothers and the social disadvantage of their children.

Sara McLanahan and Gary Sandefur's research on the effects on children of divorce, nonmarital births, single parenthood, and stepparenthood was an exercise in both ethical-egoist and utilitarian thinking. In their *Growing up with a Single Mother* (1994), McLanahan and Sandefur reported that children raised apart from both biological parents were two to three times more likely to have difficulty in school, have problems in getting a job, fail in establishing a family, and become single parents themselves.[5] Income made a difference but cut the percentages only by one half. Since nearly 50 percent of all children spend at least three years in a single-parent household, their statistics could be interpreted to say that family disruption is not good for your individual child (ethical egoism) and not good for the overall health of society (utilitarianism). These assessments were partially driven by the data but were partially a product of the model of moral reason brought to the data.

I am not suggesting that there is never a rightful place in ecclesial or public discourse for appeals to what is good for individuals or what is, on average, good for society. My point is that these moral justifications can never successfully stand alone if one wishes to act in accord with the ethic of mutuality or equal regard.

MORAL REASON AND MARRIAGE

Not only have these two teleological views played roles in the evaluation of family disruption, they have influenced recent justifications of the institution of marriage. Linda Waite of the University of Chicago has collected research showing that marriage pays. In an important 1995 article and her recent book *The Case for Marriage* (2000), she catalogues the advantages of marriage. For instance, married people live longer, have fewer heart attacks, have better psychological and physical health, have more satisfactory sex, and (most surprising of all) acquire more wealth than do never-married or divorced individuals.[6] This is true for both husbands and wives, even though marriage is slightly less beneficial for women than men. This view is far different from the one propagated by Jessie Bernard in the 1970s.

Waite's research and other studies like it are used by marriage and family educators as a new modern justification for marriage. Marriage, the logic goes, is good for your health, so like exercise, clean water, good air, and a fat-free diet, it is something you should pursue. And just as smoking, excessive drinking, and too much sun are unhealthy and to be avoided, divorce, singleness, and a disrupted family life should be shunned as well. The case for marriage as a health value is even being advanced by national governments as can be seen in the English Labour Government 1998 Green Paper on the family[7] and recent stances advanced by government documents in Australia, Canada, and now in the United States with President Bush's proposal for government-supported marriage education.[8]

But utilitarian and ethical egoist appeals that run through such admirable research as that of Professor Waite have their problems from the standpoint of the ethic of mutuality and equal regard. They tend to defend and promote marriage by demonstrating its empirical goods; they do not, as such, argue for equal-regard marriages. This raises the question, will any marriage do, even if genuine mutuality is absent? Should we settle for a high general average of physical health and wealth even though they might come with the pains of indifference, domination, or outright inequality? The logic and assessments of ethical egoism and utilitarianism do not answer these questions.

MARRIAGE AND THE LANGUAGE OF JUSTICE

Ethical egoism or utilitarianism are not the only modern forms of moral rationality. There are also deontological views associated with the great Enlightenment thinker Immanuel Kant and contemporary philosophers such as John Rawls, Jürgen Habermas, Susan Okin, and moral development psychologist Lawrence Kohlberg. Deontological views of moral reason have influenced Protestant liberalism and can be detected in recent mainline statements on sexuality and the family. Deontological moral reason holds that the morally good and right can be defined independently of the increase of nonmoral goods[9] such as health, wealth, pleasure, physical comfort, and other such goods important to modern teleologists. An act can be moral even if it leads to the decrease of these goods, such as is the case when telling the truth threatens the well-being of both ourselves and loved ones.

The core of deontological moral reason involves respect for persons as ends.[10] Kant defined personhood as the capacity for rationality. The Kantian view of moral reason conveys what Lawrence Kohlberg called a kind of "reversible logic"; it means respecting the rational agency of the other just as you expect the other to respect your own rational agency. Kantianism is a form of mutuality and equal regard.

This ethic has had a powerful influence on contemporary moral reasoning about marriage and family. However, in respecting another person as a center of moral agency, some people have interpreted this to mean accepting, and possibly even approving, whatever pattern she or he follows in the marriage, family, and sexual areas of life. This is an ethic of tolerance typical of politically liberal societies. There is no way to make comparative judgments, this view holds, about one set of goods in relation to another; this is a matter of individual choice. To respect is to accept and to accept is to approve. Kant did not have the last two steps in mind in his formulation of the categorical imperative, but Kantianism has had difficulty keeping reversible justice from drifting in this direction.

There is a reason for this. Deontological moral reason brackets, sets aside, or deemphasizes the very concern that defines teleological ethics, i.e., a concern with the nonmoral or premoral good. It has no way of handling the question of relative goods. A deontological ethic of the Kantian variety cannot tell us why some forms of human life lead to more flourishing than others; in fact, it cannot even define the nature of human flourishing. It can define justice as equal respect, but it has difficulty defining the goods that justice should equally distribute and pursue. The fairness demanded by an ethic of mutuality and equal regard are well protected by a Kantian ethic, but the good and goods also required for genuine mutuality are neglected.

Kantian deontology, however, has had an impact on contemporary Protestant studies of marriage, family, and sexuality, especially in the 1991 study titled *Keeping Body and Soul Together* prepared for the General Assembly of the Presbyterian Church (USA). Central to the argument of this document is the idea of "justice-love." "To do justice-love," the authors tell us, "means seeking right-relatedness with others and working to set right all wrong relations, especially distorted power dynamics of domination and subordination."[11] Or again, "Justice as a formal standard by which to measure relationships . . . is deeply rooted in the biblical and theological heritage."[12] In these definitions, the emphasis is on justice and the absence of domination; other issues about premoral good and human flourishing are set aside. The report uses this ethic of respect to argue for a pluralism of sexual arrangements—most notably the possibility of sexual expressions outside of marriage and in gay and lesbian relationships as long as they are just and devoid of domination and manipulation.

Allow me to bracket these two issues; my concern is not with nonmarital sex or gay and lesbian relations as such. My objective is to illustrate a type of moral reasoning often used in the contemporary American ecclesial and public debate over marriage and family. It is interesting to observe how prominent Kantian deontology is in the Presbyterian report even though never explicitly invoked. In the spirit of this form of moral sensibility, the study sets aside the teleological question of the premoral goods to be served by sexual activity. There is no discussion whatsoever of children, thought by much of Western philosophy and theology as one of the great goods of sexuality. There is an affirmation of sexuality as a gift of God; in this, at least, the unitive and pleasurable goods of sexuality are acknowledged. And indeed, there is ample justification in the Christian tradition to make these affirmations.

The potential conflict, however, between the good of sexual expression and other goods of life such as health, wealth, education, and children is not addressed in this report. The relation of sexual activity to disease, unwanted pregnancies, poverty, and the disruption of a host of other important human goods is ignored. There is no mention of the new social science information on the negative personal and social consequences of divorce, single parenthood, fatherlessness, or the strains endured by stepfamilies. The morally right action, the document argues, is basically to respect all persons in their sexual choices as long as they appear to avoid domination and exploitation. The theological and biblical justifications for this ethic, it should be pointed out, are difficult to find in *Keeping Body and Soul Together*. The ethic of justice-love is mainly grounded in the idea of hospitality to the stranger—the idea that in visiting, feeding, and clothing the stranger one is doing this as well to Jesus himself (Mt. 25:31–46).[13]

There is, it should be acknowledged, some wisdom in the ethic of justice-love. It is close, although not identical, to the love ethic of mutuality and equal regard that we discuss and amplify in our book *From Culture Wars to Common Ground: Religion and the American Family Debate* (1997, 2000), the summary book of the Religion, Culture, and Family Project.[14] But the idea of justice-love fails to provide a fully Christian ethic for either ecclesial or public family policy. It cannot resolve the reality of conflicting relative goods. It is both ethically rational and fully Christian to believe that one can respect another person or group (indeed, be in solidarity with them) but hold as well that how they have organized the sexual and procreative goods of life seriously conflict with, if not profoundly suppress, other fundamental goods. An adequate ethic of mutuality and equal regard should be able to address *both* the question of *justice* and the question of the *relative goods* likely to be actualized in various marital and family arrangements.

In short, moral rationality applied to marriage and family has two tasks, not just one. *It has the task of determining justice and it has the task of assessing relative goods.* There is a place for both the logic of the deontologist and the logic of the teleologist—both a moral logic that respects persons and a teleological logic that weighs, hierarchicalizes, and actualizes competing goods. Is there a way of bringing these two styles of moral rationality together? Is there a way of melding them into a single view of moral thinking that does not keep them in separate corners ready to knock each other down at the sound of the bell?

Paul Ricoeur is among a group of contemporary religiously minded philosophers who believe that there is a way to bring them together. He does it by reinterpreting the Golden Rule. We generally say that the Golden Rule entails the formal rule of doing unto others as you would have them do unto you. This formulation puts the accent on showing respect and reversible justice to both other and self. But this formal interpretation absorbs the Golden Rule into Kantian deontology, which is often done even in the recognized literature of moral philosophy and moral theology. But Ricoeur believes in interpreting the Golden Rule in its ancient Jewish context; when this is done, he interprets it to say that you should do good to the other as you would have the other do good to you. This formulation turns respect for the other into something much more active; it involves not only treating the other as an end but also actively helping the other to weigh, prioritize, and realize the goods of life.[15] My coauthors and I in *From Culture Wars to Common Ground* followed Ricoeur's formulation in our love ethic of mutuality and equal regard.[16] In following this more biblical tradition, we bring aspects of both teleology and deontology together. We do this, however, by subordinating teleological judgments about the relative good to deontological judgments about the just, the fair, and the right. In this, we are at odds with much of the utilitarian logic of contemporary public policy as well as the thin ethics of justice that one finds in many quarters, including the Presbyterian *Keeping Body and Soul Together*. It is very unlikely that this report kept body and soul together since it was so profoundly unable to keep together justice and the goods of life.

But even within Ricoeur's view of the Golden Rule, goods can often conflict; the willingness to actualize goods for both other and self does not tell us how to weigh and prioritize them. This means, as Ricoeur reminds us, that even within relationships of mutual respect and mutual promotion of the good, there must be exercises in what the Greeks called *phronesis*—the capacity to weigh, balance, prioritize, and resolve the violence of conflicting goods. Some goods of life are more compatible with a wide range of other goods, whereas some other goods needlessly trample and extinguish their competitors. For instance, the good of wealth, if pursued relentlessly, can trample the good of health. *Where do we turn, then, to discover the scales of premoral values that should guide phronesis or practical reason? Where do we turn to make mutuality serve both justice and the nonmoral goods of life?*

HERMENEUTIC REASON AND THE FAMILY DEBATE

I will advance two answers: 1) we must turn first to tradition and, 2) only later turn to the social sciences. To amplify these points, I turn to a discussion of the third model of moral reason—the idea of *hermeneutic moral rationality.*

By using the word hermeneutic, I am invoking the traditions of the continental philosophers Hans-Georg Gadamer and Paul Ricoeur as well as the work of the American philosopher Richard Bernstein.[17] From a hermeneutic perspective, moral reason is primarily an interpretive process. It begins with tradition; in fact, it holds that all reason is embedded in tradition. Gadamer and Ricoeur tell us that long before the teleologist starts calculating goods and long before the deontologist exercises judgments of reversible and universal justice for self and other, they both are deeply oriented by prior religiocultural traditions. These traditions provide practical reason with surrounding narratives about the meaning of life—narratives that also are *thick*. They contain hierarchies of premoral goods, general principles of justice such as the Golden Rule or Neighbor Love and more concrete patterns of practices and rules. Hermeneutic philosophy tells us that we first are conventional moral thinkers; we are born and socialized into traditions and largely live life by following their moral patterns. According to hermeneutic models, we start thinking critically about moral issues when our traditional ethical patterns are seriously challenged.

Hermeneutic models of ethics see moral reason going through at least four stages. First, we should ask, What is happening in the situation that is bringing about the crisis? How should we interpret what is happening? Second, we should ask, What are the inherited ideals that have governed our understanding of the situation and that will provide the likely preliminary answers to issues the situation raises? Third, once we understand our traditions and its ideals as well as possible, we should ask, Are they true? Can my inherited ideals stand up to criticism and various tests? Finally, once our ideals are correctly understood and tested, we should ask, How can the original problematic situation be addressed and, perhaps, transformed? This view of hermeneutic moral reason is a synthesis of the best aspects of the hermeneutic philosophies of Gadamer, Ricoeur, and Bernstein. It is a view that I have summarized and promoted in my *A Fundamental Practical Theology* (1991).[18]

Neither the utilitarian, the ethical egoist, nor the deontologist finds a prominent place for religious and cultural traditions. In fact, this tells us much about the context of the contemporary crisis of marriage and family, the *first* step of hermeneutic reason. Marriage and family are increasingly being guided by individualistic and utilitarian values and moral logics. These two modern views of practical reason are, quite frankly, culturally and religiously nihilistic; follow them and one will short-circuit, if not totally disregard, the role of tradition in moral thinking. This is what has happened in the social sciences and in policy think tanks that follow one or other of the dominant modern teleological models. The neglect of tradition also happens to the deontologist, as is the case with much of political and religious liberalism; the principle of reversible justice is used to throw into the trash heap of useless relics all history, tradition, and religious classics that seem to contradict this Kantian philosophical moral guide. *But we lose more than the wisdom and insights of the past if we follow this course. If my argument so far is correct, we lose the delicate balance between the just and the good that mutuality finally demands.*

Second, to understand hermeneutic models of moral reason, one must understand Gadamer's theory of the classic. The ideals, i.e., the aspirational symbols and goals of moral and religious traditions, depend on classics. These are the key texts, monuments, and actions that are returned to time and again because they reveal a central truth about the human condition.[19] In the case of marriage and family, the classics of the Western marriage and family tradition are found in the first two chapters of Genesis. The priestly theology of Genesis 1:27 tells us that God created humankind in His image and that both male and female carry this image. In the very next verse, God gives the responsibilities of parenthood and economic stewardship (procreation and dominion) *equally to both male and female*; God instructs both man and woman to "Be fruitful and multiply . . . and have dominion" over the fish, birds, and every moving thing on earth (Gen. 1:28).[20]

It is stunning to notice that in these few verses, we have a recasting of insights from both deontological and teleological models of moral reason. The ground of respect for persons is established in these verses, based not on human rationality, as Kant would have it, but on the image of God in all humans, both male and female. Furthermore, the grounds of respect in marriage and family are established as a narrative about God's intentions for creation. This is the ontological grounding of mutuality in the Jewish and Christian traditions, and hence for much of the fundamental mythos that has informed Western societies. In these verses as well, we find insights associated with teleological forms of reason, i.e., the realization of the goods of life. In this passage, this has to do with the goods of procreation and the goods of economic activity. According to this idealized story, these goods are also made available to both male and female. Hence, this story tells us that equality and justice do not stand in isolation from other aspects of life; they are based on God's creation of humans in God's image, a truth that functions to empower both males and females to pursue life's basic goods. These passages are the classics that have shaped much of our cultural and legal traditions about male and female relations.[21] Recent research shows that these idealized statements were not always mirrored in everyday androcentric Hebrew life, but they doubtless did function to raise new possibilities for marriage and family. And they certainly did this for succeeding generations of interpreters.[22]

But there is more. Men and women, according to the Genesis narrative, are not only entitled to joint and equal economic and reproductive opportunities and responsibilities, they also are commanded to be in communion with one another. The Yahwist theology of Genesis 2:18 gives us the words, "It is not good that the man should be alone; I will make him a helper as his partner." And in Genesis 2:24, we hear the classic words that have shaped Judaism's, Christianity's, and Islam's understanding of the unitive goals of marriage: "Therefore a man leaves his father and mother and clings to his wife, and they become one flesh." These passages are repeated by Jesus in Matthew 19:6 and Mark 10:6 and have been subject to endless commentary, giving them all the more the status of classic texts.

Several observations about these classic passages should be mentioned. These texts keep the unitive goods of marriage and family in tension with the procreative and economic goods. This tension has continued throughout the history of Christian interpretation, with the procreative goal sometimes seen as dominant while at other times the unitive was viewed as supreme. Seldom in the history that interpreted these scriptural classics, however, were the procreative and unitive completely separated from one another. In these classic narratives, justice-love is about the ordering of other goods—the goods of children, the goods of economic activity, and the goods of intimacy. Furthermore, the one-flesh relation of husband and wife in these texts took precedence over the authority of the extended family. In spite of the ambiguity of the derivation of Eve from Adam's rib,

Genesis 2:24 tells us that a man leaves his patriarchally controlled extended family and cleaves to his wife, thus differentiating the conjugal couple from the father's household and clan. The one-flesh mutuality of the conjugal couple becomes more central than the power and authority of the clan or extended family.

The continuity between Genesis 2:24, the synoptic gospels, and even such disputed classics as Ephesians 5:21–33 must be acknowledged. It is true that Ephesians never escaped completely the patriarchy of antiquity. But when compared to the honor-shame codes of the surrounding Greco-Roman world and the philosophy of male dominance found in Aristotle (whose thought provided the accepted theory of the relation of family to *polis* in Roman Hellenism),[23] even Ephesians seems to have a progressive tilt toward the ethic of mutuality and equal regard.[24] The husband and father modeled after the sacrificial love of Christ for the church fractured, although it did not completely dismantle, Greco-Roman models of male dominance. Even here, however, the deontological test of justice and equal regard (i.e., a touch of insight later given philosophical expression by Kant) can be found; husbands, we are told, should "love their wives as they do their own bodies" (Eph. 5:28). And once again, we hear in this passage the classic verse of Genesis 2:24: "For this reason a man will leave his father and mother and be joined to his wife, and the two will become one flesh" (Eph. 5:31).

These are the great texts that have shaped Western sensitivities about marriage and family, at least up until the very recent past. John Witte in his outstanding *From Sacrament to Contract: Marriage, Religion, and Law in the Western Tradition* (1997) shows how these texts also shaped much of Western law.[25] In addition, as Gadamer would suggest, these classic texts form for much of our culture the preunderstandings that shape our interpretations of what is happening to marriage and families today. Had our interpretive sensibilities not been shaped by these passages, we probably would not be perplexed by the doubling since 1960 of the divorce figures, the six-time increase in nonmarital births, and the worldwide explosion in the number of children raised without the presence of fathers.

To honestly fulfill the second step in hermeneutic reason, we must ask the question: do we really understand what these classics mean? This is the task of hermeneutic reason in its historical mode and often seen as the task of historical theology.[26] We often take this step far too rapidly. For instance, Promise Keepers and the Southern Baptist Church both are certain that the classic texts of the Old and New Testament teach a doctrine of male headship. Hence, these contemporary expressions of Christianity are antagonistic to the ethics of mutuality and equal regard and are at best proponents of soft patriarchy. Although nothing in the Bible ever completely escapes the pervasive patriarchy of the ancient world, the best scholarship shows that the Jesus movement and pre-Pauline Christianity were moving toward gender equality in fact as well as ideal. This equality was never fully accomplished in early Christianity, but it opened a theological agenda that remains for us to complete today.[27]

The *third* question of hermeneutic reason is this: can these texts really stand the test of critique? This is when we must return to some of the modern teleological and deontological models of moral reason, whether found implicit in theology or more explicitly visible in philosophy or the social sciences. Teleological and deontological models, with all of their historical amnesia of the classics of the past, still have their place. But, rather than standing on their own, they should be understood as clarifying and testing the classic patterns of our religiocultural heritage. Indeed, they should be understood as clarifying and extending the implicit deontological and teleological themes detectable, as I have suggested above, in the texts themselves.[28]

As both Paul Ricoeur and Robert Bellah have taught us, modern teleological and deontological moral rationality should be subservient to hermeneutic moral reason.[29] They should be seen as clarifying the ambiguities and self-deceptions that always exist in classic traditions. They also should envision their roles as testing and measuring how these classic traditions actually work in practice amidst the contingencies of changing circumstances. What does a religious narrative that says both male and female are made in the image of God mean within a wage economy in contrast to a herding or agricultural economy? What do equal rights and responsibilities for the goods of both procreation and economic stewardship mean in modern and postmodern economies in contrast to premodern ones? Hence, these modern models of moral reason should be seen as dependent on, yet exercising degrees of critical distance from, our religiocultural classics.

Answering such questions gets into the *fourth* moment of hermeneutic practical reason, the moment that deals most specifically once again with the concrete situation which gave rise to the original question stimulating the entire process. This is the place where reason has to weigh the relative goods at stake, try to actualize the highest and most comprehensive organization of goods, but do so within the framework of justice. This is what mutuality truly requires; it requires justice, but it also requires that we actively do good to one another.

I make this argument about the role of reason not only to assist with a better debate within the church about marriage and family issues but also to help with a better debate in secular society. Secular society must understand that the classics I have discussed have had pervasive influence throughout the cultural, legal, medical, and political traditions of the West. They were not simply the texts of the church; they were the classic texts of much of philosophy, much of Western law until recent decades, and most genres of Western imaginative literature. They deserve a place in our reasoning about family issues and our attempts to both ground and balance justice and the good in marriage and family.

NOTES

1. William Frankena, *Ethics* (Englewood Cliffs, NJ: Prentice-Hall, Inc., 1973), 14.
2. Ibid., 9–10.
3. Ibid., 17, 35.
4. Jessie Bernard, *The Future of Marriage* (New York: World Publishing, 1972).
5. Sara McLanahan and Gary Sandefur, *Growing up with a Single Mother* (Cambridge, MA: Harvard University Press, 1994).
6. Linda Waite, "Does Marriage Matter?" *Demography* 32, no. 4 (Nov. 1995): 438-507; Linda Waite and Maggie Gallagher, *The Case for Marriage* (New York: Doubleday, 2000).
7. *Supporting Families* (London: Home Office, 1998).
8. *To Have and to Hold* (Canberra, Australia: House of Representatives Standing Committee on Legal and Constitutional Affairs, 1998); Maggie Gallager, "Marriage and Public Policy: What Can Government Do?" *Policy Brief*, April 16, 2002, New York: Institute for American Values.
9. Frankena, *Ethics*, 16.
10. Immanuel Kant, *Foundations for the Metaphysics of Morals* (New York: The Bobbs-Merrill Co., 1959), 47.
11. *Keeping Body and Soul Together: Sexuality, Spirituality, and Social Justice*. A Document Prepared for the 203rd General Assembly of the Presbyterian Church (U.S.A.), 1991, 18.
12. Ibid., 149.
13. Ibid., 151.
14. Don Browning, Bonnie Miller-McLemore, Pamela Couture, Bernie Lyon, and Robert Franklin, *From Culture Wars to Common Ground: Religion and the American Family Debate* (Louisville, KY: Westminster John Knox Press, 1997, 2000), 274–282.
15. Paul Ricoeur, *Oneself as Another* (Chicago, IL: The University of Chicago Press, 1992), 219–227.
16. Browning, et. al., *From Culture Wars to Common Ground*, 276–277.
17. Hans-Georg Gadamer, *Truth and Method* (New York: Crossroad, 1982); Paul Ricoeur, *Hermeneutics and the Human Sciences* (Cambridge: Cambridge University Press, 1981); Richard Bernstein, *Beyond Objectivism and Relativism* (Philadelphia, PA: University of Pennsylvania Press, 1983).
18. Don Browning, *A Fundamental Practical Theology* (St. Paul, MN: Fortress Press, 1991), 47–58.
19. Gadamer, *Truth and Method*, 253–258.
20. For an engaging interpretation of Gen. 1:28, see Phyllis Trible's *God and the Rhetoric of Sexuality* (Philadelphia, PA: Fortress Press, 1978), 19.

21. See the following statement by John Collins in his "Marriage, Divorce, and Family in Second Temple Judaism," in Leo G. Perdue, Joseph Blenkinsopp, John Collins, and Carol Meyers, *Families in Ancient Israel* (Louisville, KY: Westminster John Knox Press, 1997), 127. " . . . there is no doubt that both the Priestly theology of Genesis 1 and the Yahwist theology of Genesis 2–3 were conducive to an ideal of monogamy. Both texts speak of one man and one woman. Neither envisages the dissolution of the union. Neither was a legal, prescriptive text, and they entailed no prohibition of divorce or polygamy. But in the postexilic period, these texts were prominently displayed at the beginning of the Torah, and we should expect that they would have had an effect on the formation of religious ideals, if not always on practice."

22. Perdue, "The Israelite and Early Jewish Family: Summary and Conclusions," *Families in Ancient Israel*, 189.

23. David Balch, *Let Wives Be Submissive* (Atlanta, GA: Scholars Press, 1981).

24. For a discussion of the honor-shame codes of the Greco-Roman world and how they provided a contextual background to early Christian thinking about the family, see Carolyn Osiek and David Balch, *Families in the New Testament World* (Louisville, KY: Westminster John Knox Press, 1997), 38–39.

25. John Witte, *From Sacrament to Contract: Marriage, Religion, and Law in the Western Tradition* (Louisville, KY: Westminster John Knox Press, 1997).

26. Browning, *A Fundamental Practical Theology*, 49.

27. Browning, et al., *From Culture Wars to Common Ground*, 134–141.

28. See Ricoeur's use of Kant to test, although not derive, the practices and narratives of traditional systems of ethics, *Oneself as Another*, 218–219.

29. Both the Kantian deontological test and scientific explanation are for Ricoeur products of the "distanciating" capacity of hermeneutic reason. For them to work rightly, they must first "belong" to an "effective history" shaped by "classics." See his *Hermeneutics and the Human Sciences*, 203–208. For a similar understanding of the relation of scientific explanation to hermeneutic reason, see Robert Bellah, "Social Science as Practical Reason," in *Ethics, Social Sciences, and Policy Analysis*, ed. Daniel Callahan and Bruce Jennings (New York: Plenum Press, 1983), 37–64.

4

+

Who Submits to Whom?
Submission and Mutuality
in the Family

Carolyn Osiek, RSCJ

The interaction of revelation and culture is a perpetual issue in the history of religious interpretation. To what extent do faithful and observant believers accommodate to cultural norms and are fully citizens of their world, and to what extent must they say "no" to some cultural norms or practices in order to affirm their identity as believers? In the New Testament, this issue is perhaps clearest in the refusal of John, author of the Book of Revelation, to countenance any compromise with the Jewish ritual prohibition against eating meat that had been part of temple worship of a false god (Rev 2:14, 20). This was his unalterable position in spite of the fact that earlier Paul, presumably having agreed to enforce this regulation (Acts 15:20, 29), played rather lightly with it in his advice to Corinth (1 Cor 8:1–13; 10:27–33). Within the New Testament itself, there is a difference of opinion on this problematic issue. It was not at all clear in the early church, any more than it is today, over which issues the question of Christian identity is most fully at stake.

There is no more important domain in which this perennial question arises than that of family life, lived day to day as we attempt to be faithful Christians in a world not wholly friendly to our intentions. Members of families constantly confront this tension between revelation and culture in their attempt to live a life of faith in the midst of a world that impinges on it with pressures to acquire, perform, compete, and value persons by their income and accomplishments. The family faces this tension with every decision to acquire a new house, new furnishings, entertainment, and the latest software. It also faces this tension as it works out relationships within the family: when does a family meal together, or

church attendance, or a family celebration take precedence over the interests of individual members? The democratic ideal of the community of
fully responsible persons fails even to describe a group of adults, much
less the intergenerational family. Family units and systems are usually
filled with subtle or overt power struggles, both horizontal and intergenerational. The real family is far from the ideal republic!

Whose word should prevail on the basis of legally or traditionally constituted authority is not so clear as it once was, since structures of authority are breaking down and changing nearly everywhere. In some cultures,
especially Asian and African and those that have not been wracked by
crises in traditions of authority, age is a determining factor, with the assumption of greater wisdom deserving of greater honor that comes with
it. Immigrants from cultures that have traditionally supported the authority of the elders, who come into Western cultures that do not support
such structures or to a much lesser degree, typically experience painful intergenerational clashes, and even in their home cultures social forces are
at work to undermine this traditional way. Because technology especially
is rapidly changing not only the way information is disseminated but also
how the world is perceived, the wisdom of the elders is often met more
with indifference than with trust.

Most cultural systems that attribute wisdom and consequent authority
to elders also incorporate a gender bias in favor of male authority, sometimes with explicit statements and beliefs in the superiority of males over
females, sometimes simply by endorsing cultural customs that reinforce
the power of men over women or the disparagement of women's participation in leadership. There is hardly a culture in existence even today that
does not in some way disadvantage women either politically or socially,
yet it is the stated goal of some to eliminate these disadvantages.

Increasingly in technological societies authority is invested only in
those with demonstrable experience and the power of economic control
over others. It follows that social and especially family systems that attempt to embody authority in legally constituted persons without demonstration of the ability to succeed find themselves in difficulty. It is no secret, for instance, that family authority structures in the United States are
in crisis.

Into the midst of this crisis has come in recent years a move toward the
restoration of "biblical values" through a return to consciously conservative ethics based on an earlier American frontier tradition of Gospel
preaching. A renewal of a form of radical Protestantism, often in the form
of "biblical fundamentalism," affirms that the Bible contains all that is
needed to lead a successful Christian life. Often included in that promise
of the good life are success and wealth. Often, however, a more realistic
and humble reading of the biblical text acknowledges that there is no

magic connection between faith and worldly success. Frequently included is a literal reading of New Testament familial authority structures from the so-called Household Codes of the Letters to the Ephesians and Colossians (Eph 5:22–6:9; Col 3:18–4:1). The renewal of biblical values has been a powerful force in conservative Christianity toward a renewal of authentic relationships, but it is nearly always plagued by the question of the submission of some to others on the basis of divinely constituted authority, especially in Western societies in which such submission is not seen as a virtue.

We are confronted here not only with the problem of revelation and culture, but of revelation and diverse cultures. The message embodied in an ancient Mediterranean culture in a coherent way is less successfully embodied in a contemporary Western culture. The ancient Jewish-Greco-Roman culture in which the New Testament was written held a hierarchical view of persons in society, in which those of higher birth were to be given social privilege and honor as the natural holders of authority. While they were also expected to excel in nobility of character, they did not have to demonstrate this in order to establish their credentials for leadership. As Aristotle says, some are born to rule, others to be ruled. In his view, only freeborn noble Greek males were born to rule, all others to be ruled, though in various ways: freeborn Greek wives with the enlightened guidance of republican government, children with the firmer hand of a monarch but with a view to their good upbringing into successful citizenship, slaves and barbarians with despotic authority (*Politics* 1.5.1258b, 1260a).

For elite Greeks, all others were barbarians—including Romans! The form of ethnocentrism of course shifted depending on the group at the center: for Romans, all but elite Greeks were included among barbarians; for Jews, all non-Jews were outsiders. The tendency of elite males to make of themselves the center of the universe is very ancient. The idea of social equality could be entertained among this elite group without extending it to all men. Some general notions of the fundamental equality of all males were raised by philosophers, but without much influence in popular thinking or political structures. The ancient societies of Athens and republican Rome that we honor as birthplaces of "democracy" were really oligarchies controlled by groups of elite males who among themselves sometimes practiced what might be called genuine democracy, but to the exclusion of all others.

The patronage system, more heavily practiced in imperial Rome, assured that social prominence and control remained in the hands of the few who could provide access to wealth and power for all others, their social subordinates and inferiors. This system cemented vertical relationships that kept different social classes from being isolated from one another. On the contrary, there was constant interaction because inferiors

needed to access their patrons and to form dependent patron-client relationships in order to get what they needed and wanted. Patrons, on the
other hand, relied on the support, public praise, and even labor of their
clients to maintain their social position and acclaim. At the top of the patronage ladder was the emperor, *pater patriae*, father of the fatherland,
who held ultimate power and therefore depended most keenly on the
adulation of his clients, most of the rest of the world.

Slavery was simply the roughest edge of this dependency pattern upon
which society was based. According to Aristotle, the slave possessed sufficient rationality to obey orders but not to understand. The large farms
and mines of Italy and North Africa owned by the state and by aristocratic
families depended largely on slave labor, but the agricultural system was
changing into one using tenant farmers, no less bound to their land and
compelled to remain there. The slavery referenced in the New Testament,
however, was in its urban manifestation of imperial and household service, which could often, *pace* Aristotle, give to certain slaves a high degree
of derivative authority even over the freeborn: the manager of an estate or
the tutor of elite children, for instance. Yet their authority was strictly del-
egated and in absolute dependence on that of their owners, to be removed
at will. Slaves were subject to despotic and arbitrary treatment, though
abuse of slaves was increasingly subject to civic control. Slaves in urban
settings usually had good possibilities to gain their freedom in young
adulthood and take their place among the freedmen/women class that
was still considered among the inferior classes but had some definite social and economic advantages. Like all slave societies, this one had built
into it severe differences among persons that could never have made it
possible to create a genuinely democratic society in which even all males
were considered to have the same rights.

With regard to women, the picture is even more clearly hierarchical. For
Aristotle, all women are fit not to rule but only to be ruled because they
possess rationality but in a defective manner. Aristotle was not the origi-
nator but the echoing voice of this pattern of female subordination, which
runs through all of ancient South European and Middle Eastern culture.
The submission of women to patriarchal rule along with children and
slaves was seen as a necessary component for the good ordering and thus
the well-being of the family. Most women at first marriage were considerably younger and less well educated than their new husbands, thus fa-
cilitating a dependent relationship. Under Greek influence in those countries most influenced by Hellenism, such as Greece, Asia Minor, and the
upper societal levels of Egypt, the elite ideal of the seclusion of women
was at least voiced, though it is not known whether seclusion was as
strictly practiced as it had been in classical Athens. Philo, the Hellenistic
Jewish philosopher of first-century Athens, says that married women

should go only as far as the outer door of the house and unmarried girls only to the inner door (*On the special laws* 3.169). Of course, this was an elite ideal that was never possible in poorer and working households.

In most cultures women are seen as the guarantors of men's legitimate offspring. To the extent that men feel it necessary to control that process and assure legitimation, women will be closely guarded. That fundamental importance of women is then domesticated and sacralized into the embodiment of family virtue and integrity. The family is only as good as its women, and the state is only as good as its families, since the family is the microcosm of the state. Thus upon women is placed the entire burden of social integrity, just as comparably, women in today's families often bear the entire responsibility for maintaining relationships in the extended family and across generations. In the culture that produced the New Testament, the subordination and submission of women first to parental and then to spousal authority was very much seen as an integral component of the integrity of the family and the state.

It follows from the above information that the concept of the person in these ancient societies was very different from what it is today in Western society. The effects of the Enlightenment, the democratic experiments of modern countries, and the psychological and technological revolutions have completely changed our ideas of what it is to be a person in community, from subordinate or ruling member of society, depending on one's birth, to free and autonomous individual with inalienable rights. For those, then, who wish to live according to biblical precepts and moral principles, an acute problem arises of transposing models of relationship from a culture with very different ideas of the person.

The respect and reverence for elders and designated leaders is expressed in the New Testament in such passages as 1 Thessalonians 5:12–13; 1 Timothy 5:1–2; 1 Peter 5:5. It is sometimes argued that a passage such as Gal 3:27–28 with its affirmation that "whether Jew or Greek, slave or free, male and female, we are all one in Christ Jesus," witnesses that New Testament authors had an essentially egalitarian view of the human person. It then follows in this argument that the subordination of some to others as given in the Household Codes is no diminishment of the dignity of the person, and therefore neither should it be for us. But Gal 3:28 is a soteriological statement, not a philosophical one. The text does not say that we are all equal, but that we are all one in Christ Jesus; that is, in the baptismal context of the text, we are all saved together without distinction of ethnicity, legal status, or sex. New Testament writers could affirm an equality of salvation without an equality of social relationships. They could hold in tension the submission of some to others on the basis of class or sex with a belief in the Christ-given dignity of every person, something which modern society finds difficult to reconcile because of the change in understanding of the person. Yet it is to this clash of understandings that biblical authoritarians would expect us to return.

Modern proponents of biblical values who wish to put forward the Household Code, with its admonitions of mutual responsibility and subordinate relationships between wives and husbands, children and parents, slaves and owners, as a God-given text to be taken at face value, engage in very selective interpretation. The admonitions to slaves and owners are of course ignored as anachronistic, though these same texts in other times in Christian history were instrumental in "proving biblically" that slavery was permissible. The exhortations to children and parents are seen to have continuing validity because minor children in any situation owe obedience to their parents by the natural ordering of society. But in the ancient society in which they were written, the "children" included adult children who owed obedience and submission to their fathers at whatever age, as long as their fathers were alive. Moreover, the legal requirement was obedience to fathers, not to mothers, so that the translation "parents" is a modern adaptation to what was really intended to mean "fathers" only.

Most of the heat and not much light is generated with regard to the first pair, wives and husbands. The texts have been much exegeted, with conclusions subject to the presuppositions of the exegete. It must be pointed out that the Household Codes themselves are strikingly different than their literary predecessors and counterparts, the Hellenistic discussions of household management. These discussions usually address only the patriarchal husband, father, and master, describing to him how he should rule his household and how he should get his subordinates, wife, children, and slaves, to acquiesce to his every desire. But the New Testament forms address both the superior and the subordinate member of each pair rather than only the patriarchal head of household as in other texts; moreover, they address the inferior members, wives, children, and slaves, first in each pair, thus granting them a degree of personhood even while affirming their subordinate status. Yet the very notion of submission of one person to another only because of sex or legal status is simply unacceptable to the modern person.

Those who would try to superimpose on the contemporary idea of person as possessed of freedom and full dignity a supposedly divinely ordained plan of subordination on the basis of sex or status contradict an element of revelation given to us by culture. This is one example—and not the only one—of a cultural insight that sheds light on the biblical text. The development of the understanding of personhood in the culture makes it impossible to continue to interpret the biblical text in the same way.

But we are still talking about the subordination, or not, of the "inferior" member. Is there a way to move beyond this problematic? The ideal alternative is consensus, in which no party has to yield to another except on the basis of thought-out positions and freely given acceptance. In the real world, this is sometimes not possible within a practical time frame or with certain personalities. Biblical writers sometimes speak of submitting to or serving one another in love. Ephesians 5:21 exhorts hearers to submit to one another out of reverence for Christ. It then goes on immediately, however, to establish patterns of submission on the basis of the Household Code. In that context, the author must have meant honoring the full humanity of each one even while working within the subordinate relationships dictated by the culture. We honor the author's intention by doing the same, that is, working for the full humanity of all within the requirements of our own culture about what it is to be a human person.

In Gal 5:13, Paul exhorts the community to serve one another through love, without specifying who serves. What did Paul have in mind? Perhaps he gives us a clue if we can return to a question with which we began: the limits of cultural accommodation and Paul's prime example, meat sacrificed to idols. He begins the discussion in 1 Corinthians 8 by the rational argument that all are supposed to have knowledge and thus be able to make their own decisions. No idol or other god has real existence. However, those with knowledge should realize that some will be confused by the sight of a well-informed believer eating this meat. So while everyone has the right to eat because the other gods do not exist, care should be taken not to cause confusion by their actions.

In chapter 10 of 1 Corinthians, Paul reminds his hearers that eating and drinking can bring blessing or condemnation, as was the case with the Israelites in the desert. He then affirms that one cannot actually assist at the worship of another god and still share the cup and bread of Christ. He tells them, probably repeating back what they have said, that "everything is lawful," though some judgment should be exercised. They can eat anything without raising questions and freely accept dinner invitations from unbelievers, unless it is a case of giving scandal to a weak believer. Do they object that they have the freedom and the right to do what they please? Yes, it would seem so. But there is another chapter between chapters 8 and 10. In chapter 9, Paul veers from the subject in a typical rhetorical digression to give an autobiographical reflection on his own freedom and right to insist on material support from the Corinthians, a right he does not make use of. He then adds that he tries to be whatever he can to whomever, abrogating his rights, preferences, and even marks of identity in order to win others. So the not-so-subtle message is: yes, you have rights. Yes, you can exercise them. But if you were to take me as an example, you would see that not all your rights have to be exercised. It won't kill you once in a while, for the sake of someone else, to forego a right, or even a desire.

Here is a message that is perhaps more timely than all the discussion of submission, pro and con. Can we learn to relate to each other, not hierarchically nor antihierarchically, but with the give and take that characterizes mature relationships in which persons are secure enough to establish a rhythm of taking and receiving, of ceding and affirming? Can we leave behind the language of hierarchy and submission and still be certain that we are living biblical values as we seek to be "servants to one another through love" (Gal 5:13)? If we can do this, we will be able to leave a legacy to our children and grandchildren that will enable them too to build families of love and support.

II

MUTUALITY MATTERS IN MARRIAGE

5

Between Rhetoric and Reality: Women and Men as Equal Partners in Home, Church, and the Marketplace

Herbert Anderson

When Phyllis and I were married in 1964, I assumed that at least three things would be constant in our relationship: 1) I would be the primary wage earner in the family; 2) if there was a difference of opinion in such things as buying a car or moving to a new home, for example, I would cast the deciding vote; and 3) I would be the most widely known person in the public arena of church, except perhaps in our local congregation. All these assumptions were true for my father all his life. None of these things is true for me today. For over 20 years, as the result of decisions we made together, Phyllis has been the primary wage earner. Her income made it possible for me to do what I loved to do—teach pastoral care—at a school that I loved: Catholic Theological Union. When the topic of the "man as breadwinner" has come up in conversations, I quickly deny that it bothers me that my wife provides the primary income. I lie. I was grateful for her support but mildly embarrassed that I was not the primary provider.

Secondly, two years after we were married, I decided to go to graduate school. I hauled Phyllis and our one-year-old son, Joel, across the country away from her family with very little financial security. I certainly cast the deciding vote. Phyllis was not happy about leaving a parish where she had come to have a significant role as the minister's wife. My inclination to take over was clearly operative in the early years of the marriage. When our children were eight and ten, Phyllis was gone for most of the summer as part of her preparation for ordained ministry. I had full responsibility for the house and children. We discovered that I was more willing to take over what had previously been her work than she was willing to give it up. When I think about those times, they seem very far away. Although I have gradually learned to share power and delight in role changes, my father would not understand if he were alive, sometimes the old myths still whisper and I long for the time when men still had the last word. I have also become aware that love does not guarantee a just marriage.

Phyllis is more widely known than I am in the Evangelical Lutheran Church in America and among theological educators because of the remarkable work she has done. I am delighted to be introduced as Phyllis Anderson's husband. Her public role has added much to our life together. It has also changed our more private roles in the marriage. Because my wife's work over the last two decades often required a lengthy commute, extensive travel, and long, demanding hours, I chose to be the primary cook. Perhaps it would be more accurate to say that I took over as primary cook. It is something I love to do. I gain particular satisfaction from preparing dinner parties for large groups. Recently, I have become aware that a kind of injustice has evolved in the distribution of roles as Phyllis cleans the toilets and I prepare the food. People do not heap praise for clean toilets as they do for elegant, homemade meals, particularly prepared by a man. I have transformed the more private role of househusband into a public activity. No matter how much we change, things stay the same. It is an ongoing task to keep balance and maintain justice as roles continue to shift in a marriage.

Most people who, like myself, were married in the '60s had been raised in families in which mutuality was occasional and the gender roles in marriage were traditional and frequently lacking equality. My story identifies only a few of the many changes that have revolutionized the roles of men and women at home and at work and in the church. Men have discovered deeper dimensions of their humanity that do not depend on dominance. Fathers are more likely to be involved in nurturing their children and maintaining the household. Men are eligible to take time away from the workplace to care for children, and fathers may be given custody of children in a divorce court. Husbands are are more willing to acknowledge and defer to the wisdom or greater earning power of their wives. The result of this revolution has been a multiplication of role possibilities for both women and men that will not be reversed. These new patterns of relating will continue to be modified as information technology makes it possible to do some kinds of work from almost anywhere and as we explore further the implications of the democratization of marriage and family roles.

Greater flexibility and mutuality in gender roles in marriage and family living have not, however, diminished the rate of divorce in this society. In her book *The Divorce Culture*, Barbara Defoe Whitehead argues that "our divorce-culture" has created a low-commitment culture in which breaking bonds is commonplace for human relationships.[1] While I agree that the reluctance to make and keep commitments is problematic for being married or living in community in this society, it alone does not explain the continuing high rate of divorce in this society. The rhetorical vision of justice and equality in the workplace has been slower to be established in the home not only because change cannot be legislated but also because the changes touch deeper issues of intimacy and power. As a result, there is still a significant gap between possibility and actuality, between rhetoric and reality. We know that love is not enough to diminish this gap when increased autonomy for women in marriage diminishes in men the desire for intimacy. What is needed for marriage to endure is a shared vision of a just relationship sustained by the practice of mutuality. The aim of this chapter is to explore such a vision of equal regard *and* mutual love between women and men at home, at work, and at church.

ORIGINS OF THE PRESENT DILEMMA

The changes described above have not happened overnight. Patterns of family living that began with industrialization have continued to evolve under the influence of the free-market economy in the twentieth century. The movement of men from working at home to a world of work as a consequence of industrialization has been paralleled in this century by the move of women from domestic labor at home to wage labor outside the home. As a result, there is greater potential for equality for women and men in both the public and the private spheres of human life. For women, this push for equality has been furthered by the convergence of American individualism and greater economic independence. When the internal relations of a family are no longer maintained by social and economic imperatives, when women no longer need to stay in a marriage for economic reasons, the binding element of a marital bond is mutual affection. That is to say, intimacy and communicative affection have become the primary bases for sustaining bonds in the modern marriage. This companionate understanding of marriage is not, however, something that we set out to create. It simply evolved over time as a consequence of other changes that happened as work and home became separable spheres of influence.

Although the split is no longer absolute between the private world of family, presided over by women, and the public world of work, leisure, and church, dominated by men, traditional expectations that give primacy to public roles dominated still by men continue to influence the worlds of family, church, and work. Changes in role patterns for women and men within the privacy of family happen more slowly. Within the home, there is a fundamental difference in perception of the changes that have in fact occurred. In 1993, for example, the Families and Work Institute surveyed dual career couples regarding the division of parenting responsibilities. "We share it 50–50" was the response of 43% of the men and only 19% of the women. This discrepancy of perception is not simply because men are myopic; it reflects an insufficient understanding of parental tasks and a reluctance to become regularly mindful of the responsibilities of nurturing children. Rhona Mahony argues persuasively that what is needed is a reformation in the sexual division of labor in the home that is negotiated by the two people who live together. It is possible for both women and men to achieve greater mutuality but it is difficult. The sad truth, Mahony observes, is that by the time the sun sets on the typical woman's wedding day, "she has already done nearly all the negotiating over chores and child care that she will ever do."[2] In this sense, changes in role definition for women and men in marriage are often more rhetoric than reality.

Despite her pessimistic observation, Mahony believes that practical equality between women and men is not a dream anymore, but women, she says, have to make it happen. I agree with Mahony's hopeful analysis of the current situation but not her future plan. Men today do more housework and parenting than they used to, but it is not equal and it is still often described by women and men alike as "helping women with the housework" or "babysitting the children." Moreover, as long as the responsibility for change in the family remains with women, maintaining a marriage and parenting children will be a woman's thing to do. Women feel guiltier than men about work-related absence from the family and therefore are more likely to choose to cut back their careers. If, however, children are not getting enough time from parents, that is a family issue for men and women alike. The movement from rhetoric to reality in the practical equality between women and men is and must be as much the responsibility of men as it is of women. Greater equality in marriage is a consequence of a shared vision and the practice of mutuality.

Couples who are determined to work toward an equal division of household and parenting responsibilities often find themselves torn by the limits of time. Even when the intent is to establish equality, there is simply too much to do and not enough time in which to do it. Sometimes we are caught in tensions of our creation because we have programmed too many activities or too much enrichment for our children. In order to meet all of our appointments, children are expected to accommodate themselves to adult schedules. Some couples run out of time because they need to work two, three, and four jobs to afford a house they never have time to enjoy. The application of cost-benefit analysis from economic theory is perhaps the most pernicious factor undermining our best intentions to realign the gender distinctions between the public and private spheres and establish equality of responsibility between women and men at home as well as at work. The "cost" of attending a daughter's soccer game or taking a son's scout group to a baseball game is compared with the "benefit" of meeting a new client. Even when we do not consciously ascribe economic value to human interactions, the fact that we schedule family time like work time makes it easy to confuse them and then measure them both according to cost-effective market standards.

IS YOUR FAMILY WRECKING YOUR CAREER?

Perhaps the most disturbing observation about the tension between work time and family time has come from German sociologist Ulrich Beck. He has observed that a free-market economic model presupposes a society without families or marriages. The free-market model of a society presupposes a society in which everyone (women and men alike) is free and available for the market. "The market individual is ultimately a single individual unhindered by a relationship, marriage or family....[In fact] a fully realized market society is also a society without children—unless the children grow up with mobile, single-parent mothers and fathers."[3] A market model of society presupposes that everyone who works in the market is free to respond to the demands of the market. According to Beck, and I am inclined to believe that he is right, the crisis of the family today is built into the organization of modern, industrial, market-driven societies. It is not surprising, therefore, that the family is a constant juggling act of disparate, multiple ambitions, requiring maximum mobility on the one side with the obligations of being married and raising children on the other side. A society that rewards people for selfishness should not be surprised that it faces a crisis in families. If both women and men are equally devoted to the marketplace and its demands, children will obviously suffer. But so will the marriage, even if there are no children.

An article in *Fortune* magazine with the title "Is Your Family Wrecking Your Career?" illustrates this tension between family and work. Families are a liability in the corporate world. Several studies indicate that well-educated men with working wives are paid less than men whose wives stay at home. The ultimate male status symbol today may be a wife that does not work. You must be very talented to overcome the damage to your career that comes from having a family or a wife who works. "In a world built on just-in-time, the ideal employee is the one who's always available, not the one who's constantly torn. In a world that's a village, the corporate hero is the one free to fly to Singapore on a moment's notice, not the poor schlep who has to get home to relieve the nanny."[4] Although changes have occurred, like flextime, job sharing, or personal leaves, the old demands for single-minded devotion by the corporation have not changed, even though both women and men are in the workplace. As long as parents are the only ones making choices about balancing work and family, children will suffer. Joel Anderson develops this theme more fully in a subsequent chapter in this section.

If having work that demands too much of men is a problem for some families, not having work at all continues to be a dilemma for others, black men in particular. While the percentage of black women in the work force has continued to grow in recent years, middle-aged black men are often out of work because a factory closed or moved or because they cannot translate their skills into today's jobs. Many service jobs require skills these men do not have. Nationally, more than twice as many black men are out of work as white men. The instability created in families when men cannot work is magnified in the black community. In the new economy, emerging poor black men are worse off than black women. It is difficult to insist that black men take responsibility for supporting their families when they can't get jobs. The chapter by Homer Ashby on father absence in the African-American family explores this complex issue in depth.

Achieving greater equality in gender roles in marriage is a complicated task. Although we have declared as a society that children benefit from two parents who are actively involved in their lives, we have not created an economic environment that makes such a parenting ideal easily achievable. Even when husbands and wives are determined to work toward a just marriage, there are contending forces in the larger society that continue to whisper old patriarchal themes. The family simply does not have the clout to demand what it needs in the face of current economic pressures and political realities. Robert Bellah is correct to observe that the "task of restoring family life, whatever form the family may take, cannot be the family's alone."[5] The future of the family and the future of the society are the same agenda. In the same way, society's change cannot be separated from individual and familial transformation. This is also a way of affirming the fluid boundaries between the public and private spheres.

I propose three changes that need to occur in marriage in order to foster the practice of mutuality and transform to reality the rhetoric of equality in marriage: recognizing the other in marriage; making negotiable promises; and adding justice to affection at the core of marriage. From a Christian perspective, the possibility of actualizing these changes is increased if couples learn how to practice reconciliation in daily family living. Just love is maintained when listening and forgiving are as natural as breathing.

RECOGNIZING THE OTHER

Marriage is sustained by paradox. The central paradox of marriage is found in holding in vital tension the human needs for intimacy and for autonomy. One manifestation of this paradox is suggested by Rainer Maria Rilke's observation that "a wonderful living side by side can grow up, if they [the couple] succeed in loving the distance between them which makes it possible for each to see the other whole and against a wide sky."[6] Distance makes intimacy possible, but it does not guarantee that it will happen. Living side by side does not always make for clear seeing of the other. Couples may rather see what they would like the other to become or a mirror image of themselves or the other as an object to be used. Couples who are able to love the distance that exists between them are more likely, however, to see clearly the uniqueness of each partner. Each person in a marriage may be a fully defined self, but the recognition of that unique self by the other is a necessary prelude to a just relationship. Distance (that makes it possible to see the other clearly) also enhances the possibility of intimacy. The power of mutual love, Paul Wadell has observed, (p. 18) is that "we see and still love, know and still embrace."

The experience of being recognized is not only a prerequisite for community; it is fundamental for human growth and identity. Recognition precedes empathy and is a prelude to mutual respect. What begins in infancy in the interaction between a newborn child and its mother is a lifelong need for human folk. Marriage becomes a context for growth if two people are able to see one another "whole and against a wide sky." Jessica Benjamin suggests that "recognition is that response from the other which makes meaningful the feelings, intentions, and actions of the self."[7] When we are recognized by someone on whom we depend for the validity of the self, we are confirmed in our identity and encouraged to act as a subject. Marriages that endure and flourish have achieved a kind of mutual recognition between husband and wife that honors the spouse as a unique and separate subject. When each partner is able to see the particular gifts of his or her spouse, domination is diminished and the possibility of equality is increased. In order to increase the possibility of equality for women and men in marriage and at work, husbands need to practice recognizing their wives in order to see them "whole and against a wide sky." Once the distinctive gifts and abilities of women are recognized, they can be actualized and honored both at home and in the marketplace. *Remembering Babylon*, a novel by David Malouf, is about the unexpected visit of Gemmy, a shipwrecked British cabin boy raised by aboriginal people, who wanders into a British settlement in northern Australia in the mid-nineteenth century. To the people of the settlement, Gemmy was not a black person, but he was not a white person either, rather an unsettling combination of "monstrous strangeness and unwelcome likeness." One of the people most affected by Gemmy was Jock McIver. Because of his encounter with Gemmy, the tall grass through which he had always walked now had "tips beaded with green" that he had not seen before. He also sees himself, his neighbors, and his wife more clearly than ever before.

He had turned his full gaze upon her—that is what she felt. He wanted to know now what her life was beyond what he saw and had taken for granted, a shift washed and shaken to make it soft, food on the table; to inquire into her affections. It was amazing to him—that is what his tentativeness suggested—that he had known so little and had not looked.[8]

Even when they were first courting, Jock had not seen her so clearly, this woman he loved so dearly. Like Jock McIver, many men know little about the women we live or work with, and yet we do not look or ask in order to understand more. Because men do not always see their wives and other women clearly, women easily become objects rather than subjects, people whose uniqueness is covered over by role definition and stereotypes. Recognition is a prelude to equal regard between men and women because it helps us see the gifts each one brings to our common life and work together. It is also a prelude to empathy. If the desire to be heard and understand accurately and without judgment is understood as mutual in marriage, then each partner will seek to see clearly and confirm the experience of the other without fear of losing voice or power. Partners in marriage are more receptive to each other's experience if they are confident that their own story will be understood and validated as well. At its best, marriage is a community of mutual recognition and reciprocal empathy.

In order truly to see one another clearly, however, we must begin with the presumption of equal worth. This presumption overcomes fear of the stranger, engenders curiosity about the other, and promotes the kind of disciplined listening to one another that leads to understanding. This willingness to see the other "whole and against a wide sky" also carries with it the possibility of surprise. Instead of imposing preconceptions on those with whom they live and work, men and women alike will need to be prepared to receive something new, something unexpected, some unthought-of possibility. Marriages that endure and flourish have achieved a kind of mutual recognition in which husbands and wives each honor the other as a separate and unique subject, worthy of respect and equal regard. In this sense, mutuality precedes intimacy.

MAKING NEGOTIABLE PROMISES

It is a truism to say that we live in a time of rapid change. Scientific discoveries about the mysteries hidden in genes and the dissemination of information through technology have changed how we think about human beings and how human beings think. It is difficult to imagine that the present trajectory of change will diminish in future decades. In one sense, the changing roles of women and men comprise simply one small dimension of change in our time. Changes in the way we think about women and men in marriage, in the church, and in the workplace nonetheless evoke strong emotional response because they challenge long-standing assumptions about the gender-specific nature of social roles. My own struggle to accept the reality that Phyllis was the primary wage earner illustrates the point. It was important for me to continue to mourn the loss of male privilege even as I came to understand that being the breadwinner does not determine my identity as a man. For me, there was new freedom in discovering that I could share the responsibility of providing for the family. While men have always been protectors of the hearth, they have never been the only providers.

One of the gifts of this time of rapid change is that it has sensitized us to the ordinary change that continues to be part of daily family living. Families change because people change and because the social context changes as well. Sometimes those changes are negative and destructive; other times they are inevitable and constructive. Most of the time, however, change in a family's patterns of interacting is messy and disruptive. Families or individuals that spend time and energy resisting change or railing against it are not likely to plan for the kind of accommodation or adaptation that is necessary to adjust to the demands of modern family living. The family has a future in part because it has always been able to change its patterns of interaction in response to changes in the larger society. And because the family continues to change, it will always be characterized by a lot of "controlled disorder" and some grief. When families are unable to mourn the ordinary losses that come from ordinary changes, they are more likely to insist on remaining rigid and inflexible in order to maximize continuity.

The kinds of changes that once marked shifting family forms and functions over long periods now occur within the lifetime of a marriage. Because we can regularly anticipate changes in roles and disruptions in living that will destabilize the family, we need to understand that renewing our mutual promises will be necessary in order to keep the marriage covenant alive. "Promising again is an act of creative fidelity because we see and understand implications and dimensions of the initial promise we could never have anticipated when we first made it."[9] When my wife and I married, she thought she was marrying someone who would always be a parish pastor. For myself, I did not imagine I was marrying someone who would become a national leader in theological education. Even when the gender roles in a relationship continue to follow traditional patterns, people are less likely to stay in the same occupation for a lifetime. Changing jobs is itself a destabilizing factor for many families because new work routines disrupt established patterns of daily living.

In order to accommodate the inevitable and sometimes necessary changes that occur in marriage, couples need to practice making promises that are time-limited, situational, circumstantial, and frequently renegotiated. Obviously, these promises build on the primary promises of love, respect, and mutual recognition that are foundational for marriage. Promising again and again within marriage presumes the art of negotiating in which the clear communication of needs and wants is coupled with the capacity for empathy and understanding the partner from his or her point of view. If one parent agrees to stay home with young children so the other can invest fully in a career opportunity, that is a situational promise that need not last for the duration of a marriage. If one spouse accepts a major volunteer assignment at their church to head up the building fund drive, the couple may agree to forgo certain social activities for the length of the campaign. When one partner sets aside his regular golf schedule while the other recovers from surgery, that is a time-limited response to a particular circumstance. If modern marriages are to move toward greater equality of roles and work opportunity for both partners, couples will need to develop the capacity to negotiate, modify, and then give up circumstantial promises.

Finally, however, in order to survive the kind of fundamental changes that occur in marriage and the workplace today, we need to discover the possibility of transformation that moves beyond adaptation. Promising again and again is an intentional, relational act that defines the self and honors the other. It is an act of mutuality that rests on the willingness of two people to recognize each other as people of worth, each with particular gifts and a unique story. Both mutuality and adaptability are necessary in order to live through the changes that are inevitably a part of modern family living. Adaptation, however, is not enough. Transformation is necessary. Transformation, change in a deeper and more enduring sense, is grounded in the conviction that the continuity of a family is in God's ongoing creative work. "Transformative change unites the soul of a marriage with a longing for the new thing that God is doing."[10] It presumes the possibility of a radically different way of perceiving, thinking, and interacting within a family. Perhaps the most fundamental transformation in marriage is the commitment to a just relationship that Pauline Kleingeld proposed in the second chapter.

ADDING JUSTICE TO LOVE AT THE CORE OF A MARRIAGE

Seeing the other in marriage clearly and seeing role changes for women and men in the home and workplace as a sign that God is doing something new will require that the marital promise include not only a commitment to love one another but also a commitment to be just with one another. This is perhaps the most fundamental transformation needed in marriage in our time. In an earlier chapter, Pauline Kleingeld has proposed in an earlier chapter that we view marriage essentially as

> not only a matter of love, but also of justice. It is necessary to move beyond the ideology—historically rooted in an era of male dominance—according to which marriage is a matter of love only, at the exclusion of justice. On the view I am proposing, married couples ideally would think of themselves as sharing at least two overarching aims: a loving marriage and a just marriage.[11]

What Kleingeld is proposing fundamentally changes the framework for negotiating role equality in marriage. It is not simply that two people who love each another seek to work out some arrangement regarding role responsibilities that is acceptable, beneficial, and even fair for everyone involved but that the commitment to work for justice for each partner in the relationship is part of the marital bond. Seeking justice is not antithetical to loving one another. It is the shared goal of life together.

The positive changes made in the larger society and in many marriages today have not eliminated injustice from marriage nor eradicated injustice toward women in the church and at work. We all know stories of pain and disappointment. Household labor studies consistently show that women continue to do more housework than men. Women are paid less than men for the same or equivalent work. Men whose wives do not work outside the home have higher salaries and are promoted more quickly in top management positions. Men are themselves sometimes penalized in the workplace if they attempt to balance their work responsibilities with child care. Still, unless men do assume more responsibility at home, greater opportunity for women in the workplace may make it seem like women are taking over everything. It is necessary to continue to work for laws and policies that will make it easier for justice to prevail in the workplace and in marriage, but that is not sufficient. Just laws do not guarantee just action. Husbands and wives will work together toward a just division of household responsibilities only if both partners in a marriage care that their marriages are just. As Kleingeld argues,

> If justice is to be an important aspect of marriage, it needs to be able to unite spouses instead of structurally pitting them against each other...Once couples regard "a just marriage" as a shared goal, they move beyond the model of two competitively bargaining individuals and replace it with a model of two spouses committed to a shared effort to achieve justice.[12]

Because this commitment to a just marriage will also seek for a balanced sharing of power and mutuality of influence in a relationship, it is one way to strengthen marriage and diminish divorce.

Couples who are determined to work toward a just division of household and parenting responsibilities still find themselves torn by the limits of

time. Even when the intent is to establish equality of responsibility in a relationship, there is simply too much to do and not enough time in which to
do it. Some couples run out of time because they need to work two, three,
and four jobs to afford a house they do not have time to enjoy. Sometimes
husbands and wives are caught in tensions of their creation because they
have programmed too many activities for themselves or too much enrichment for their children. Moreover, valuing efficiency in the marketplace has
created a new tension in the home because mutuality and shared roles are
not efficient. Because the schedule is so tight, no one can afford to get sick
and children are expected to accommodate to adult schedules. As a result,
husbands and wives overlook each another to make everything happen.
However, justice requires a second look. A quick glance on the run is not
long enough to see the other clearly enough to honor his or her gifts.

The application of cost-benefit analysis from the economy is perhaps the
most pernicious factor undermining our best intentions to realign the gender distinctions between the public and private spheres and establish
equality of responsibility between women and men at home and at work.
Attending a daughter's soccer game or taking a son's scout troop to a baseball game is determined along with the benefit of meeting a new client.
Even when we do not consciously ascribe economic value to human interactions, the fact that we schedule family time like work time with calendars
and spread sheets makes it easy to confuse them and then measure them
both according to our cost-effective market standards. The commitment to
form a just marriage and in turn a just family will be strengthened by a tran-
scending faith perspective. It is more likely that both husbands and wives
will be free to live responsibly for the common good if human stories are retold and commitments to justice are made in the light of the Divine Story of
God's desire for justice for humankind.

The aim of God's justice is a network of human relationships inseparable,
even though distinguishable, from love. Because God's love is both gracious and just, human love that mirrors the love of God is also just and loving. "Just love," as that phrase is being used in this collection of essays, depends on a willingness of all persons in the family to regard each other as
persons of worth, renew relations when they are broken, and restore the imbalance of power. The family is transformed into a "crucible of grace," as
Paul Wadall describes it in chapter one, through the regular practice of forgiveness and reconciliation.

PRACTICING JUSTICE IN THE FAMILY

The commitment to justice does not eliminate the need for sacrifice. The demands of the world of work and the demanding work of being married

and being a family regularly exceed our finite energies and time. Compromise is inevitable. No one can "have it all" if a marriage is to be just. And no one does all the accomodating if the love is mutual. The deeper meaning of sacrifice is not about giving up our freedoms or our preferences but giving them over to a larger reality. That larger reality is a marriage of love **and** justice. If both partners in a marriage are committed to a just relationship, then no one person will do all the accommodating. Within a marital bond committed to justice, the admonition from Paul about sacrifice becomes one appropriate way to work toward justice: "Do nothing from selfish ambition or conceit, but in humility regard others as better than yourselves. Let each of you look not to your own interests, but to the interests of others" (Phil 2:3–4). If both husband and wife are committed to forming a just marriage, then the willingness to set aside our needs for the needs of others becomes a positive expression of a common bond. Sacrifice deepens a marital bond as long as each person in a relationship is committed to justice. When one partner does all the accommodating or when the sacrifices are not evenly distributed over time, the marriage is not just.

Justice in marriage and family living is an act of restoration. Walter Brueggemann has observed that justice means sorting out what belongs to whom and returning it to them. Returning possessions or giving back land is the easiest way to think about restorative justice. In marriage and family living, however, justice as an act of restoration will prompt men and women to sort out what roles and virtues belong to everyone (rather than one gender) and giving them back. The television marriage of Archie and Edith illustrates the point. Like most traditional marriages, it was assumed in the Bunker marriage that Archie was always right but a little bad. Edith, on the other hand, was the "bearer of the good" even though she was usually wrong. This delineation of roles and virtues trapped Edith and Archie in patterns of behavior that in turn reinforced unjust sterotypes and limited growth.

When certain virtues or particular roles are attached to one gender and not another, both women and men are deprived of the possibility of human fullness. Marriages in which one partner overfunctions while the other is free to underfunction reflect this same unjust distribution of capabilities. In order to achieve a just marriage in which all the virtues are available to everyone, it is necessary for men and women alike to determine what does not belong exclusively to them and then return it to their common life. When justice is added to marriage, wives and husbands will commit to give back virtues not uniquely their own, cancel debts that continue to destabilize the marital bond, honor the unique gifts each brings to their life together, take time for a second look, and redistribute power.

Justice occurs in marriage when power is shared. When women and men are both empowered to speak and influence choices that are made, mutuality flourishes and conflicts are settled quickly. When mutuality is absent and power is out of balance, then decisions about who initiates sex, how money is spent, how clean the bathrooms must be and who cleans them, which relative to visit at Christmas, or the use of leisure time all become occasions for anger or hurt or both. When a husband insists that "I may not always be right, but I am never wrong" he is not a likely candidate for sharing power. Mutuality in marriage builds on a willingness to forgo the realization of one's own interests or intentions for the sake of a larger vision or in deference to the other's needs. By contrast, preoccupation with rights fosters hostility and separation rather than a deeper commitment to justice. Fostering mutuality in marriage depends on seeing one another's gifts clearly while working simultaneously for a just relationship

Working toward justice for women and men in marriage is seldom easy. It presumes trust, clear communication, and a shared, equal commitment to a just marriage. It depends on the capacity of each partner to articulate his or her own wishes and desires and hear clearly the hopes and dreams of the other. Misunderstanding creates barriers not easily overcome. Occasional egoism may prompt one partner to present needs in a distorted way. My own recent discovery of an imbalance in roles in my marriage between cooking for parties and cleaning toilets points to the need for constant attentiveness to the distribution of family tasks with justice in view. The absence of empathy impedes the willingness to make common cause with one's partner for a deeper vision of a just relationship. In the final analysis, however, justice in marriage is not only something we achieve. It is something we discover. "What makes justice different for those who follow Christ is that it is something that is given rather than earned. For Christian persons in marriage, it is impossible to separate justice from gratitude."[13]

THE NEED FOR ONGOING RECONCILIATION

The struggle for a just marriage is complicated by a social reality in which the constraints and conventions that have kept marriages together are increasingly dissolving. In this society, the myths supporting the vision of a father who works outside the home and a mother who works to keep the home and raise children have been challenged by the feminist movement of the last decades and undermined by an economic environment in which it is less and less possible to support a family on one income. The decline of job stability for those whose salaries were sufficient to support a family further erodes the possibility of sustaining traditional roles for women and men either at home or in the workplace. Around the globe, traditional functions for men have ordinarily included providing meat through hunting, protecting the village, and initiating young boys. In most traditional societies today, hunting is not permitted, police protect the family or clan, and boys are educated in schools. It is important not to overlook the profound grief that accompanies these changes as we consider new role patterns for women and men at home and in the workplace.

In a subsequent chapter, Joel Anderson observes that seeking to return to traditional role patterns for women and men at home and at work is not really an option in modern industrial societies. "Aside from the fact that returning to more traditional approaches would involve unconscionably disproportionate sacrifices from women, it would not actually eliminate the need to make complex and conflict-ridden decisions."[14] When a couple picks the traditional male-breadwinner/female-homemaker pattern today, the modern understanding of mutual and just respect requires that it be a choice made by equals. Couples who make a commitment to form a just marriage will inevitably experience unexpected conflicts and unseen rocky shoals that will require a wide array of skills and virtues that must be developed and practiced. These include recognizing the other, empathic listening, the ability to postpone gratification, clear expression of wishes, renegotiating previous promises, and a short-term memory that does not always keep score.

Because conflict and disappointment and grief will be inevitable dimensions in the life of a couple who seek to establish a just marriage, men and women will need to learn how to practice reconciliation in advance. Reconciliation, as I mean it here, is more than restoring relationships broken by conflicts over contending views of what is just: it is a way of living and thinking that seeks to promote a peaceable environment in which husbands and wives might sort out very complex and competing demands on their time from work and home. Within a peaceable environment, bonds of trust can be safely rebuilt. Such reconciliation cannot be achieved in haste. It does not ignore past or present injustice. If, however, women and men tend toward reconciliation and justice, it is possible that they will find new ways to work together for the common good.

Seeing the other whole, making negotiable promises, and loving justly all require radical changes in our views of men and women at home and work. In order to see in a new way, we need to be prepared for surprise. Tending toward the other may be the beginning of mutuality. In Malouf's novel, Jock McIver was surprised to see the tips of grass beaded with green. He had been among the tall grass before, but it was as if he were seeing it for the first time. In order to see new roles for women and men at home and at work and in the church, we will also need to be transformed by the experience of mutuality. That transformation is most likely to occur when we live gently with the contradictions of our lives.

NOTES

This essay is a revised version of an article that first appeared in *Word and World* (Volume XVII, Number 4, Fall, 1997) and is used here with the premission of the editor.

1. Barbara Defoe Whitehead, *The Divorce Culture* (New York: Alfred A. Knopf, 1996).

2. Rhona Mahony, *Kidding Ourselves: Breadwinning, Babies, and Bargaining Power* (New York: Basic, 1995), 5.

3. Ulrich Beck, *The Risk Society: Towards a New Modernity* (Newbury Park, CA: Sage, 1992), 116.

4. Betsy Morris, "Is Your Family Wrecking Your Career?" *Fortune*, March 17, 1997, 72.

5. Robert N. Bellah, *The Good Society* (New York: Alfred A. Knopf, 1991), 260.

6. Rainer Maria Rilke, *Rilke on Love and Other Difficulties*, ed. John Mood (New York: W. W. Norton, 1975), 28. For a fuller development of the implications of "recognizing the other" in marriage, see Herbert Anderson, *Jacob's Shadow: Christian Perspectives on Masculinity* (Louisville, Ky: Bridge Resources, 2002), 87–98.

7. Jessica Benjamin, *The Bonds of Love: Psychoanalysis, Feminism, and the Problem of Domination* (New York: Pantheon, 1988), 12.

8. David Malouf, *Remembering Babylon* (New York: Vintage, 1993), 108–109.

9. Herbert Anderson, David Hogue, and Marie McCarthy, *Promising Again* (Louisville, KY: Westminster John Knox Press, 1995), 27.

10. Ibid., 122.

11. Pauline Kleingeld, "Just Love? Marriage and the Question of Justice," *Social Theory and Practice*, 24:2 (Summer 1998): 269. Also see chapter 2 in this volume.

12. Ibid.

13. Herbert Anderson and Robert Cotton Fite, *Becoming Married* (Louisville, Ky: Westminster John Knox Press, 1993), 154.

14. Joel Anderson, "Is Equality Tearing Families Apart?" *Applied Ethics: A Multicultural Approach*, 2d edition, ed. Larry May, Shari Sharratt, and Kai Wong (New York: Prentice-Hall, 2002). Also see chapter 7 in this volume.

6

✛

Gender Narratives and the Epidemic of Violence in Contemporary Families

Christie Neuger

INTRODUCTION

It is not an overstatement to suggest that we are in a time of tremendous transition concerning many dimensions of family life. In the midst of these transitions many fear the breakdown of core values. Some of these core values are: a single, lifelong commitment to a partner of the other sex; procreation and care of the young; certain "biologically decided" sex roles which most efficiently support the life and growth of the family; and family units which carry and convey through time the moral life taught and supported by the Church. While there is a deep concern that the structure and tasks of the family are in jeopardy, we are also aware that culture is changing and, along with it, the shape of families. The Church sometimes finds itself in a dilemma as it seeks to be both gatekeeper of family values and source of liberation and empowerment for the marginalized, including women. This essay will explore the power of gender roles in family and culture and their implications for family violence. It will also consider the responsibility of pastoral care and counseling professionals to help re-shape the formative narratives, which can implicitly engender and support such violence.

DEFINING FAMILIES

In the past forty years, the Church has borrowed heavily from the normative sociological definition of the family put forth by Talcott Parsons and others. This definition was a functionalist one that suggested that the family itself is part of the larger social fabric and works to contribute to the betterment of the whole and to serve the needs of the society. Pauline Boss and Barrie Thorne suggest that it was in part the context of the 1950s, with its postwar emphasis on stability and equilibrium, that supported the popularity of Parsons' paradigm.[1] Parsons suggested that women and men have different, inevitable functions to play in family life as the family carries out its two main functions of socializing the young and providing emotional support for its members. Women, by nature, have the expressive roles. The family is their emotional domain and they are responsible for the nurturance and care of family members. Men, by nature, have the instrumental roles and they provide the structural support for the family and bridge the gap between the private/domestic world and the public world.[2] According to Parsons, deviation from these natural roles creates dysfunction and instability for families. Thus, it is important for all of society to support this role division for the sake of the greater good.

This theory of family life was—and in some contexts still is—extremely popular and has played an ongoing role in sociological theory building and in the popular mind. This is despite the fact that this bifurcated family has never been the only, or even most common, family form. African-American women, for example, have always been likely to be both mothers and workers. In actuality, families composed of two never-divorced parents, children at home, Dad at work, and Mom at home make up less than 10% of families in the United States today. Still, this "traditional" family form is influential when establishing norms and expectations for family life today.

In recent years there has been considerable challenge to this image of the normative family. The perpetuation of this normative vision in the face of a different reality causes numerous problems. This is especially true for women who try to meet the demands of this normative model even while living a different family lifestyle. As Susan Moller Okin, in *Justice, Gender, and the Family*, states,

> The fact that society seems no longer to have any consensual view of the norms and expectations of marriage is particularly apparent from the gulf that exists between the continued *perception* of most men and women that it is still the primary responsibility of husbands to "provide for" their wives by participating in wage work and of wives to perform a range of unpaid "services" for their husbands, and the *fact* that most women, including mothers of small children, are both in the labor force *and* performing the vast majority of household duties.[3]

Because this traditional definition of marriage tends to blur, and even obscure, many of the crucial issues in the lives of women, feminists have taken a leadership role in broadening and studying definitions of the family. Since we live in a culture in which most people pass through a significant variety of family forms over their life cycle, it is important to acknowledge that families take on different shapes and structures and that this is good and valuable.

That being said, I will focus the rest of this essay on women in the "traditional" family structures of husband, wife, and children. I do so, not only because it is the most common in terms of operating assumptions, but also because it has serious political, social, physical, and psychological ramifications for women. Philip Blumstein and Pepper Schwartz studied and interviewed people from a variety of family types to assess attitudes and practices in those families. They found that in heterosexual marriages, traditional (functionalist) mores about the woman maintaining the home and providing emotional nurturance and the man providing and controlling the family finances are still dominant. The problems that emerge for women in this kind of arrangement are not so prevalent in cohabiting heterosexual couples and are even less so in committed lesbian relationships. The power arrangements in these two latter family forms are considerably more equal. They are also less affected by cultural sexism than are those in the traditional marriage structure, which was defined to serve the needs of the larger patriarchal society.[4]

WOMEN IN FAMILIES

Sociologists, psychologists, and theologians have made a serious mistake in adopting a functionalist view of family life that, by its very definition, separates the private/domestic sphere from the public world. In doing so we neglect to understand the relationships between husbands and wives in the home in the broader context of relationships between men and women in the culture. We have seen the higher rates of depression in married mothers than in single women but have neglected to understand the connections between loss of power and increased domestic responsibility. Thus, Rachel Hare-Mustin notes that, "Despite the idealization of women's mother role, there is consistent evidence that children have a negative effect on the mental health of women, a fact many family therapists seem oblivious to. Paradoxically, with the birth of each child, the mother's power in the family diminishes relative to that of her husband."[5] Ronald Taffel and Rosemary Masters conducted an extensive study that points to five key variables affecting a woman's likely success in achieving emotional health in therapy. She is more likely to succeed in therapy if she has *fewer children*; if she has *older children* rather than younger; if she has *autonomous economic viability*; if she has a *career or a plan for a career*; and if she has an *empathic support network.*[6] Unfortunately these characteristics which foster the ability to achieve mental and emotional health are not the ones fostered by traditional structures of marriage or, often, by the Church.

Susan Moller Okin states the problem clearly when she says,

> Marriage and the family, as currently practiced in our society, are unjust institutions. They constitute the pivot of a societal institution that renders women vulnerable to dependency, exploitation, and abuse. When we look seriously at the distribution between husbands and wives of such critical social goods as work (paid and unpaid), power, prestige, self-esteem, opportunities for self-development, and both physical and economic security, we find socially constructed inequalities between them, right down the list.[7]

There is strong evidence that married women have a shorter life expectancy than unmarried women whereas married men have a longer life expectancy than do unmarried men. The group of women most at risk for depression is married women who do not work outside the home and have three or more children under the age of twelve. In addition, there is the compounded problem that women sometimes work two shifts—one at home and one at work—so that fatigue plays a pervasive role in their psychospiritual distress. The private, domestic realm has always been considered to be women's place and the pressures on maintaining relationships and keeping the hearth and home inviting and nurturing are immense—even when both spouses work. For women who have been raised in the church, too often pressures come from biblical and theological interpretations that hold women responsible for the home without giving them direct power and authority or access to the public realm. Both the church and the larger culture teach women to use indirect power in order to run their home with harmony and peace and, indeed, teach them to sacrifice much for the sake of domestic tranquility.

On the other side of the story, many women have strong needs for connection, and married women often find their greatest meaning and self-esteem in their roles as mothers and wives. When I have asked married career women where they find personal meaning, it is generally in their family. The reality that marriage is structurally oppressive for women in psychological, spiritual, social, economic, and physical ways does not mean that women do not seek life in families or wish to be married. Even women who recognize the oppressive quality of an institution that has been normalized to meet the needs of a patriarchal culture know that there are the important rewards of intimacy, commitment, connection, and nurturance. The real task for people who work with women and men in traditional families—pastors and counselors included—is to help empower them; to help husbands and wives to restructure marriage in ways that take seriously the cultural disempowerment for women; and to educate people who will be forming families about the realities of sexism (and racism and classism) as it impacts family life.

Traditionally, women who became depressed or troubled because of family responsibilities, family violence, or family dysfunction have been counseled—either alone or with their spouse—toward the goal of better adjustment. Since the home is the place where women are held responsible and since women tend to feel over-responsible when relationships are not working successfully, most often it is the woman who brings the problem to the counselor. Even if it is the pastor who notices in a home visit that there are problems in the family, he or she tends to start with the wife/mother as the access route to the whole family. Usually women feel enough guilt (and fear of abandonment) that they will take as much responsibility and blame as is offered to them, and then work with single-minded determination to fix a problem that belongs at least to the whole family and more likely to a culture that endorses unequal power and responsibility in traditional marriage.

MEN IN FAMILIES[8]

The separation of domestic and public lives that characterizes the framework of contemporary families and can be so oppressive for women probably isn't good for men either. Over the past two decades there has been a considerable amount of gender-conscious research that has focused on masculinity and men's psychological and spiritual health. Ron Levant writes that these new attempts to understanding masculinity "have provided a framework for a psychological approach to men and masculinity that questions traditional norms for the male role, such as the emphases on competition, status, toughness, and emotional stoicism, and that views certain male problems (such as aggression and violence, homophobia, misogyny, detached fathering, and neglect of health) as unfortunate but predictable results of the male role socialization process."[9]

James O'Neill suggests that there are six patterns that are a result of gender socialization in men. Those are:

- Restrictive emotionality
- Socialized control, power, and competition
- Homophobia
- Restrictive sexual and affective behavior
- Obsession with achievement and success
- Health care problems

He goes on to note "how men are socialized produces sexist attitudes and behavior that explains much of the personal and institutional sexism in society."[10] O'Neill suggests that normative masculinity sets up persistent worries about personal achievement, competence, failure, status, upward mobility, and wealth and career success in men's lives as well as a drive to obtain authority, dominance, and influence over others. There is an emphasis on striving against others in competitive ways. Restrictive emotionality suggests that men have difficulty and fears about expressing feelings and difficulty finding words to express basic emotions.

In a similar vein, Ron Levant argues that emotionality is socialized out of boys very intentionally and this has four major consequences. First, boys develop a form of empathy that he calls "action empathy" which is the ability to see things from another's point of view in order to predict what they will "do" (not what they feel) and is usually employed in the service of the self (different from emotional empathy). Second, boys become strangers to their own emotional life and most develop at least a mild form of alexithymia (not having words for emotions). Men who are in the presence of an unrecognized emotion often experience only the bodily sensation of its physiological component. Third, boys pour their vulnerable emotions out through the channel of anger—one of the few emotions boys are encouraged to express. And, fourth, boys learn to channel their caring emotions through the channel of sexuality.

We need to recognize some of the important negative consequences for men of gender role strain. For example, probably all four of the gender role conflict factors correlate positively with depression in men, and restrictive emotionality correlates positively with depression at all life stages of men. Higher levels of gender role conflict correlate positively with low self-esteem. In race studies, men from European-American, African-American and Hispanic races all reported problems with success, power, and competition, restrictive emotionality, and conflicts between work and family relations. Results of several studies indicate strong correlations between gender role conflict and negative attitudes toward help-seeking.[11]

Other consequences include the fact that women live, on average, seven years longer than do men, and gender-related lifestyle choices are part of this (e.g., between the ages of fifteen and twenty-four, men die at three times the rate of women mostly because of violent death among male youth). Women are more prone to anxiety disorders and depression, but men show more evidence of antisocial personality disorder and alcohol and drug abuse.[12] And men participate in violence in very destructive ways that can be clearly related to gender role training. In a recent study of 518 college men, 34% reported that they had engaged women in unwanted sexual contact, 20% reported they had attempted unwanted intercourse, and 10% reported they had completed unwanted intercourse.

46% said that they were at least somewhat likely to force sex if they wouldn't get caught.[13]

There are important implications of these gendered realities for the epidemic of intimate violence, especially violence in families.

MALE-FEMALE VIOLENCE IN INTIMATE RELATIONSHIPS

The statistics about violence in families are staggering. The United States Justice Department recently released a comprehensive study on the price of violence in our society. It attempted to include the costs of domestic violence and child abuse in addition to the kinds of violence more typically studied. The report found that "child abuse and domestic violence account for one-third of the total cost of crime."[14]

According to Margi McCue, "[Domestic] abuse may be the single most common etiology for injury presented by women, accounting for more injury episodes than auto accidents, muggings, and rapes combined. A review of 3,676 records randomly selected from among female patients presenting with injury during one year, revealed that forty percent of the women's injury episodes were identified as resulting from a deliberate assault by an intimate. Nineteen percent of the women had a previous history of abusive injury."[15] The American Medical Association estimates that four million women suffer severe assaults by boyfriends and husbands each year and that one in four women will be abused in her life. Estimates in a variety of studies range from two million to eight million women assaulted every year by partners and up to one in two women being abused sometime in her life.

According to the Bureau of Justice, intimates commit thirteen percent of all rapes, robberies, and assaults. Men are more likely to be the victims of violent crime in general (by a ratio of twenty-six men: nineteen women) but women are more than ten times more likely (ninety-two women: eight men) to be the victim of violence by an intimate. It is important for those engaged in pastoral care or pastoral counseling to recognize the impact this reality has for women—whether they are directly victimized or only victimized by knowing their risk of being abused by someone they love or have loved.

Women who are in battering relationships tend to look diligently for an explanation that explains a presumably aberrant situation. Lora Lempert suggests that "violence is not a generally expected marital interaction. Cultural expectations of love and marriage do not include the 'stories from hell' that are the lived experiences of abused women. It is the unexpected nature of the violence, its seeming unpredictability, that makes it difficult to assimilate."[16] As a result, women look for an explanation that fits their core narrative. Piera Serra writes, "If the woman perceives the violence she is subjected to as the expression of her partner's inner world, and she considers the act as a symptom or a message, she will tend to disregard her own suffering and physical helplessness. Most of the women we interviewed who were still living with their partners interpreted their partners' violent behavior as a sign of distress."[17] The impact of this mind reading and pro-other interpretation is that it gets in the way of moral evaluation and self-care. Psychologically, it also gives the woman the illusion that she still has a chance of fixing this problem in the relationship (which of course is not a problem in the relationship at all, but a problem in her spouse). Lempert suggests that "women in a battering relationship cannot afford to relinquish beliefs that they exercise some control, however minimal, over their lives because their survival depends on those beliefs and on continued use of whatever personal power they possess. With the erosion of these personal and social resources comes increasing demoralization."[18]

Serra concludes her discussion by stating that women turn to outsiders to help end the violence so as to preserve the relationship. Yet most caregivers—whether police, clergy, counselors, or friends—help only by suggesting that she leave the relationship; they do not feel they have the authority or right to make the batterer stop battering. Thus, when the batterer expresses contrition, mild affection, or even just temporarily ends the violence, she takes this as a sign of change and the bonding between them that may result is usually more satisfying than any outside help has been.[19] In this way, her training to be relationally responsible, to sacrifice self-interest for other care, and to hope for nurturing and love if she follows the gender rules are often temporarily enabled in the period between violent episodes by the batterer himself.

When considering men's gender training and its relationship to violence in marriages, it's notable that numerous studies have linked the inability to express vulnerable feelings with a strong tendency to engage in interpersonal violence. Other studies have been able to make clear linkages between socialization for aggression and interpersonal violence.[20] Wayne Ewing writes, "When the question is raised, 'who is the male batterer?' the answer is sometimes given, 'everyman!' Without pushing too quickly, let me simply point out here that this observation is accurate."[21] Numerous studies have shown that the psychological profiles of violent men (rapists or batterers) are not significantly different from the psychological profiles of the general population of men. Male gender training, which is facilitated by families and other important institutions, is related to high risk for interpersonal violence. In fact, Ewing goes on to say, "The teaching of violence is so pervasive, so totally a part of male experience, that I think it best to acknowledge this teaching as a civic, rather than as a cultural or as a social, phenomenon. Certainly there are social institutions that form pieces of the total advocacy of violence: marriage and family; ecclesiastical institutions; schools; economic and corporate institutions; government and political institutions."[22] He concludes, "I used to think that we simply tolerated and permitted male abusiveness in our society. I have now come to understand rather that we advocate physical violence. Violence is presented as effective. Violence is taught as the normal, appropriate and necessary behavior of power and control."[23] Certainly not all men (or even most men) are emotionally and/or physically violent in their intimate relationships. However, all men who don't engage in family violence must actively resist cultural narratives of maleness that would predispose them toward it. And, men must be willing to protest actively against the kind of culture that makes it likely for them to be violent with intimate partners. If men want to be seen as nonviolent, it is important that they take a clear stand against family violence.

The issues of power and hierarchy are a foundational part of understanding domestic violence. We must not fall into the mistake that many battered women make that battering is primarily a symptom of personal distress or dysfunction of her male partner. Michael Kaufman writes, "Men's violence against women is the most common form of direct, personalized violence in the lives of most adults and . . . is probably the clearest most straightforward expression of relative male and female power."[24]

Ewing writes, "The ruling paradigm for male supremacy remains to this hour, physical violence."[25] And, it is often effective. McMahon and Pence have studied men who batter. They conclude, "when asked, violent men are quite clear about what it can accomplish: 'she would listen,' 'she would drop the order for protection,' 'next time she'd think twice.' Such men benefit from their violence. How much more seductive are explanations that say a man's violence is an expression of his insecurity or impulsiveness."[26]

Gender training and performance within this context of power differences forms a powerful narrative that may well support family violence by men against women. It helps us understand that the work of pastoral care and counseling needs to include the reshaping of these cultural, formative narratives, not just working with the idiosyncratic stories of individual perpetrators and victims. The deconstruction of "complementary" gender roles in families and for families will contribute to the possibility that men and women, boys and girls, may be more able to live out their full humanity in partnership with one another and may help reduce the violence that is a part of so many families' lives.

NOTES

1. Pauline Boss and Barrie Thorne, "Family Sociology and Family Therapy: A Feminist Linkage," in *Women in Families: A Framework for Family Therapy*, ed. Monica McGoldrick, Carol Anderson, and Froma Walsh (New York: W. W. Norton, 1989), 79.

2. Ibid., 79.

3. Susan Moller Okin, *Justice, Gender, and the Family* (New York: Basic Books, 1989), 139.

4. Philip Blumstein and Pepper Schwartz, *American Couples: Money, Work, Sex* (New York: Pocket Books, 1983), see especially the epilogue and conclusion.

5. Rachel T. Hare-Mustin, "The Problem of Gender in Family Therapy," in *Women in Families*, 65.

6. Ronald Taffel and Rosemary Masters, "An Evolutionary Approach to Revolutionary Change: The Impact of Gender Arrangements on Family Therapy," in *Women in Families*, 122.

7. Okin, *Justice, Gender, and the Family*, 136.

8. Some of this material appears in a prior form in Christie Neuger, "Narratives of Harm: Setting the Developmental Stage for Intimate Violence," in *In Her Own Time*, ed. Jeanne Stevenson-Moessner (Minneapolis, MN: Fortress, 2000).

9. Ronald Levant and William Pollack, "Introduction," in *A New Psychology of Men*, ed. Ronald Levant and William Pollack (New York: Basic Books, 1995), 1. Herbert Anderson develops similar themes in *Jacob's Shadow: Christian Perspectives on Masculinity* (Loiusville, KY: Bridge Resources, 2002).

10. James O'Neill, Glenn Good, and Sarah Holmes, "Fifteen Years of Theory and Research on Men's Gender Role Conflict: New Paradigms for Empirical Research," in *A New Psychology of Men*, 171.

11. O'Neill, Good, and Holmes, 188–191.

12. Richard Eisler, "The Relationship between Masculine Gender Role Stress and Men's Health Risk: The Validation of A Construct," in *A New Psychology of Men*, 207–225.

13. Gary Brooks and Louise Stevenson, "Understanding the Dark Side of Masculinity: An Interactive Systems Model," in *A New Psychology of Men*, ed. Ronald Levant and William Pollack (New York: Basic Books, 1995) 284.

14. Donaldson, Lufkin and Jenrette *Newsletter* (May 1996): 13.

15. Margi Laud McCue, *Domestic Violence: A Reference Handbook* (Santa Barbara, CA: ABC-CL10, 1995), 81.

16. Lora Bex Lempert, "A Narrative Analysis of Abuse: Connecting the Personal, the Rhetorical, and the Structural," *Journal of Contemporary Ethnography* 22:4 (1994): 428.

17. Piera Serra, "Physical Violence in the Couple Relationship: A Contribution toward the Analysis of the Context," *Family Process* 32:1 (1993): 25.

18. Lempert, 432.

19. Serra, 29.

20. Carol Ember and Melvin Ember, "War, Socialization, and Interpersonal Violence," *Journal of Conflict Resolution* 38:4 (1994): 633.

21. Wayne Ewing, "The Civic Advocacy of Men's Violence," in *A New Psychology of Men*, 304.

22. Ibid., 304.

23. Ibid., 304.

24. Michael Kaufman, "The Construction of Masculinity and the Triad of Men's Violence," in *Men's Lives*, 3rd edition, ed. Michael Kimmel and Michael Messner (Boston: Allyn and Bacon, 1995), 17.

25. Ewing, 301.

26. Martha McMahon and Ellen Pence, "Replying to Daniel O'Leary," *Journal of Interpersonal Violence* (September 1996): 452–455.

7

✛

Is Equality
Tearing Families Apart?

Joel Anderson

Let me begin with what I take to be two basic truths. First, social inequality between the sexes should be eliminated. Second, anything that systematically undermines the possibility for healthy, stable, fulfilling family life should be eliminated as well. Put positively, a good society must be *both* pro-equality and pro-family.

On its own, neither position is particularly controversial. Treating women as inferior to men clearly denies them their dignity and moral worth. Insofar as the majority of society's rewards go to men solely because of their sex, women are victims of injustice. Similarly clear intuitions hold with regard to the importance of stable, caring, mutually rewarding marriages and families. Assuming (as I do here) that "married couple" and "family" are understood broadly, as including both traditional and nontraditional household arrangements,[1] what is at issue is one of the most basic forms of social relationships around which individuals build their understanding of the good life. A society that denied its members something that is so widely held to be an essential component of a life worth living would be gravely depriving them. Properly understood, then, a "decline of the family" would pose a genuine threat to human well-being.

My concern here is with the perceived conflict between pro-equality and pro-family approaches. Those who have fought hardest for gender equality often view "pro-family" rhetoric with suspicion and even hostility. And those who have worried most about the decline of the family often view campaigns for gender equality with a similar degree of suspicion and hostility. In this essay, I examine this second set of worries, put forward by a range of social critics and philosophers whom I will label "neotradition-alists."[2] I shall be focusing on three ways in which promoting equality is thought to contribute to the disintegration of families. In each case, these neotraditionalist critics argue that the egalitarian policies of feminists entail further social developments—specifically, genderless parenting, self-ish individualism, and competing agendas—social developments that are tearing families apart. I shall be arguing that this entailment is rarely plausible, and that even when it is, the risks of social fragmentation should not overshadow the importance of gender equality.

Before continuing, a brief clarification is in order with regard to what it means to say that the family is "in decline" or is being "torn apart." I do not mean this as simply a matter of a demographic shift from "intact" families (a couple in their first marriage and their children) to single-parent families and "stepfamilies." Unless one assumes that particular structures for living together are ordained by God or biology, it is an open question whether the increase in single-parent households or common-law marriages represents a problem. What clearly would represent a problem, however, are developments that threaten to rob family life of its meaning and purpose. If, for example, the very point of families is to provide a context in which family members are nurtured, cared for, socialized, etc., then a lack of contact between family members represents a decline of the family. In this sense, a family can be torn apart even without a divorce. Being torn apart is thus also a matter of degree. Again, however, what would be problematic is not that a particular form of household is on the decline,[3] but that people are having trouble maintaining the interpersonal commitments about which they care deeply. On the broad understanding assumed here, the breakup of an unmarried couple can be an instance of family disintegration.

There is mounting evidence that the family is suffering from social fragmentation: half of all marriages end in divorce; "in disrupted families, only one child in six, on average, saw his or her father as often as once a week in the past year";[4] and "parents had roughly 10 fewer hours per week for their children in 1986 than in 1960."[5] None of this demonstrates that we should return to the past, but if some degree of stability and integration is a necessary condition for the sort of family life that so many people deeply value, then the criticisms raised by neotraditionalists must be taken seriously.

EQUALITY AND GENDERLESS PARENTING

Neotraditionalist critics of egalitarian feminism sometimes claim that promoting equality involves endorsing the idea of a genderless family in which breadwinning, homemaking, and childrearing are divided evenly between husband and wife.[6] Neotraditionalists then argue that eliminating distinctions between the role of father and mother forces both men and women to deny essential components of the identity of parents, which is not only bad in itself but also denies families the much-needed stability and complementarity provided by the male-breadwinner/female-homemaker model.

Arguments for this position come from a wide range of viewpoints. In an unusual convergence with neotraditionalists, some feminists hold up motherhood as the distinctive feature of what it is to be a woman.[7] The parallel argument is found, for example, in the work of David Blankenhorn, who argues that fatherhood is central to masculinity.[8] I shall focus on this latter discussion.

Neotraditionalists have taken issue with the ideal of the sensitive, caring, supportive "New Father" who changes half the diapers and whose sense of self-worth depends as much on his homemaking as his breadwinning.[9] Against this ideal, they argue that it is vitally important to recognize the distinctiveness of a father's contribution to the family, especially as a good provider and a strong protector. According to these critics, recognizing this is important for three reasons.

First, if we eliminate the differences between what it means to be a father and what it means to be a mother, we will lose the benefits of diverse role models within the family. For example, some studies have shown that men tend to inspire adventurousness, assertiveness, and risk-taking in their children, whereas women tend to be more risk-averse and protective. If, as seems plausible, children need to learn to balance these two modes of behavior, then it would be a genuine loss if this diversity were eliminated.

Second, as with many social organizations, the family benefits from functional differentiation, that is, from having a diversity of roles and functions that complement one another, rather than having everyone performing the same roles. On these grounds, neotraditionalists hold, for example, that children do best in a situation in which the authority figure of the father contrasts with the sympathetic ear of a mother.

Third, neotraditionalists argue that by telling men that they must think of themselves as homemakers, proponents of gender equality exacerbate family disintegration by leaving men feeling that they have nothing special to contribute.[10] Without the feeling of masculine pride that comes from being a good provider and a role model of strength in the family, it is argued, men's attachment to the responsibilities of fatherhood is diminished. And genderless parenting denies men this feeling of pride.

These neotraditionalist arguments all attempt to link genderless parenting to the depletion of crucial resources for healthy families. Though

some critics might go so far as to claim that this means we should rein-
state the traditional, male-breadwinner/female-homemaker family as the
normative model, the more moderate position is that the differences between men and women should be accepted, thereby "allowing" women
to choose full-time homemaking without guilt and men to focus on breadwinning without shame.

There are several difficulties with this line of argument. To begin with,
it is not entirely clear that promoting equality between men and women
requires eliminating the distinctive roles of mothers and fathers. "Genderless" parenting does not deny that there will be role differences ("father" and "mother") but only that parents should not be trapped in one
role or the other. Thus one can maintain the diversity of roles on which
neotraditionalists insist, while keeping open the question of *who* must fill
the roles. Neither of the first two arguments has given us reason to think
that men should not be "mothers" nor women be "fathers."

The third argument does aim to provide such reasons. At this point,
neotraditionalists often appeal to claims about what is "natural." They re-
ject the idea that men can be "mothers" and women can be "fathers."
Given how much of what gives humans their dignity is the ability to re-
frain from doing "what comes naturally," such direct appeals to nature
are generally dubious. Even so, many people are impressed with the pur-
ported "brute fact" that women are more emotionally attached to their
children, so that they have a much harder time leaving them in the care of
others, and are much more reluctant to put young children in child care.[11]
Assuming, charitably, that there is empirical evidence for a persistent and
fairly general trend, would this show what the neotraditionalists want it
to show? Not necessarily. For it might turn out that the persistence of this
phenomenon may be traceable to inequalities that have much more to do
with socialization than with chromosomes.

Consider, for example, Rhona Mahony's suggestion that women's
"headstart effect" can be overcome through the use of "affirmative action
for fathers."[12] Mahony acknowledges that pregnancy often gives mothers
an inevitable "headstart" over fathers when it comes to their emotional attachment and sensitive attunement to the infant, but she stresses that what
happens after the birth is not biologically predetermined. Typically, of
course, mothers' headstart leads to quicker and more successful responses.
Even without the greater degree of coaching and encouragement women
generally receive from female friends and relatives, the headstart effect can
quickly lead to a situation in which mothers are able to quiet a child
quickly and fathers feel frustrated by their difficulty living up to the standards of mothers. Even when a couple is resolved to share the parenting,
Mahony argues, there are unintentional mechanisms that tend to snow-
ball, so that after only a few months it becomes much more efficient for

mothers to take over the greater share of the childcare. This may look like a "natural" outcome, but biology does not determine this outcome beyond the "headstart effect." In fact, if fathers are given long periods of time in which they have sole responsibility for the young infant, there is every reason to expect that such "affirmative action" will correct the balance or possibly even tip it in the other direction. Before large numbers of fathers have had the opportunity to become equally expert with their children, speculation about what men and women "naturally" want is a poor basis for legitimating practices that perpetuate the unequal status of women.

In this connection, we must be very clear about what is at stake for women in the present discussion. Neotraditionalist attempts to restore the idea that women and men have specific roles to play as mothers and fathers threaten to reentrench the situation in which women who have the primary childcare responsibilities see their chances diminished of later returning to interesting jobs. As recent discussions of "mommy tracks" and "glass ceilings" have made clear, being the primary caregiver for their children often hinders women on the job front, both by restricting the amount of time they can devote to their work and by making them less attractive candidates for being promoted to positions of responsibility.[13] I shall return to this point below.

EQUAL NEGOTIATING POSITIONS

A second set of neotraditionalist suspicions about the egalitarian agenda regards the destabilizing effects of focusing on equality of power. Here the argument is that, although some equality of power in the family is probably a good thing, it should not become a dominant principle. The family, it is argued, follows a different logic than that of politics or business. It is a place of unconditional love and fidelity, a "haven in a heartless world."[14] This climate of love and trust is destroyed by a focus on equal power and equal negotiating positions.

Neotraditionalists do not advocate inequality. They agree with egalitarians that wives should be equal before the law, should be able to own and inherit property, and (for the most part) should not be required to submit to the wishes of their husbands. What they object to is the stronger position taken by egalitarians.

According to this egalitarian position, genuine equality demands both a commitment to equalizing power imbalances as much as possible and an adequate awareness of one's relative power in the relationship. If we care about equality, we must be concerned with how the choices that spouses make are shaped in subtle ways. Unless the negotiating positions are equal, the appearance of fair decision making may be easily misleading.

Furthermore, and this is the importance of *awareness*, even if neither spouse perceives a problematic imbalance, that may simply be because some spouses may be in such a vulnerable position that they cannot *afford* to think about their inequalities.[15]

To understand the egalitarian position, it is best to focus on the difficult decisions that families inevitably face, because it is there that subtle differences on a person's negotiating position can have a huge impact. Take the case of young parents making decisions about who will cut back on his or her hours at work (or quit altogether) in order to care for the newborn, when both spouses are in careers that they love but that will be jeopardized if they cut back on work. Equality demands that the interests of each spouse should weigh as much as those of the other (which is not to say that the only fair outcome is a fifty-fifty split). That requires, in turn, that it is a genuinely open question whether the mother or the father will go part-time to take care of the babies. But if, as is very often the case, the husband's more established career provides a better income or he has little idea how to take care of children by himself, then the wife's negotiating position is seriously weakened. Even if the spouses love each other, this disparity can influence the decision making. Whether the mother wants to or not, the "obvious" thing to do will be for her to cut back on her hours and thereby jeopardize her career. In this way, even among spouses who love each other, an unequal negotiating position can deny women the opportunity to have their career plans adequately considered.

In a similar way, ensuring equal negotiating positions requires guaranteeing that divorce is not available to one spouse on more advantageous terms. This point is important, because when family conflicts arise, they are played out against the background of the possibility of that the marriage may break down. The possibility of divorce gives partners not only a way of escaping an unacceptable position—not insignificant in a world of marital rape and spousal abuse—but also a way of increasing the chances of their criticism being taken seriously. As Albert O. Hirschman observes, "The chances for voice to function effectively as a recuperation mechanism are appreciably strengthened if voice is backed up by the *threat of exit*, whether it is made openly or whether the possibility of exit is merely well understood to be an element in the situation by all concerned."[16] Thus, the equal availability of an "exit option" may actually serve to *prevent* divorce by ensuring that both men and women have a threat at their disposal that will ensure that their voice gets heard.

Beyond formal access to divorce, it is crucially important that the consequences of divorce are equally costly. Otherwise, the negotiating position of one spouse will be stronger. Currently, men's exit options are generally better than those of women: "income for mothers and children declines on average about 30 percent, while fathers experience a 10 to 15 percent increase in their incomes in the year following the separation."[17] The causes of this disparity are complex, but they surely include not only lax enforcement of child support payments but also the fact that while fathers were improving their employment position, mothers have often focused on childcare and housekeeping rather than job experience and networking. Whatever the reasons, however, in this situation of unequal negotiating positions, when the disagreements are intense or the decisions of great consequence, women's awareness that they will be the bigger losers in a divorce can make them willing to tolerate treatment that their husbands would not tolerate. This is a serious form of inequality in their relative negotiating positions.

For neotraditionalists, this egalitarian requirement that couples be vigilant about their relative negotiating positions (and that one work try to establish equal negotiating positions) risks increasing marital instability, for the more a couple focuses on the equality of their negotiating positions, the more they are likely to undermine the climate of trust, commitment, and self-sacrifice that makes families both stable and worthwhile. From this perspective, when spouses start closely monitoring who is taking advantage of whom or thinking about who will lose out in a divorce, they introduce ways of relating to each other that are antithetical to good marriages (as well as being symptomatic of deeper problems). This is often expressed by saying that the culture of the public world of contracts and self-interest has invaded the private domain of the family, where a distinctive culture is to be cherished.

> The goals of women (and of men, too) in the workplace are primarily individualistic: social recognition, wages, opportunities for advancement, and self-fulfillment. But the family is about collective goals that by definition extend beyond individuals: procreation, socializing the young, caring for the old, and building life's most enduring bonds of affection, nurturance, mutual support, and long-term commitment.[18]

Without this commitment to the larger whole, it is argued, families lack the glue that holds them together, and they tend to disintegrate as soon as sacrifices are required. On this view, if family members are focused on making sure that they get their share, they will have trouble weathering the short-term conflicts that inevitably arise.

But does equalizing negotiating positions between spouses really lead to the sort of self-interested culture that tears families apart? Ultimately, this is an empirical question, but given the complexity of the issue and the sort of data needed, some philosophical analysis may help to clarify which hypotheses are most plausible. The answer to this question will certainly depend, in part, on the sorts of families that one has in mind. Here we can distinguish three different cases.

(1) In some families, the negotiating positions will be roughly equal. When spouses must make choices that jeopardize their chances of career advancement and financial independence in the future, the sacrifices are made equally; various arrangements are in place to ensure that neither spouse will end up benefiting financially from a divorce; and, when applicable, childcare responsibilities are distributed in a way that their emotional investment in the children and expertise in childcare is likely to be fairly decided on an equal basis. (This last point is important: if a father has a much easier time losing custody of his children in a divorce, this can make the mother relatively vulnerable in negotiations.) In such cases, an awareness of their equal negotiating positions seems likely to strengthen the stability of the family, for spouses will know that *even when they are not getting along*, they are not in a position to take advantage of the other. Of course, equality of negotiating positions is not sufficient to hold a marriage together, but there is no reason to think that if a couple knows that their interests are balanced, this will threaten their mutual love.

(2) In families where inequalities of power are actually exploited, the different issue arises as to whether keeping the family together is really the best option. I said at the outset that family disintegration is usually something that no one wants, and it is bad for that reason—but not always. If we care about human dignity and autonomy, we must recognize that only if people are aware of the possibility of inequality arising in a relationship will they have any chance of correcting a situation in which someone is taking advantage of them. In a family with young children, of course, the choice to end a marriage often represents a tragic situation, and neotraditionalists are right to point out that parents may have an obligation to accept some sacrifices for the sake of maintaining a tense but stable situation at home. But a situation in which it was typically *women* who made the sacrifices would be a situation of indirect sexism and would deserve moral condemnation.

(3) The neotraditionalist objection is perhaps on its best footing in cases in which there are unequal negotiating positions, but the more powerful spouse does not exploit the other. If the power imbalance is *temporary*—say, if one parent loses a job—then it may well be just a matter of family members needing to take the long view and to trust that advantages will balance out over time. In a situation of lasting and structural inequality, matters may also seem benign, as long as both spouses feel that they have an equal say. An insistence that spouses be aware of the imbalance may then seem unnecessarily risky to the relationship. As long as we are talking about *adequate* and not *maximal* awareness of relative negotiating positions, however, the greater danger, I would suggest, lies in being blind to the presence of serious inequality. For an awareness of it allows both spouses to be attentive to the ways in which they may inadvertently slide

into patterns that they would not have accepted if their negotiating positions had been equal. Furthermore, only with an awareness of such imbalances is it possible for spouses to make a moral appeal to each other based on a special vulnerability, which itself can contribute to marital stability.

This last point can be generalized. If neotraditionalists are concerned with genuine stability in a relationship, they would do well to acknowledge the ways in which genuine equality provides a basis that is at least as stable as the reliance on traditional family models. To ensure that the stability is more than skin-deep conventionalism, some awareness of and concern with spouses' relative negotiating positions is vitally important.

EQUALITY OF INDIVIDUAL OPPORTUNITY

The third neotraditionalist criticism that I wish to consider focuses, like the one just discussed, on the threat that increasing individualism poses to the family. The central suspicion is that feminist egalitarianism undermines the stability of families by allowing the centrifugal forces of the labor market to affect the family more brutally than ever before. Neotraditionalists suggest that, in the push for women's equality, traditional assumptions about the family have been dismantled, taking with them one of the best bulwarks against the divisive demands of the labor market.

In order to examine this claim, we need to understand something of the importance of freedom of choice, especially with regard to the choice of occupation. Historically, the process of industrialization has led to fundamental transformations of family life, for example, in nineteenth-century Europe.[19] Whereas the vast majority of people in preindustrial societies had no choice of occupation (to the point that their role, usually as peasant, was prescribed by the metaphysical world order), in modern industrial societies the possibilities for choice expanded both in scope and significance. The modern view emerged that free choice of occupation is an important basic liberty, one that guaranteed the opportunity for self-realization. Freedom of choice—and particularly freedom to choose one's occupation—thus became a fundamentally important moral claim of modern individuals. What is at issue is the very possibility of leading one's life as one's own. Only if people could choose their line of work could they truly be free to develop their own sense of individual identity and self-worth.

Women were, of course, long denied this freedom. Men planned their careers, and women planned their weddings. Insofar as that is still the case, promoting equality will indeed demand that the roles available to women be expanded so as to be equal with that of men. As a general proposition, few would deny that women have an equal moral claim to the possibilities for self-determination and self-realization as men. What feminists have shown, however, is that developing the social conditions under which this is a reality calls for significant transformations. In particular, it involves eliminating the automatic assumption that women will be the ones staying home to care for small children. For as long as employers have reason to believe that young women are more likely to leave the work force (or request a shift to a part-time position), decline positions that require overtime or travel, and take time off to care for a sick relative, employers have significant economic incentives to invest in training and promoting men rather than women, thus reducing women's opportunities for self-realization.[20] Rectifying this situation is not, it should be noted, a matter of making special accommodations to women but of realizing more consistently the principles of a free labor market.[21]

As neotraditionalists point out, however, the labor market does not operate on the basis of family-friendly principles.[22] Especially in a world in which global competition is intense and labor unions are relatively weak, the labor market often demands, for example, that workers relocate to find work and that they put in extra hours if they are to remain competitive. The German sociologist Ulrich Beck follows out this line of thought to its logical extreme:

> Ultimately, the market model of modernity presupposes a society without families or marriages. Everyone must be free and independent for the requirements of the market, in order to secure his or her existence.... Accordingly, a fully realized market society is also a society without children—unless the children grow up with mobile, single-parent fathers and mothers.[23]

Given this, even some feminists have recently discussed the costs to women (and their families) of their entry into the labor market, even if it is something that equality demands.[24] Neotraditionalists tend to blame these costs on feminists' campaign for equal opportunity. But it seems far more accurate to say, as Beck does, that this transformation was a matter of artificial barriers to women's participation in the workplace finally being removed.

Whatever the cause, having both men and women in the labor market has added strains on the family as a result of the increasing number of difficult decisions that must be made. The more options people have, the more complicated the task becomes of trying to coordinate cooperative relationships. As a result of the constant demands to communicate needs and arrive at agreements, the potential for conflict rises dramatically. Take the case of being relocated for a job. In a world in which tradition clearly dictates that the family will move wherever the father's job takes him, no decision really needs to be made. There may still be unhappiness and conflict about the move, but the source of the conflict is situated outside the family. As those traditional assumptions crumble, it becomes a contingent matter how families should resolve such situations. Simple appeals to "how we have always done things" must be replaced by the hard work of finding a way to take everyone's needs into consideration. As a result, to quote Beck again, "The family becomes a constant juggling act of disparate multiple ambitions among careers and their requirements for mobility, educational demands, conflicting parental obligations, and bothersome housework."[25] If this is what women's equality of opportunity brings us, neotraditionalists ask, is it really worth it?

With regard to what women's full participation in the labor market has *taken away*, the critics argue that given how promoting equality involves challenging traditional assumptions about how parental responsibilities will be divided, the egalitarian agenda may be undermining the very bulwark that it needs against the centrifugal pressures of the labor market. When women did not insist on working outside the home, they argue, family stability was less threatened by employers' demands for mobility, because the pressures were again construed as lying *outside the private sphere of the family*. On this view, the head of household faced the competitive, interest-based public world, but came home to a world free of competing agendas. Furthermore, the traditional family model also provided clear roles and expectations, such that much less was open to the sort of debates that can tear families apart.

The difficulties with this neotraditionalist line of argument lie both in what it advocates and what it fails to advocate. On the first count, the neotraditionalist proposal that we restore our faith in certain traditional assumptions about the family—such as the model of men as family providers—is not really an option available in modern industrial societies. Aside from the fact that returning to more traditional approaches would involve unconscionably disproportionate sacrifices from women, it would not actually eliminate the need to make complex and conflict-ridden decisions. Once "how we do things" has become a contingent matter, every form of traditionalism is a *neo*traditionalism. You have to argue for it, or at least choose it. Today, when a couple picks the traditional male-breadwinner/female-homemaker pattern, the modern understanding of mutual and just respect demands that it be a *choice* made by *equals*—and that it be done in a way that does not jeopardize future possibilities for self-determination.

What neotraditionalists overlook are the posttraditional alternatives. Since industrial societies have been based on the assumption that only half of the potential work force would participate, it is not really all that surprising that fundamental changes are needed as part of the shift to genuinely full employment (that is, of both men and women). There are numerous proposals regarding *structural changes* that can be made in the way in which homemaking and breadwinning are distributed.[26] For example, some have proposed policies that would enable couples to participate effectively in the labor market *as couples*.[27]

Much of the appeal of the call for retraditionalization is based on the assumption that people will necessarily be overwhelmed by the complexities of a world without traditional gender roles. Talk of "disorientation" is common here. Such talk is premature, however. With the appropriate support, there is clearly room to increase people's capacities to handle these complex new decisions, not simply as individuals but also as families, concerned with their well-being as families. If families are to find their way through the inevitable conflicts, they will need a wide array of skills, virtues, and practices that must be developed and sustained themselves. These include, for example, capacities to listen sympathetically and express oneself clearly, commitments to ensuring that no one is inadvertently silenced and that even unconventional solutions are given due consideration, and clearly established (but revisable) procedures for family deliberations. This could empower individuals to build and maintain their families amidst growing complexity.

Although providing a full blueprint for change is beyond the scope of the present essay, these brief sketches serve to highlight the possibilities for responding effectively to contemporary challenges to family stability without having to follow the neotraditionalists in compromising a commitment to equality.

There is no denying the difficulties involved in keeping a family together today, and many of these challenges result partly from the increasing equality of men and women. But it would be a narrow-minded mistake to say that the current challenges are generated by demands for gender equality. Rather, they are part of the larger challenge posed by living in a world in which the artificial constraints of tradition and conventions are increasingly dissolving. What I have argued here is that, as we face these challenges, neotraditionalism only presents us with a false dichotomy between genuine gender equality and a supportive climate for stable family life. Critics of feminist egalitarianism would have us choose between pro-family and pro-equality positions. Fortunately, even in complex modern societies, that is one decision that no one has to make.[28]

NOTES

This essay first appeared *Applied Ethics: A Multicultural Approach*, 2nd edition, ed. Larry May, Shari Sharratt, and Kai Wong (New York: Prentice-Hall, 2002) and is used with permission of the copyright holder.

1. In "Of Mothers and Families, Men and Sex", Marilyn Friedman provides a suitably broad definition of "family" as an "enduring household based on inter-

personal commitment," which rightly includes homosexual couples. I shall focus on heterosexual couples, however, since I am concerned with gender equality and thus on relations between men and women.

2. In this essay, "neotraditionalism" represents a composite portrait of positions defended by a wide range of authors, most typically by the members of The Council on Families in America and the Institute for American Values. See the essays collected in *Rebuilding the Nest: A New Commitment to the American Family*, ed. David Blankenhorn, Steven Bayme, and Jean Bethke Elshtain (Milwaukee, WI: Family Service America, 1990); and *Promises to Keep: Decline and Renewal of Marriage in America*, ed. David Popenoe, Jean Bethke Elshtain, and David Blankenhorn (Lanham, MD: Rowman & Littlefield, 1996). Although the positions I outline are typical of this approach, my concern here is with widely held viewpoints rather than the claims of particular authors.

3. After all, social critics in the past decried the breakdown of the extended family and the rise of the nuclear family.

4. Barbara Defoe Whitehead, "Dan Quayle was Right," *The Atlantic Monthly*, April 1993, 65.

5. Janet Z. Giele, "Decline of the Family: Conservative, Liberal, and Feminist Views," in Popenoe (et al.), *Promises to Keep*, 91.

6. E.g., Susan Moller Okin, *Justice, Gender, and the Family* (New York: Basic Books, 1989).

7. E.g., Nel Noddings, *Caring: A Feminine Approach to Ethics and Moral Education* (Berkeley: University of California Press, 1984); and Virginia Held, "Feminism and Moral Theory," in *Women and Moral Theory*, ed. Eva Feder Kittay and Diana T. Meyers (Totowa, NJ: Rowman & Littlefield, 1987), 111–128.

8. David Blankenhorn, *Fatherless America: Confronting Our Most Urgent Social Problem* (New York: Basic Books, 1995).

9. In addition to Blankenhorn's *Fatherless America*, see Bruno Bettleheim's earlier piece, "Fathers Shouldn't Try to Be Mothers," *Parents Magazine*, October 1956.

10. This is the main theme of Blankenhorn's *Fatherless America*. It is also a prominent message in various recent "men's movements," including the Promise-Keepers and the Nation of Islam's Million Man March.

11. Rhona Mahony, *Kidding Ourselves: Breadwinning, Babies, and Bargaining Power* (New York: Basic Books, 1995), 107–109. For a contrasting approach, which views the greater attachment of mothers as a fact of "genetic wiring," see Danielle Crittenden, "Yes, Motherhood Lowers Pay," *The New York Times*, August 22, 1995.

12. Mahony, *Kidding Ourselves*, 102–106. It should be noted that the biological headstart effect is absent in the case of adoptive mothers.

13. See, e.g., Mahony, *Kidding Ourselves*, 14–17.

14. Christopher Lasch, *Haven in a Heartless World* (New York: Basic Books, 1977).

15. See Okin, *Justice, Gender, and the Family*, ch. 7; and Laura Sanchez and Emily W. Kane, "Women's and Men's Constructions of Perceptions of Housework Fairness," *Journal of Family Issues* 17 (1996): 358–387.

16. Albert O. Hirschman, *Exit, Voice, and Loyalty: Responses to Decline in Firms, Organization, and States* (Cambridge, MA: Harvard University Press, 1970), 82.

17. Whitehead, "Dan Quayle Was Right," 62. See also Lenore J. Weitzman, *The Divorce Revolution: The Unexpected Social and Economic Consequences for Women and Children in America* (New York: The Free Press, 1985). For a discussion of how this affects women's negotiating position, see Mahony, *Kidding Ourselves*, ch. 3. It should be noted that different issues affect the very poor: insofar as welfare assistance is restricted to unmarried mothers, the breakdown of a marriage may leave men with even fewer resources than women (with custody).

18. David Blankenhorn, "American Family Dilemmas," in Blankenhorn et al., *Rebuilding the Nest*, 10f.

19. For an excellent analysis of this development, see Elisabeth Beck-Gernsheim, "Auf dem Weg in die postfamiliale Familie: Von der Notgemeinschaft zur Wahlvervandtschaft," in *Riskante Freiheiten: Individualisierung in modernen Gesellschaften*, ed. Ulrich Beck and Elisabeth Beck-Gernsheim (Frankfurt: Suhrkamp, 1994), 115–138.

20. Felice N. Schwartz makes clear what it currently costs companies to ensure that mothers make their way into the executive ranks in "Management Women and the New Facts of Life," *Harvard Business Review* (Jan./Feb. 1989).

21. Ulrich Beck, *Risk Society: Toward a New Modernity* (London: Sage, 1992), 176–181.

22. Robert N. Bellah, "The Invasion of the Money World," in *Rebuilding the Nest*, 227.

23. Beck, *Risk Society*, 191.

24. Even feminists such as Judith Stacey have expressed concerns here: "Feminist enthusiasm for female autonomy encouraged women's massive entry into the postindustrial labor market. This, in turn, abetted the corporate deunionization strategies that have accompanied the reorganization of the U.S. economy." Stacey, *Brave New Families: Stories of Domestic Upheaval in Late Twentieth Century* (New York: Basic Books, 1990), 12f.

25. Beck, *Risk Society*, 184.

26. E.g., Okin, *Justice, Gender, and the Family*, ch. 8; and Mahony, *Kidding Ourselves*, ch. 9–10. Neotraditionalists make some of these proposals themselves but see structural change as far from sufficient to counter the pressures toward social fragmentation: see, esp., The Council on Families in America, "Marriage in America: A Report to the Nation," in Popenoe et al., *Promises to Keep*, 310.

27. Beck, *Risk Society*, 194–204.

28. I would like to thank Larry May, Pauline Kleingeld, Herbert Anderson, and Don Browning for comments on earlier drafts.

8

Navigating between Cultures: The Bicultural Family's Lived Realities

K. Samuel Lee

If our assumption . . . is to regard the other as an individual or culture or religious tradition of equal worth, we need to be able to set the other at [a] distance and imagine a world quite different than our own. Even when our understanding is partial, even if our presumption of the other's equal worth is fleeting, it is a beginning. Even that beginning, however, is risky. When we really listen to the story of another, when we enter as fully as possible in to [sic] the world and experience of someone we presume to be a stranger, we will be changed. And even if we are not changed, our vision of the human has been expanded by every story we hear. *We may discover in the end that the stranger is not dangerous: empathy is.*

—Herbert Anderson[1]

Korean American families today face difficult and distinctive questions about the nature of love because of the particularities of their historical and social context. Most troubling, can a theologically conceived notion of familial love from a monocultural context be applied to a multicultural context? More specifically, what happens to the concept of biblical love, construed as *agape* (sacrificial love) and *caritas* (mutuality), when multicultural dynamics are added to the theological equation? How is the experience of mutuality in marriage expanded by bicultural partnership? In this essay, I shall address these questions about familial love within the Korean American bicultural family via the concept of cultural identification.[2]

On the surface, the Korean American family is confronted with seemingly opposing and contradictory cultural forces that cannot be reconciled. The Korean American family has been influenced by a worldview fashioned from centuries of hierarchical Confucianism. At the same time, it is going through structural renovation because of the experience of living in the highly individualistic North American culture. The Korean traditional familial practice is often perceived as putting more emphasis on sacrificial love of family members for the collective, while the North American familial practice calls for mutuality of individuals in familial relations. I shall argue in this essay, however, that this apparent contradiction between hierarchy and mutuality results from the theoretical construction that allows only the forced choice of *either-or* between the bicultural dimensions in which Korean American families live.

Privileging one set of cultural practices over another in the bicultural family's life falls short of the ideals of mutuality. In contrast to the *either-or* model, I propose for the Korean American family a *both-and* model which regards both cultures as sources of strength for bicultural family living.[3] Enhancing familial love in bicultural families requires a kind of cultural mutuality or mutual respect for the contributions of both cultures. Below I shall describe the concept of cultural identification, the two cultural identification models, how familial love may be best understood as a function of both agape and caritas in the Korean American family, and implications for pastoral theology.

CULTURAL IDENTIFICATION

Within the field of individual developmental psychology, the concept of identification has been regarded as a mechanism of limited usefulness. In his study of American youth, Erik Erikson emphasized understanding identity and identity formation instead.[3] In the context of cross-cultural psychology, however, cultural identification has been regarded as an important concept. Psychologists E. R. Oetting and Fred Beauvais state that cultural identification is a concept deriving from cultural process theories in contrast to cultural content theories.[4] Cultural process theories examine formalistic aspects in cultural transitions, such as the process of marginality,[5] acculturation,[6] and the concept of cultural stake,[7] while cultural content theories examine culture-specific behaviors, attitudes, and beliefs, such as childrearing practices and gender role differences.

Oetting and Beauvais observe that cultural identification is an important concept when studying multiple cultures in contact with one another, especially for ethnic minorities. Individuals with minority status are often pulled between two cultures and report conflicting self-identity, values, attitudes, beliefs, or loyalty, all of which are considered influential factors in shaping the overall pattern of one's cultural adaptation. In this society, one must choose, whether voluntarily or involuntarily and whether consciously or unconsciously, ways to identify himself or herself with their traditional and often devalued ethnic culture or with the esteemed American culture. Furthermore, the latter is usually regarded as the norm according to which all other cultures are judged. According to Oetting and Beauvais and partially confirmed by my own study, the ways of being in relation to cultures, or cultural identification, have important bearing on how successfully or unsuccessfully a person may function in a given society.

Oetting further develops the idea of cultural identification as an underlying long-term personality trait that has bearing on one's cognition, emotions, and behaviors.[8] He describes culture as a functional organism that interacts with the person. The individual experiences the culture in terms of its demands and its responses or rewards and punishments. Cultural identification depends upon the pattern of cultural demands and responses and the degree to which the person's and the culture's needs are met as they continue to interact with each other. Accordingly, "cultural identification develops and is maintained through interactions with the environment" similar to other personality traits.[9]

More specifically, Oetting offers the following four-step model to illustrate how the culture and the person interact, leading to either the maintenance or decline of one's cultural identification:

Step 1: Culture presents demands

Cultural demands are requirements made of people when they interact in specific cultural contexts. These requirements run the entire gamut of cultural content. Examples include using language appropriately; expressing the "right" cultural attitudes; using gender-appropriate gestures; playing defined roles in ceremonies; or engaging in culturally approved child care, work, or play.

Step 2: Actions respond to demands

Culture-related actions are designed to meet these cultural demands and include nearly every behavior that occurs within or in relation to social contexts: for example, speech, dress, posture, attention, walking, dancing, typing, driving, painting, and elimination.

Step 3: Culture responds to the person's actions

The culture evaluates whether these actions meet cultural requirements and responds accordingly. Cultural responses can be simple verbal and nonverbal communications. They can include objects such as money or clothing, symbols such as rank or a marriage tattoo, or actions. Most importantly, when the person behaves in ways that meet cultural demands, the culture responds in ways that the culture views as positive.

Step 4: Needs are met through culture's responses

For a cultural response to be truly reinforcing, it must meet the cultural needs of the person. Culture-related needs can be as fundamental as the need for food, water, shelter, and social exchange or as peripheral as the desire for a new pair of designer jeans. All these needs, even the most basic ones, are met in today's world through cultural interactions. Culture provides the context in which these basic human needs are met.[10]

Issues of cultural identification were experienced in my own family as we went through different stages of the family cycle. For instance, my daughter, who was born in Arizona, was raised at home with the Korean language intentionally spoken. She started to attend a predominantly European American preschool in Los Angeles at the age of three. Until this point, we had always called her by her Korean (middle) name, Aujean. On the first day of her preschool, when she asked to introduce herself, she used her American (first) name, Christina—the name that we had not used much in our family.

Even for a three-year-old toddler, it was evident what the culture demanded of her. Her culture-related action was designed to meet the cultural demand. Toward this end, she needed not to appear to be exotic, uncommon, or strange. Presumably, her identification with the dominant culture of her class resulted in acceptance by others; her use of the American name also helped her feel at one with the rest of her class. Thus, her need to belong on the first day of preschool was met through her intentionally chosen culture-related action. Having met her personal need, her culture's response continues to shape the way she identifies with the cultural context in which she functions.

Of course, our family continues to call her by her Korean name. Once in a while, Christina wonders aloud whether she should use her Korean name. Perhaps she will confront the ambivalence of American culture before she intentionally bestows a name on herself when she becomes an adult. The ambivalence comes from an American culture that demands that she be American but simultaneously demands that she stay within her ethnic enclave, regardless of the fact that she was born in the U.S. and is as much an American as anyone. Embedded in this societal ambivalence is the covert pressure that coerces individuals to choose between the two cultures—either American or Korean culture.

Most Korean American families, however, have no choice but to live in two different cultures. Like trying to swim in water that contains a mixture of elements, many people deal with this by parsing out certain cultural elements, as if different cultural demands can be neatly isolated within lived experience. They try to operate with one set of assumptions in one context and another set of assumptions in another context rather than realizing that the elements cannot be so neatly separated. In the next section, I review two models of cultural identification that illustrate these divergent options.

TWO CULTURAL IDENTIFICATION MODELS: LINEAR VS. ORTHOGONAL

The Korean American family, like many other ethnic minority families in this society, lives under the dominant influence of the Anglo-Saxon-European-American culture that assumes being American is better than remaining Korean. Between two seemingly contradictory cultural forces, the Korean American family is expected either to become more American (thus less Korean) or remain more Korean (thus less American), thereby leaving no alternative way of considering one's bicultural identity. This understanding of cross-cultural identification is based on the linear or zero-sum model wherein the family's cultural identification with two cultures always adds up to zero.

Oetting and Beauvais present several types of the linear cultural identification model. The linear cultural identification models, though various in type, share the belief that two cultures stand at the opposite ends of a continuum and that it is obviously better to move toward the dominant culture. Moreover, identification with one culture cancels out identification with the other culture.

The way in which Korean American immigrants represent their generations in terms of numeric value is a prime example of the prevalence of this linear cultural identification model. Parents (born in Korea) are called "first generation" and children (born in the U.S.) "second generation." The term "1.5 generation" refers to children who are born in Korea but grow up in the U.S., thus usually bilingual and bicultural. The "1.5 generation" Koreans who stand between two generations are regarded as caught in between two cultures, marginalized from both cultures and often confused about their identity. The "1.5 generation" Korean Americans are not quite American or Korean and are said to suffer from the anomie (absence or lack) of identity because they cannot locate themselves on the mutually exclusive line between the two cultures.[11]

According to the linear model, one might hypothesize that the bicultural family would be inherently problem-ridden because of the seemingly irreconcilable cultural differences, and that the "1.5 generation" Korean Americans would suffer more than other generations from "acculturation stress."[12] Oetting and Beauvais tested these hypotheses with Native American and Hispanic American populations, and I have duplicated the study with a Korean American population.

The results of our studies, however, indicate that the linear cultural identification model is inadequate to explain the lived experience of the bicultural family. These studies suggest instead that bicultural identification is best understood using an orthogonal model or using a two-dimensional model with "x" and "y" axes. In other words, identification with American culture is independent from identification with Korean culture and vice versa rather than operating on the same singular line. Furthermore, statistical analysis indicates that persons who suffer most in a bicultural environment are those who lack identification with any culture, that identification with both Korean and American cultures is a source of strength, and that identification with both cultures has additive and positive effects on one's mental health status. Not surprisingly, the persons who measured most favorably on a mental stress scale were those with the strongest identification with both Korean and American cultures, presumably those who are like the "1.5 generation" Korean Americans in the linear model.

These findings suggest that there is no reason to privilege one culture over another in a bicultural experience in so far as one's mental health is concerned. More importantly, if identification with each culture contributes to the well-being of individuals, the biculturality of the Korean American family should be encouraged and fostered. This mixing of cultures more closely resembles the lived reality of the bicultural family than the "either-or" linear model.

This analysis of cultural identification has important implications for how love is understood and expressed in Korean American families. Stated simply, defining familial love as either agape (sacrificial love) or caritas (mutuality) resembles too closely the linear model in understanding love. Such conceptions create impossible tensions for Korean Americans who inhabit two cultures with different assumptions about love. In the next section, I propose a way to resolve the tension between agape and caritas generated by the linear model and experienced within the Korean American bicultural family.

FAMILIAL LOVE IN THE
KOREAN AMERICAN FAMILY: AGAPE VS. CARITAS?

Every cross-cultural study must acknowledge the critical and theoretical research quandary generated by the Malinowskian Dilemma. The Dilemma states that elements within one cultural system can only be understood in its own cultural terms.[13] Similarly, Emile Durkheim recognized that no cultural facts can be understood when they are detached from their cultural context. And Clifford Geertz used an onion metaphor to speak about culture. According to Geertz, the cross-cultural comparisons are strenuous because the researcher's explication of a culture is like peeling the outer layers of an onion. When the researcher gets to the "bottom" or the root meaning of a given cultural construct, such as familial love, he or she is left with a series of disjointed layers that function as the context out of which meaning is construed.

In other words, familial love as understood within the American cultural context cannot be directly correlated with or understood as familial love within the Korean cultural context. This implies that a sound cross-cultural study should not privilege one culture over another. This also reveals the serious limitations of the linear model described above due to its value-laden evaluation of minority cultures.

If this is the case, how does one compare a concept across two cultures? I would argue that this question itself challenges the limits of a Western Platonic idealism that inclines to discriminate and even segregate taxonomies rather than to appreciate the complexities of life. Rather than evaluative comparison, appreciating the differing ideals of familial love within respective cultures is a better starting point. In cross-cultural discussion, such appreciation would promote a "both-and" rather than an "either-or" choice.

In recent years, North American pastoral theologians have pointed out the importance of mutual love and the problems of sacrificial love. As much as I support the need to work against the long-standing patriarchal oppression of women, I would argue that extreme emphasis on mutuality or equality alone ignores the multivalent complexity of human relationships. Granted that all human beings are equal in worth, person-to-person relationships are shaped by various essentials as well as socially constructed variables, such as age, developmental and acquired disabilities, religion, ethnicity, socioeconomic status, sexual orientation, indigenous heritage, national origin, and gender.[13] The concept of mutuality alone cannot cover the many complexities of human identity and relationship. In a different but related argument in another chapter in this book, Bonnie Miller-McLemore considers the ways in which age and developmental stages of family members mitigate the concept of mutuality and demand a modification of common understandings in light of the "transitional hierarchy" between parents and children.

Does an analogous move need to be made when considering bicultural families? How can the Korean American family effectively resolve the tension between Confucian hierarchical influence and the more individualistic and egalitarian influence of North American culture? Even the way the question is stated reflects the "either-or" dilemma of monoculturalism. Whether or not this tension can be successfully resolved, the bicultural family already lives in the bicultural reality. Pushing people to choose between two cultures is like demanding that people breathe in only a certain element that the natural breathing process cannot separate. Such coercion only results in what Paulo Freire calls "cultural violence" against the minority members of a society.[14] The "empirical principle" of pastoral theology honors the lived experience of the bicultural family. Rather than seeing the Korean American family as a problem that needs solving, trusting the lived experience of struggling families provides an alternative framework for determining theological norms.[15] Moreover, many majority persons who live within a monocultural world limit their full life potential when they remain in their "monocultural encapsulation."[16]

RECONCEPTUALIZING FAMILIAL LOVE IN A BICULTURAL CONTEXT

To conceptualize the bicultural experience more clearly, theologian Jung Young Lee proposes the concept of "complementary dualism" over the "conflicting dualism" of Western philosophy.[17] The concept of complementary dualism derives from the Asian yin-yang philosophy, which Lee describes "as a hermeneutic key" to understanding the Korean "cosmo-anthropology." The yin-yang philosophy views the world as complemented by seemingly conflicting forces of yin (negative) and yang (positive).

The conflicting dualism approach to familial love represents it dualistically, positioning agape over/against caritas. In some cases, this view of family love has created an "either-or" choice that actually undermines existing familial relationships.[18] The linear cultural identification model embodies such dualism. When a researcher follows the linear model in collecting empirical data on how familial partners regard agape and caritas, the researcher asks this type of question:[19]

On the following scale of 1 to 5 (1=agape and 5=caritas), how would you rate yourself in relation to your partner?

Agape				Caritas
1	2	3	4	5

This type of question presupposes that agape and caritas are opposites, conflicting in nature, and a matter of an either-or choice. This is a zero-sum model because to be more agape-like means to be less caritas-like and vice versa. Stated in different terms, this question implies that agape and *caritas* are analogous to elements, such as water and fire, thus representing concepts that have a nullifying effect on each other. In one respect, water and fire have physical properties that seem oppositional because they do not mix well. In another respect, however, they are totally different physical matters that are not oppositional in nature and cannot be directly compared. Likewise, laying the assumptions of conflicting dualism over the concepts of agape and caritas can easily distort how lived reality is perceived.

The orthogonal cultural identification model suggests a different type of question:[20]

On the following two scales of 1 to 5 (1=minimal and 5=maximal), how would you rate yourself in relation to your partner?

Least Agape-like   Most Agape-like
1   2   3   4   5

Least Caritas-like   Most Caritas-like
1   2   3   4   5

Here two separate questions are used in recognition that one's identification with agape is not necessarily correlated with one's identification with caritas. If, in fact, these two concepts describe the opposite (not oppositional) and complementary (not conflicting) sides of the same coin, there is theoretically no reason for these two concepts to correlate linearly with one another. Both, I would argue, are good, important, and complementary virtues in a theologically and psychologically healthy family.

How then might the Korean American family understand the tension between Confucian hierarchy and egalitarian North American culture? If biculturality is desirable and contributes to the well-being of individuals, both influences must be viewed not in terms of conflicting dualism but in terms of complementary dualism. As opposite sides of the same coin, these two visions of reality are inseparable both in bicultural living and familial love. The wisdom garnered from cross-cultural experience recognizes that both views of familial love possess good and important values and, when taken as complementary, more fully embody human life.

In a collection of essays, *Is Multiculturalism Bad for Women*, feminist political scientist Susan Okin raises a difficult question.[21] Other feminist thinkers in the book rightly admonish Okin that multiculturalism and feminism must not be juxtaposed in conflicting dualism. Yet, at the same time, the question points out how certain unjust cultural practices can be perpetuated in the desire to respect cultural diversity. Okin is absolutely correct in calling many patriarchal cultures unjust because they suppress the necessary and faithful navigation between complementary values that must be foundational for healthy and just familial relationships.

The same question might be posed for the Korean American bicultural family. Can the traditional Confucian values coexist with egalitarian values? The question is misleading, however, because such values coexist already, whether one likes it or not. Better stated, the question should ask: How can both the traditional Confucian culture and the Western egalitarian culture support and complement each other for healthy and just familial relationships? Both Korean and American cultures, I believe, have values and practices that can contribute to nurturing a healthy family. At the same time, both cultures are in need of continuing transformation to rid themselves of oppressive elements. Values advocated in a culture can always become perverted in practice. In the name of love, a familial partner may be pressed to live the life of self-sacrifice unjustly. In the name of love, a familial partner may demand equal regard in such a way as to disregard the self-giving that is also foundational for the Christian understanding of familial love. Furthermore, families should be protected from the enslaving extremes of cultural assumptions. The relationship itself, as source of both mutual and sacrificial love, deserves safeguarding. Faithful navigation between the Korean and the American cultures (or between the virtues of agape and caritas) remains the task of the bicultural family, rather than the selective breeding of monocultural values. As argued earlier, such a practice of selective cultural breeding is an impossible task that resembles the effort to parse out certain elements from the air in our natural breathing process.

IMPLICATIONS FOR PASTORAL THEOLOGY

I have argued that the linear model of cultural identification, or the conflicting dualistic mode of thinking about lived reality, is unhelpful in describing multicultural family life. Moreover, the pastoral theologian must examine critically Christian doctrines in light of lived reality. Often, doctrinal and theoretical frameworks streamline the complexities of lived experience, thus presenting a shallow, if not distorted, account of reality. A bicultural examination can deepen the pastoral theologian's appreciation of the richness of human life because the seemingly conflicting worldviews force her or him to examine the very basic assumptions that have been taken for granted. In this regard, multicultural examinations of human life and belief systems have much to offer because they will keep us more faithfully on our creaturely toes before our Creator. The pastoral theologian's task is not to reduce the messiness of lived reality to satisfy the human mind's need for clarity to the point of idolatrous reductionism. It is rather to show appreciation for the Creator's complicated and intricate design already embedded in the human lived experience. The pastoral theologian will discover in the end that the multicultural stranger is indeed not dangerous: empathy, or a faithful and multicultural engagement with the stranger is—and wondrously so.

NOTES

1. Herbert Anderson, "Seeing the Other Whole: A Habitus for Globalization," *Mission Studies* 14:1–2 (1977): 40–63.

2. I use in this essay the definition of the Korean American bicultural family as the immigrant Korean family that typically consists of the first generation parents and the "next generation" children who are either born in the U.S. or came to the U.S. before their teenage years, thus being more American than Korean in their cultural identity. The importance here is not necessarily in the generational difference but in the existing reality of two cultures in the family's life. Therefore, intermarriage between Korean and non-Korean persons can also be considered as the Korean American bicultural family.

3. See the following selected references for more thorough reviews of these two models: E. R. Oetting and Fred Beauvais, "Orthogonal Cultural Identification Theory: The Cultural Identification of Minority Adolescents," *The International Journal of the Addictions* 25:5A and 6A (1990–91): 655–85; E. R. Oetting, "Orthogonal Cultural Identification: Theoretical Links Between Cultural Identification and Substance Use," *Drug Abuse Among Minority Youth: Advances in Research and Methodology*, Monograph 130 (Bethesda, MD: National Institute on Drug Abuse Research, 1993), 32–56; and K. Samuel Lee, "Korean American Cultural Identifications: Effects on Mental Stress and Self-Esteem," Ph.D. dissertation (Tempe: Arizona State University, 1995).

4. Erik Erikson, *Identity: Youth and Crisis* (New York: W. W. Norton, 1968).

5. Oetting and Beauvais, 656.

6. E. V. Stonequist, "The Marginal Man: A Study in Personality and Culture Conflict," in *Contributions to Urban Sociology*, ed. E. W. Burgess and D. J. Bogue (Chicago: University of Chicago Press, 1963), 327–45.

7. E.g., J. Berry and R. Annis, "Acculturative Stress: The Role of Ecology, Culture and Differentiation," *Journal of Cross Cultural Psychology* 5 (1974): 382–406; J. Berry and U. Kim, "Acculturation and Mental Health," in *Health and Cross-Cultural Psychology: Toward Applications*, ed. P. R. Dasen, J. W. Berry, and N. Saartorius (Newbury Park, CA: Sage, 1988), 207–36; J. Berry, U. Kim, T. Minde, and D. Mok, "Comparative Studies of Acculturative Stress," *International Migration Review* 21:3 (1987): 491–511; J. Berry, U. Kim, S. Power, M. Young, and M. Bujaki, "Acculturation Attitudes in Plural Societies," *Applied Psychology* 38 (1989): 185–206; J. Berry, J. Trimble, and E. Olmedo, "Assessment of Acculturation," in *Field Methods in Cross-cultural Research*, ed. W. Lonner and J. Berry (Newbury Park, CA: Sage, 1986), 291–349.

8. F. N. Ferguson, "Stake Theory as an Explanatory Device in Navajo Alcoholism Treatment Response," *Human Organization* 35:1 (1976): 65–78.

9. Oetting, 33ff.

10. Ibid., 33.

11. Ibid., 34–5.

12. Based on my research, my preference is to call 1.5 generation the "trans-generation" and, together with second-generation Koreans, "next-generation" Korean Americans.

13. Berry and Annis, 382–406.

14. Walter Goldschmidt, *Comparative Functionalism: An Essay in Anthropological Theory* (Berkeley: University of California Press, 1966), 7ff.

15. This list of variables is represented as the acronym ADDRESSING by Pamela Hays, *Addressing Cultural Complexities in Practice: A Framework for Clinicians and Counselors* (Washington, DC: American Psychological Association, 2001).

16. Paulo Freire, *Pedagogy of the Oppressed* (New York: Seabury Press, 1970).

17. James N. Poling, "Sexuality: A Crisis for the Church," in *Pastoral Care and Social Conflict*, ed. Pamela Couture and Rodney Hunter (Nashville, TN: Abingdon, 1995), 116. Poling applies the empirical principle in the context of human suffering. I use the term more liberally, applying it to the undeniable lived reality of human experience.

18. Gilbert Wrenn, "The Culturally Encapsulated Counselor," *Harvard Educational Review* 32 (1962): 444–49.

19. Jung Young Lee, *The Trinity in Asian Perspective* (Nashville, TN: Abingdon, 1996), 23.

20. The extreme example of this situation is reviewed by Bonnie Miller-McLemore's critique of Carter Heyward's radical understanding of mutuality.

21. This question is for the purpose of illustration only. Operationalizing the concepts of agape and caritas for a social scientific study would be a much more involved task.

22. The previous footnote comment is also applicable here.

23. Susan Okin, "Is Multiculturalism Bad?" in *Is Multiculturalism Bad for Women?* ed. Joshua Cohen, Matthew Howard, and Martha Nussbaum (Princeton, NJ: Princeton University Press, 1999), 8–24.

III

MUTUALITY MATTERS
IN THE FAMILY

9

✛

Sloppy Mutuality: Just Love for Children and Adults

Bonnie Miller-McLemore

Theologians have long debated the role of self-sacrifice in Christian love and, more recently, in family life and gender relationships. In recent years, many theologians have joined the general democratizing trends by challenging submission, obedience, and sacrifice as key Christian ideals and endorsing Christian mutuality as essential. Mutuality has become a common way for theologians from a variety of persuasions to talk about a more just love, a love that combines affection and justice.

In all this discussion, however, neither Christian nor secular scholars have given much thought to children.[1] Almost all those who argue for equality or mutuality in families are talking about mutuality between adults. But what does love look like when the participants are not adults alone but parents and children? Whereas traditional theology idealized sacrificial love for everyone but often exacted more from women and children in submission to the rule of husband and father, recent proponents of mutuality assume mutual love ought to apply to all relationships without distinction.

I initially found myself disturbed about what I have come to call "sloppy mutuality" while reading a highly controversial book by Episcopal priest and lesbian feminist theologian Carter Heyward, *When Boundaries Betray Us*.[2] I begin the chapter by reviewing her claims and the controversy she sparked because her book raises serious questions about prevalent conceptions of mutuality. In her indiscriminate championing of mutuality, however, she is not alone. While I lift up some troubling oversights in her analysis, my intent is not to dismiss her work. Rather she deserves appreciation for daring to enrich the conversation by telling her own story, even if she raises more questions than she herself can answer. Her book provides the impetus to move toward a richer understanding of mutuality more inclusive of children, parents, and other relationships of temporary inequality. Mutuality, I will argue, needs to be understood differently in situations of temporary "transitional hierarchies," especially those involving children and those who care for them. Families must maintain a balance and tension between self-sacrifice and self-fulfillment, autonomy and connection. My task in this chapter is to amplify this in terms of what it means for children.

A YEARNING FOR MUTUALITY

In *When Boundaries Betray Us*, Heyward takes the ideal of Christian love as mutuality to an extreme. Divided into three parts, the book tells the story of the cataclysmic fallout from Heyward's intense desire for a two-way friendship with Elizabeth Farro, the pseudonym for Heyward's former lesbian feminist psychiatrist, and Farro's refusal, silence, and rebuff. The first part chronicles the process of "wounding in therapy," divided into four periods between February 1987 and September 1988. During these eighteen months, Heyward moves from a sense of deep spiritual and erotic connection with Farro to growing tensions and finally to an abrupt severing of relations. Heyward desires more than the traditional therapist-client relationship; she wants mutual intimacy. Farro eventually makes clear that this will never happen. The more Farro refuses the more Heyward pursues her until the whole enterprise falls apart. Heyward terminates treatment and Farro denies further contact.

The final two sections interpret the falling out, first from Heyward's own perspective, and then by five "experts" and friends, including feminist and lesbian therapists, Heyward's partner, and a male priest. All of these respondents seem prepared to testify on Heyward's behalf. For the most part, they defend her criticism of therapeutic standards of distance between therapist and client. Their statements of support make it all the more difficult to suggest that Heyward may have overlooked certain aspects.

Heyward's overt agenda is an important one: to subject the values and rules of therapy to serious questioning. Is therapy genuinely healing when conducted in an atmosphere of detachment and objectivity that demands a strict separation of personal and professional agendas between client and therapist? Or do these very definitions establish a hierarchy of power that makes real healing impossible and even abusive?

In arguing for the latter, Heyward questions the entire assumptive world of therapy. Her critique actually extends the general criticism of the "power-relations in white western patriarchy" that prize a hierarchical "power-over" instead of a mutual "power-with." She challenges as *"un-*

ethical any so-called ethic that rules out the cultivation of genuinely mutual relation anywhere in our lives."[3] Genuine Christian love, she believes, cannot occur within the constraints of hierarchy and artificial boundaries. There is something inherently untrustworthy and even abusive about healing and growth that is not shared mutually by both parties. For "abuse" is "not simply a matter of touching people wrongly." It is equally a matter of "withholding intimacy and authentic emotional connection from those who seek our help." Abuse takes place when therapists fail "to make right-relation" or refuse "to touch people rightly."[4] Hence the therapeutic boundaries and hierarchies of nonmutual traditional therapy ultimately betray clients.

A second agenda, more covert and difficult to arbitrate fairly, troubles the water. In publishing the book, Heyward still wants to reach her psychiatrist, even if Farro has refused further contact. She seems to want to say, "You must know how much you have hurt me and yet how much I have learned despite you." In essence, she still wants to know whether Farro experienced their relationship as "mutually empowering." Did Farro admire and need her as much as she admired and needed Farro?

This personal plea colors over and makes an impartial reading of her theoretical plea to challenge therapeutic boundaries almost impossible. In writing the book, Heyward herself crosses over conventional boundaries. She not only undercuts the premises on which therapy rests. She reveals the inner workings of Farro's so-called "private practice" and exposes her own psychological merger with Farro, her anger, wounds, and confusion of emotional, spiritual, and sexual needs, her more recent struggles with bulimia and alcoholism, and her disturbing memories of molestation in early childhood. Most peculiar, she ultimately recants these memories, attributing them instead to a "transpersonal" experiencing of the violence inflicted on other women, girls, boys, and marginalized men.[5] Here and in general, the book projects an intense, at times almost unbearable, yearning for recognition in the face of an abyss of silence and pain.

DO BOUNDARIES ALWAYS BETRAY US?

It is no wonder therefore that Heyward did get a response, but not the one she may have wanted. With all the emotional catharsis going on, few groups or individuals can read the book without immediately choosing sides—pro or con boundaries and pro or con Heyward. The book sparked a minidebate, spread across two 1994 issues of *Christian Century*, between Heyward and Marie Fortune. Two other major review articles appeared each taking almost diametrically opposed positions. The discussion ultimately culminated in a book appropriately titled *Boundary Wars*.[6]

Fortune reviews the book from her perspective as someone well known for combating clergy sexual abuse. Proper boundaries do not betray clients, she argues, but instead preserve a safe space for therapeutic work in which the client need not think about taking care of the therapist. She worries in particular that the effort to level the therapeutic playing field will simply give license to those ministers and therapists already inclined to violate the vulnerability of those they help.[7] In a subsequent issue, Heyward reasserts her main contention: professional codes ought not prevent a therapist from choosing friendship with a client.[8] In the final retort, Fortune insists that boundaries can be flexible but should not be fluid, especially in relationships with power differences.[9]

Although the *Christian Century* exchange ended there, Heyward managed to get the last word. In 1995 she delivered a paper entitled "Fear Raging among Us: Boundaries, Vulnerabilities, and Psychotherapy" at a special session on the question of boundaries at the American Academy of Religion. She once again disputes the sacrosanct character of "professional boundaries" and suggests that they delude us in their promise of "safety" and lull us into a pretense of safety when in reality they divide and conquer. Heyward eventually incorporates this argument into a book of essays.[10]

As this summary demonstrates, the question of boundaries and abuse has dominated the discussion. The therapeutic issues are certainly worth identifying briefly, if only to lift up the complexity of the book. I believe, however, that this discussion of boundaries has seriously sidestepped a more troubling issue—the question about the nature of mutuality. I will return to this issue momentarily.

A review article in *The Journal of Pastoral Care* written by three psychologists, a clinical social worker, two clergywomen, a spiritual director, and a "wisewoman" is the most accusatory of Heyward herself. The authors suggest that she is a "deeply wounded person" in the grip of a powerful but almost wholly unrecognized transference.[11] She fails to realize just how little she knows about therapy and, more serious, how little genuine self-reflection she has done on the unconscious sources of her pain despite her obsessive personal rumination. Instead she "uses the book to punish the therapist" and displays the intense "addictive displacement patterns of early alcohol recovery."[12]

While this characterization unfairly pathologizes Heyward on points about which she herself is partly aware, Heyward does provide grounds for criticism. She seems so enmeshed in a powerful alterego or twinship transference that she collapses differences between herself and Farro and assumes that everything she feels is also shared by Farro.[13] From the very first phone call, Heyward writes that she "sensed [Farro] felt the same way" as Heyward feels, that Farro "had experiences not unlike mine," and that they therefore were potential "soulmates" and "sister-sojourners."[14]

She seems to want not just mutuality but fusion. Moreover, in the very therapeutic language Heyward rejects, she dramatically "acts out" her needs outside the therapy by writing and publishing the book rather than exploring her needs for affirmation and companionship through the conversation of the therapy itself.

Another review article by pastoral theologian Roy Herndon Steinhoff-Smith, however, takes almost exactly the opposite stance. Not only does he defend Heyward and indict Farro, he comes close to ridiculing his own colleagues—those "pastoral professionals" who have, in his opinion, missed Heyward's point entirely. The psychiatrist *does* abuse Heyward, he insists, through a failure to respect her "agency" and by inflicting pain. The ultimate culprits then are those pastoral theologians who have "interpreted *When Boundaries Betray Us* as an act of war and responded to her with all the weapons at their disposal. They diagnosed Heyward as nothing but a sick client [and] ignored anything Heyward wrote that did not support their characterization of her as a demonic enemy."[15] Unfortunately, this extreme characterization of his own only serves to further intensify and stereotype the "boundary wars" rather than clarify them.

SteinhoffSmith is right, however, about problems on Farro's side. The psychiatrist does seem "fumblingly ambivalent and inconsistent," as one reviewer puts it.[16] It is not clear that the conversations between them, as retold by Heyward, were "therapy" to begin with. Good psychoanalytic therapy is not based on the gratification of desires and wishes but on their analysis and understanding. A transference relationship is powerful precisely on this score: It evokes formative emotional experiences from pivotal early encounters but within the space of the "holding environment" of therapy where ideally the trauma, failures, disappointments, and frustrations become food for thought rather than simply being reenacted. One cannot help but wonder how such an intense transference went unanalyzed. Even if this account merely reflects Heyward's own biased representation, Farro did have the greater responsibility to salvage the conflictual relationship rather than to act out the conflicts in real life herself. Sadly, for many reasons, she did not do this.

Nonetheless, while these therapeutic problems need to be recognized, the argument over boundaries and abuse has also misled us. I believe there are more substantive cultural, moral, and theological issues at stake here. I am inclined to agree with pastoral theologian Joretta Marshall who says that to dismiss Heyward as therapeutically inept or personally overinvolved "does an injustice" to Heyward's analysis.[17] And, I would add, simply to blame the therapist or those "pastoral professionals" who responded leaves other important questions lurking in the margins. The entrapment of Heyward and Farro (and everyone else) in this debate suggests that another problem—muddled understandings of mutuality—may be part of the difficulty. The use of the term mutuality is unquestionably, as one review puts it, the "most central confusion in the book"[18] or the "core of the controversy" as another says.[19]

DO SLOPPY CONCEPTIONS OF MUTUALITY BETRAY US?

In earlier publications Heyward pioneered theological efforts to redefine Christian love in terms of mutuality.[20] Yet in her diatribe against therapeutic boundaries and throughout the responses, mutuality seems ill defined and sloppily understood. Genuine love, she says, should not rule out mutuality "anywhere in our lives."[21] The need to qualify and nuance this view becomes most apparent when the participants under consideration include children.

Here and in discussions of just love in families at large, it is interesting to note how seldom children are mentioned. Children simply do not figure into the equation. Yet their presence is often precisely what makes just love between spouses and partners especially difficult. Moreover, the relationship between parent and child is commonly transposed on all sorts of hierarchical relationships, such as the one that causes Heyward so much turmoil, and on other relationships, such as teacher-student and minister-parishioner. That Heyward and so few respondents mention children and mutuality therefore is especially curious. It seems exceptionally important that this question receive attention.

One of the few references to children appears when Fortune uses them as an example to argue that every relationship need not be mutual to be authentic, intimate, or meaningful. Adults, she asserts, "should not be asking children to meet their emotional and sexual needs in the same way that they ask their adult partners to do so."[22] This position makes sense. Heyward counters by insisting simply that "parent-child relationships need to be mutually empowering."[23] This also makes sense. Part of the problem here is that mutuality takes on different meanings in different contexts. Fortune, Heyward, and others banter around the term but it is not entirely clear that everyone is talking about the same thing or even using the term in the same way all the time. Fortune means sexual and emotional intimacy. Heyward refers to shared power and agency. Others use the term to talk about equal regard or respect; and still others mean shared responsibility. Does mutuality mean mutual intimacy, equal power, agency, or regard, or shared responsibility and just love? Or isn't it more accurate to say that it means all of these in different times and places?

Consideration of children forces us to recognize that Christian conceptions of mutuality must be multivalent and responsive to constantly changing circumstances and personal development and that we must articulate more clearly what we mean when we use the term. To deal with mutuality's many meanings, we must pay better attention to several commonly overlooked dimensions: the reality of temporary inequality and "transitional hierarchies"; the role of duty, responsibility, authority, and even sacrifice on the part of the adult and qualified self-centeredness on the part of the child; and finally the inevitability of failure, harm, and reconciliation.

Transitional Hierarchy

Most advocates of mutuality fail to note that it cannot be applied across the board to all relationships without qualification. Hierarchy in and of itself has become a bad word; it is often narrowly equated with authoritarianism and sometimes with patriarchy. Yet the conflict surrounding Heyward's book makes clear that we need to recognize the reality of "transitional hierarchies," a temporary inequity between persons, whether of power, authority, expertise, responsibility, or maturity, that is moving toward but has not yet arrived at genuine mutuality. She herself seems to have this in mind when she writes, "If a healing relationship is *not moving in a more fully mutual direction*, it becomes abusive, just as any other significant human connection does."[24] Power-over relationships then are not destructive in and of themselves; they are harmful when they are "unchanging."[25] Transitional hierarchies then need not be inevitably either authoritarian or patriarchal.

Unfortunately, the question of what love looks like in the midst of life's temporality, where people grow, change, and die, has not received much attention from moral theologians and philosophers. The few attempts in practical and moral theology to address this in the past several years, therefore, represent important contributions.

In *From Culture Wars to Common Ground*, I along with my coauthors argue that the meaning of just love in families must be "determined in the concreteness of specific contexts within the human life cycle." Christian love as mutuality "means different things for different family members at different points in family and individual life cycles."[26] When pastoral theologian Herbert Anderson traces the ebb and flow of pastoral care over the life cycle in his five-book series on families, he also points to the changing dynamics of just love.[27]

In an earlier pivotal essay, theological ethicist Christine Gudorf stands alone in 1985 in attempting to understand the nature of Christian love and justice in the midst of the unfolding developments of parenting. While rearing one biological child and two adopted medically handicapped children, she finds common Christian views of love and childrearing inadequate. In particular, she lifts up the evolving nature of mutuality. Apparent initial sacrifices on her and her husband's part are always undertaken with "expectations that the giving would become more mutual." Even her definition of love is itself cast developmentally: "love both involves sacrifice and aims at mutuality."[28]

In other words, the measure of mutuality is partly determined by *where it is moving*. Elsewhere Gudorf argues that parents cannot presume they have a timeless right to a relationship with a child. Parenthood as a mutual relationship is always in "process."[29] More recently she has recognized the two-way nature of this process. The parents' continued development, including resolving leftover issues with their own parents, has a tremendous impact on children. Gudorf discovers, for example, that her need to control her first son during his teens simply continued her struggle for freedom from her own overly controlling parents. Recognizing this allowed her to quit working out her problems through her son.[30]

In short, mutuality is an ideal in process and a term that resists essentialist definitions. The fact that Christian love as mutuality cannot be fully realized in every relationship at every moment does not *ipso facto* rule that particular relationship abusive or wrong-headed. Marshall and Fortune go one step further. Marshall is "leery of mutuality as the normative base for every relationship."[31] They both argue that not all relationships need be mutual or move toward mutuality. As Fortune comments, "there just aren't enough hours in the day."[32] While this could not be more true, I would prefer, in contrast to Marshall, to keep mutuality as a generic way to talk about the norm of Christian love while more carefully differentiating among its many forms both within the family and in its more public dimensions.

Duty, Responsibility, Authority, and Sacrifice

The presence of transitional hierarchy points to another important consideration: what one reviewer describes as the "complexity of finding mutuality in a relationship where one party has more responsibility and, presumably, more experience than the other." Heyward at least raises this seldom-addressed issue but "offers little useful guidance."[33] Making finer distinctions in the application of mutuality in quite different kinds of relationships is one small step toward rendering theological discussions of mutuality less sloppy. Moral agents are not always like-minded adults but women, men, and children in various stages of development. They are not the static, independent, and mature people often presumed in many discussions about just love but rather children who have needs and cannot fully reciprocate and adults who in their care for children need the support of others and appropriate means to meet their own needs.

Lest we forget, children are different from adults. Immediately after Heyward says that parent-child relationships should be mutually empowering, she equates this relationship with "friendships, spousal and lover relationships, and professional healing relationships."[34] This quick slide from child-adult to adult-adult relationships collapses some important distinctions. Mutuality, it is assumed, applies just as well to the relationship between teacher-student, therapist-client, and parent-child as it does to adults on more equal footing. Many efforts, not just those of Heyward, to spell out the meaning of just love ignore the temporary inequalities and differences between actors in transitional hierarchies, especially those between parent and child.

At the very least, children are physically and cognitively less developed. And depending on one's perspective—with grace, luck, or hard work—most adults hope to reach greater moral and spiritual maturity than children. Physically and cognitively, children may not even be capable of the kind of inverse thinking required for genuine mutuality in which one can think and feel oneself into the other's skin. Morally and spiritually, children, like adults, certainly have and deserve the kind of moral agency that SteinhoffSmith adamantly believes Farro and "pastoral professionals" deny their clients. But rich resources in the Christian tradition would argue that children should not be held as morally responsible or as morally culpable as adults who have far greater means and opportunity to perfect their abilities to do good or evil.[35] Understanding these differences may help us understand the dynamics of other transitional hierarchies in which one person temporarily has more expertise or authority and bears greater moral and spiritual responsibility and liability until the relationship shifts to one of more complete mutuality.

Recognition of differences heretofore overlooked or denied between children and adults leads to several insights. In transitional hierarchies, the child must be allowed greater latitude in self-indulgence. One cannot demand mutuality of a child (or of anyone unable or unwilling, for that matter). Developmentally, children and adolescents need to experiment with a wide range of roles and desires, exercising what psychologist David Gutman has described as the "omnipotentiality" of youth.[36] Self-assertion, self-aggrandizement, and outright selfishness are necessary as part of the gradual evolution toward a life that brings together self-fulfillment and self-giving as mutually critical components of equal regard. Although parents must make difficult, discerning choices about when to indulge and when to override desires, for the most part this discrepancy between adults and children warrants a gracious leniency on the part of the adult toward the child's neediness and wants. Children, in other words, deserve to be heard and seen in ways that previous history and social mores have denied them. This also applies to therapy. One might even suppose that Farro could have indulged Heyward's requests just a bit more without risking the overall purpose of therapy to understand rather than enact desires.

Upon having children, parents enter a period of "transitional renunciation" which puts at least an initial check on the kind of self-absorption and self-indulgence allowed children and youth.[37] Especially during the first few years of a child's life, parents must restrict their own needs to meet the more acute and pervasive needs of a vulnerable child. A certain kind of temporary self-giving becomes requisite. From her vantage point as a parent of three boys, pastoral theologian Brita Gill-Austern argues that we need to "resist the increasingly wide-spread tendency to condemn all forms of self-giving. Christian self-sacrifice is not pernicious by definition." Indeed, persons who strive for just love in families must reckon with the reality that the "care of children requires self-denial and sacrifice of the kinds of ego gratification" often found outside the family.[38] Self-giving has an essential role to play in sustaining those in dire need. The key question then becomes how to distinguish life-giving from life-denying sacrifice. One determines this by asking whether it remains subordinate to and in the service of a greater mutuality and abundant life. Does the sacrifice, in essence, lead to more just and loving relationship?

This question is critical because exaggerated ideals of sacrifice set up destructive dynamics between parent and child in which the pretense of sacrifice covers over the many ways in which the parent uses the child to meet his or her own needs. Parents do better to admit the desires and hopes they harbor in relationship to their children. Gudorf argues that her love for her children was never completely selfless, disinterested, and detached from self-affirmation and self-love. Her parenting efforts "rebounded to our credit"; "failure to provide for them would have discredited us." Even more powerfully, from the beginning her children "gave to us," not only of themselves but also by making of the parents new and different people.[39]

Theological ethicist Barbara Andolsen provides helpful criteria to ascertain when Christian sacrifice is "legitimate." There is place for sacrifice, she argues, when practiced by the privileged on behalf of the oppressed, when a party in greater need has a *prima facie* claim on others, and when occasions of sacrifice can be balanced out over the long run.[40] Behind all this lies an implicit Christian eschatological vision. The overall intent behind such qualifications in sacrifice is the intent and hope to create a world in which suffering is vanquished and sacrifice is not necessary.

Mutuality between parents and child is different from mutuality in adult relationships in yet another way. While children may initially get most of their needs met through the parents, parents cannot depend on children alone to meet their needs. As Gudorf asserts, "it is dangerous for adults to attempt to fill personal needs exclusively through parenting. We need to have other avenues for nurturing, for intimacy, for community involvement, for activity, outside parenting, if we are to avoid using a child for our own ends." Moreover, under all circumstances, the parental role is "a constantly diminishing one in the life of a child."[41]

In my own explorations of maternal knowing, I also observe that parents must have ample space and time for self-absorption of their own, "uninterrupted by nagging thoughts and guilt about caring for others."[42] A parent's ability to maintain this fine balance between self-giving and self-gratification depends upon wider systems of support, not just the other partner but schools, neighborhoods, churches, and so forth, that care for and support the caregivers. It is no wonder, therefore, that in the pursuit of just love in families a good deal of attention has gone to and must continue to be directed at political, economic, and practical strategies that secure these wider supports.

Affirmation of a nonexploitative, nonpatriarchal hierarchy suggests one final qualification in conceptions of mutuality. Maintaining mutuality does not always involve positive affirmation, affection, and friendship. It sometimes requires correction, judgment, tutoring, and accountability. Indeed, this coheres with those images in both the Hebrew scriptures and the New Testament of an acceptable, righteous anger on the part of God, Jesus, and the faithful. It also coheres with what Reformation theologians described as the importance of mutual consolation and mutual discipline. The person with more knowledge or experience—often but not always the parent—has a greater responsibility to challenge the perception or the action of the other person when it misses the mark. Even if parents lack knowledge and experience, parents by the sheer fact of adulthood itself still have an obligation to look after children for their own sake that is not and should not be entirely reciprocal. This does not, once again, rule out the importance of mutual empowerment between parent and child but it does cast the nature of equal regard between parent and child in different terms.

Failure, Harm, and Reconciliation

Many feminist theologians who have investigated psychological and religious dynamics of domestic violence and abuse have naturally refrained from moving too quickly to a policy of forgiveness and reconciliation.[43] However, mutuality over the long haul means repeated failure and injury and hence leads almost inevitably to questions of pardon and grace. Attending to the fallen nature of human existence is perhaps Christianity's most distinctive contribution.

SteinhoffSmith criticizes what he sees as the altruistic "power over" ethic of the "pastoral professionals" by contending that humans cannot "exercise power over others without doing evil."[44] I would add, however, that humans cannot achieve mutuality or "power with" others in an entirely pure way either. In his essay on moving from rhetoric to genuine equality, Anderson names some of the causes behind what religious types would simply call "sin": "occasional egoism," "misunderstanding," "the absence of empathy," "hostility and separation." Reckoning with the harsh realities of implementing mutuality in daily life ultimately requires clearing a way for the advent of forgiveness and the grace of reconciliation, whether this comes through the formal Christian rituals of religious confession or through the nonconfessional, nonreligious means of deliberate, respectful conversation. "In final analysis," Anderson observes, "justice in marriage is not something we achieve. It is something we discover. . . .[F]or those who follow Christ . . . it is something that is given rather than earned. For Christian persons in marriage, it is impossible to separate justice from gratitude."[45] Granted some social activists, liberationists, and feminists would hear this as an escapist, pie-in-the-sky pronouncement from someone with power and privilege. But it is, in truth, a statement of experienced Christian faith uttered by someone who has had to wait on justice and has learned to wait on grace.

This does not mean that hard work is not involved in just love. Couples must work to foster the kind of "peaceable environment" into which respect, acceptance, and grace can move.[46] Once again, mutuality is more a verb than a noun; it describes an always-evolving process rather than an object that people obtain. To offer a provocative example, some acts of lovemaking are closer to the ideal of mutuality than others.[47] Or on the more mundane level, moment by moment the just distribution of child and household labor almost always falls more heavily on one partner than the other. People need to measure just love over the long haul rather than minute by minute, act by act. In an early essay on anger in the work of love, Beverly Harrison herself, Heyward's partner and theological ethicist, asserts "we must learn what we are to know of love from immersion in the struggle for justice."[48]

In *From Culture Wars to Common Ground*, we describe Christian mutuality as a "strenuous ethic," requiring respect for the selfhood and dignity of the other, which must be taken as seriously as one expects the other to respect or regard one's own selfhood. It also requires pursuing the welfare of the other as vigorously as one pursues one's own. Mutuality as equal regard does not appear overnight. It requires a complex process of "intersubjective communication and mutual decision" about its concrete enactment in the lives of those involved.[49] It includes but subordinates moments of sacrifice, evolves as people change and develop in their relationships, and finally, its achievement is not fully within human power but always occurs within the realm of the common good or, from a Christian perspective, with the coming of God's influence.

Making finer distinctions in the many variations and forms of mutuality in different kinds of relationships and under the finitude and tumult of life's daily circumstances is one small step toward rendering Christian discussions of mutuality less sloppy. Mutuality is a multivalent reality. Its subjects include children and the child in all of us.[50] When such complexities are acknowledged, Christian understandings might have the power to influence and reshape our culture into one more supportive of just love in families.

NOTES

1. I address this question at greater length in *Let the Children Come: Reimagining Childhood from a Christian Perspective* (San Francisco: Jossey-Bass, 2003), upon which parts of this chapter are based.

2. Carter Heyward, *When Boundaries Betray Us: Beyond Illusions of What is Ethical in Therapy and Life* (New York: HarperCollins, 1993).

3. Heyward, *When Boundaries Betray Us*, 10, her emphasis.

4. Heyward, *When Boundaries Betray Us*, 10.

5. Heyward, *When Boundaries Betray Us*, 157.

6. Katherine Hancock Ragsdale, ed., *Boundary Wars: Intimacy and Distance in Healing Relationships* (Cleveland, OH: Pilgrim, 1996).

7. Marie M. Fortune, "Therapy and Intimacy: Confused about Boundaries" (a review article of Heyward, *When Boundaries Betray Us*), *The Christian Century*, May 18–25, 1994, 524–26.

8. Carter Heyward, "Boundaries or Barriers: An Exchange" (a response to Fortune's review), *The Christian Century*, June 1–8, 1994, 579–80.

9. Marie M. Fortune, "Boundaries or Barriers: An Exchange" (a response to Heyward's response), *The Christian Century*, June 1–8, 1994, 580–82.

10. Carter Heyward, *Staying Power: Reflections on Gender, Justice, and Compassion* (Cleveland, OH: Pilgrim, 1995). There is one final quasi-interchange between Fortune and Heyward in *Boundary Wars* where they both have articles (Fortune, "The Joy of Boundaries," 78–95 and Heyward and Beverly Harrison, "Boundaries: Protecting the Vulnerable or Perpetrating a Bad Idea," 111–28).

11. Pamela Cooper-White, Marilyn Coffy, Jan Baltz, Jan Sollom-Brotherton, Marilyn Steele, Ida Thorton, and Nancy Ulmer, "Desperately Seeking Sophia's Shadow," *The Journal of Pastoral Care* 48, no. 3 (1994): 287 (287–302).

12. Cooper-White et al., "Desperately Seeking Sophia's Shadow," 300, 301.

13. See Heinz Kohut, *How Does Analysis Cure?* Arnold Goldberg, ed., with the collaboration of Paul Stepansky (Chicago and London: The University of Chicago Press, 1984), 193.

14. Heyward, *When Boundaries Betray Us*, 24–25.

15. Roy Herndon SteinhoffSmith, "The Boundary Wars Mystery," *Religious Studies Review* 24, no. 2 (April 1998): 141 (131–42).

16. Sheila Bienefeld, "Look Back in Anger" (a review of Heyward, *When Boundaries Betray Us*), *The Women's Review of Books* 11, no. 7 (April 1994), 7 (7–8).

17. Joretta Marshall, "Review of Heyward, *When Boundaries Betray Us*," *Journal of the Society of Pastoral Theology* 4 (1994): 123 (121–23).

18. Cooper-White et al., "Desperately Seeking Sophia's Shadow," 288.

19. Christie Cozad Neuger, "Review of Heyward, *When Boundaries Betray Us,*" *Princeton Seminary Bulletin* 16, no. 3 (1995): 382 (381–84).

20. See Carter Heyward, *The Redemption of God: A Theology of Mutual Relation* (Lanham, MD: University Press of America, 1982); *Touching Our Strength: The Erotic as Power and the Love of God* (San Francisco: Harper & Row, 1989).

21. Heyward, *When Boundaries Betray Us*, 10, my emphasis.

22. Fortune, "Therapy and Intimacy," 525.

23. Heyward, "Boundaries or Barriers: An Exchange," 579.

24. Heyward, "Boundaries or Barriers: An Exchange," 579.

25. Heyward, *Staying Power*, 9, cited by SteinhoffSmith, "The Boundary Wars Mystery," 138.

26. Don S. Browning, Bonnie J. Miller-McLemore, Pamela D. Couture, K. Brynoff Lyon, and Robert M. Franklin, *From Culture Wars to Common Ground: Religion and the American Family Debate* (Louisville, KY: Westminster John Knox Press, 1997), 154.

27. See the entire series coauthored by Herbert Anderson, "Family Living in Pastoral Perspective," all published by Westminster John Knox Press (1993–1996).

28. Christine E. Gudorf, "Parenting, Mutual Love, and Sacrifice," in *Women's Consciousness and Women's Conscience: A Reader in Feminist Ethics*, eds. Barbara Hilkert Andolsen, Christine E. Gudorf, and Mary D. Pellauer (San Francisco: Harper & Row, 1985), 181–82 (175–91), my emphasis.

29. Christine E. Gudorf, "Dissecting Parenthood: Infertility, in Vitro, and Other Lessons in Why and How We Parent," *Conscience* XV, no. 3 (Autumn 1994): 21 (15–22).

30. Christine E. Gudorf, "Sacrificial and Parental Spiritualities," in *Religion, Feminism, and the Family*, eds. Anne Carr and Mary Stewart Van Leeuwen (Louisville, KY: Westminster John Knox Press, 1996), 295–98 (294–309).

31. Marshall, "Review of Heyward," 122.

32. Fortune, "Therapy and Intimacy," 526.

33. Bienefeld, "Look Back in Anger," 8.

34. Heyward, "Boundaries or Barriers: An Exchange," 579.

35. See, for example, the chapters on Augustine, Aquinas, Luther, Calvin, and others in Marcia Bunge, ed., *The Child in Christian Thought* (Grand Rapids, MI: Eerdmans, 2000).

36. David Gutman, *Reclaimed Powers: Toward a New Psychology of Men and Women in Later Life* (New York: Basic Books, 1987), 194, cited by Browning et al., *From Culture Wars to Common Ground*, 293.

37. See Browning et al., *From Culture Wars to Common Ground*, 292–95.

38. Brita L. Gill-Austern, "Love Understood as Self-Sacrifice and Self-Denial: What Does It Do to Women?" *Through the Eyes of Women: Insights for Pastoral Care*, ed. Jeanne Stevenson Moessner (Philadelphia: Westminster John Knox Press, 1996), 315, 318 (304–21).

39. Gudorf, "Parenting, Mutual Love, and Sacrifice," 177–78, 181.

40. Barbara Hilkert Andolsen, "Apage in Feminist Ethics," *The Journal of Religious Ethics* 9, no. 1 (1981): 80 (69–83).

41. Gudorf, "Dissecting Parenthood," 22.

42. Bonnie J. Miller-McLemore, *Also A Mother: Work and Family as Theological Dilemma* (Nashville, TN: Abingdon, 1994), 164.

43. Herbert Anderson and Bonnie J. Miller-McLemore, "Pastoral Care and Gender" in *Pastoral Care and Social Conflict*, eds. Pamela D. Couture and Rodney Hunter (Nashville, TN: Abingdon, 1995), 99–113.

44. SteinhoffSmith, "The Boundary Wars Mystery," 136.

45. Anderson, "Between Rhetoric and Reality," 385.

46. Anderson, "Between Rhetoric and Reality," 386.

47. For a powerful look at this question, see Mary D. Pellauer, "The Moral Significance of Female Orgasm: Toward Sexual Ethics That Celebrates Women's Sexuality," *Journal of Feminist Studies in Religion* 9, no. 1–2 (Spring/Fall 1993): 161–82.

48. Beverly Wildung Harrison, "The Power of Anger in the Work of Love: Christian Ethics for Women and Other Strangers," in *Making the Connections: Essays in Feminist Social Ethics*, ed. Carol S. Robb (Boston: Beacon, 1985), 8 (3–21), first published in *Union Seminary Quarterly Review* 36 (1981): 41–57.

49. Browning et al., *From Culture Wars to Common Ground*, 153; see also chapter 10 where these ideas are expanded.

50. Herbert Anderson and Susan B. W. Anderson, *Regarding Children: A New Respect for Childhood and Families* (Louisville, KY: Westminster John Knox Press, 1994), 10–11.

10

Over the River and through the Woods: Maintaining Emotional Presence across Geographical Distance

Pamela D. Couture

I remember vividly the day Grandma Louise died. I was thirteen. We had spent the afternoon at her house. After Sunday dinner, we played Tripoley around the dining room table. Since we lived only twenty minutes apart by car, and Dad, Grandma, and Grandpa worked in the family business, we visited frequently. Grandma made sure that my brother, Jeff, and I learned card games, especially canasta, so we could all play together. Grandma was a great teacher—I remember her on her knees, teaching me to read blocks with letters by adding consonants to the word "in"—tin, kin, sin. "Grandma, What's sin?" was my first theological question. The day she died, we had been playing Tripoley. Grandma was a careful dealer, and Jeff, at nine, both looked and acted the part of the card shark. His tie was pulled loose and askew as he leaned over the table, collecting his chips. I admired how quick he was at math—not my gift. We drove home that evening, and as soon as we arrived Grandpa was on the phone saying that Grandma had collapsed. My father frantically left the house to be with my grandparents. I prayed hard that night and at one point was overcome with a sense of peace that she was with God. In the morning, our minister confirmed that she had died. It was my first intense grief.

Grandma Paula, my maternal grandmother, died in the middle of my qualifying exams for my Ph.D. at the University of Chicago. The Saturday before the exams were to begin, my mother called to say that grandma had been admitted to the hospital and was failing rapidly. The University of Chicago graciously allowed me to begin my exams two days late so I could fly to see my grandmother. The large extended family of my maternal grandparents had always lived in northern New Jersey, and when my mother went off to Ohio to college and married my father, and my father began a family business with his parents, she was the first to move out of state. So, Grandma and Grandpa made regular car trips across the Pennsylvania Turnpike between Ohio and New Jersey, and the family always joked about how to get rid of the state of Pennsylvania to make the trip shorter. One year, as Jeff and I anticipated their arrival with excitement, we built a toll booth and waited at the end of the driveway to charge a quarter when they arrived. I earned early my early "junior stewardess wings" flying from Cleveland to Newark. When we arrived in New Jersey, Grandma always made Hungarian stuffed cabbage, mashed potatoes, and green beans. Many summers Grandma and Grandpa rented a cottage at the New Jersey shore and we happily packed a number of extended family relatives into a few rooms, sleeping wherever. I envied my aunt, uncle, and cousins who lived within walking distance of Grandma and Grandpa. When Grandma died, after my second qualifying exam, we took pictures of the extended family around Grandpa, filling in around him as if to make the family whole in a new kind of space.

In geographical proximity or across distance, Jeff and I grew up with rituals of games, visits, and vacations with grandparents. In *Mighty Stories, Dangerous Rituals: Weaving Together the Human and the Divine*, Herbert Anderson and Edward Foley write, "rituals are essential and powerful means for making the world an habitable and hospitable place. They are a basic vehicle for creating and expressing meaning. They are an indispensable medium by which we make our way through life."[1] They contend that informal family rituals of childhood help a child to become socialized into a family and develop as an individual within that family. In this article I explore one possible logical development of their conclusions: if rituals of childhood help offspring socialize and individuate, rituals of adulthood help adult children who are separated from their families across geographical distance maintain emotional presence and connection.

In a recent conversation, Herbert Anderson and I spoke about an experience that we were each anticipating: grandparenting across geographical distance. Both of us would have much preferred to live in proximity with our adult children and their families, so we were both interested in ways to maintain emotional presence across geographical distance. This article arises from that conversation. I emailed colleagues in the four professional societies of which Herbert and I are both members, asking for stories of rituals that help them maintain relationships with their parents or with their adult children across geographical distance. Seventeen persons replied.

Perhaps the starkest question raised by this sample is, "How are our family connections being shaped by face-to-face contact and communication through evolving technology?" A second question that stands out in this sample is, "How are family connections being shaped both by verbal communication and by common activities that facilitate family interaction and enjoyment?" Our colleagues shared stories that are most easily classified in two types of communication: communication using evolving technology and face-to-face communication. Of the communication enabled by technology nine mentioned email; eight mentioned telephone (a ninth included a patch through a ham radio operator and a tenth mentioned cell phones); eight write letters regularly (two mentioned general letter writing, two others write monthly letters, and four others write weekly letters); three send cards and another sends e-cards; one faxes; one family contributes to a family web page; and two send web pictures; two draw or send cartoons. To maintain face-to-face communication five share major holidays with parents; five vacation together; three mentioned visiting parents and two mentioned receiving visits from parents on a regular basis; four attend regular family reunions; three combine family visits with business travel; two visit at birthdays; two gather the family at vacation homes; one visits at school breaks; one mentioned enjoying and sharing time with each others' friends. All three families in the sample who cross international boundaries combined technology and face-to-face communications, using technology in addition to visiting and vacationing internationally.

Almost all respondents in this sample who offered vignettes related to their communication rituals with their parents had left home in early adulthood and never lived within proximity of their parents again. A few of the respondents who wrote about maintaining relationships with their adult children did report that their families regathered and lived within closer proximity after a time of geographical separation. In *Leaving Home* Herbert Anderson and Kenneth R. Mitchell describe in depth the successes and the impediments in the differentiation process as adult children journey into the world. This article offers a view from the other side: once they have separated, what do adult children and their parents do to maintain their familial identifications and connections? It provides a glimpse of *basic patterns of care* that families use to maintain multuality across geographic distance.

RITUAL COMMUNICATIONS

The theme of "regular weekly contact" emerged strongly in vignettes that follow. In most of these cases letter writing figures significantly. The original weekly letter writing sometimes evolves into other kinds of contact, including telephone and email; in one case the weekly contact seems to have begun by telephone. But one respondent's weekly letter writing has been maintained over four decades, and the author uses his experience with his parents to build relationships with his daughters as they leave home. In the first vignette a line emerges that indicates the way that the respondent tries to recreate the emotional sense of home[2] by the way in which he conducts the communication:

> Every Saturday morning [my mother and I] talk by phone. Usually she calls me because this is more convenient for her—especially given the three-hour time differential. This "ritual" has been essential to nurture our relationship. I usually sit and sip a cup of coffee while we talk, so that it seems to me more like a morning conversation over the kitchen table. . . . My mother and I used to correspond regularly by letter—commonly weekly. Gradually this pattern has shifted to more phoning and less written communication.

In a second story, the respondent uses his own means of establishing connection to assist his daughters in their differentiation, and example of "letting go with grace"[3]:

> My mother and I have been in weekly communication by letter every since I left Helena, MT to go to college in St. Peter, MN. We have continued this practice for forty-two years. I address my letter to my mother and father, but my mother is the only one who writes the letters from their end. When our daughters were seniors—one at the University where I teach and the other in high school—I began the practice of writing each of them a letter in anticipation to their moves to Florida and Bloomington, Indiana . . . . I continued this practice with both of them for 5+ years until they moved back to Indiana. The youngest daughter and I have moved to using e-mail as our form of contact at a distance.

In the third, the respondent demonstrates that one who has left can emotionally "go home again"[4] with the aid of evolving technology:

> My parents have fairly consistently written weekly letters—both of them contributing. About four years ago we all got on e-mail and now I receive frequently, less consistent, but more notes by e-mail. My father retired about the time I was writing full-time on my dissertation and we shared morning notes at least four times a week. I told him that personal e-mail was something that helped me get going each day and he was my most regular contact.

In the fourth, the respondent demonstrates the combination of face-to-face and evolving technological contacts through which "our sense of home across geographical distance" seems to be emerging:

> I haven't lived closer than a two day drive to my parents . . . . since I was eighteen. My father died fifteen years ago. My mother and I use the phone

about once a week to keep in touch. They, and now she, travel frequently around the country to their six children. We have reunions about once a year, so I see her on average twice a year. We never use the mail except for special day cards and business. This is about the same for my adult son....We visit there about twice a year and they do the same, so we average seeing each other four times a year. We talk on the phone very Sunday and sometimes during the week e-mail occasionally. Mail only for cards, packages, and business.

Another woman reports that her parents consider "the only proper way to communicate respectfully to be long letters written with a fountain pen, and written regularly, say once a week! And this is indeed how they keep in touch with me, every week," though she is not so inclined. One respondent who usually corresponds with his son through email says that there is something special about "pen in hand," and he occasionally succumbs to the urge to handwrite a letter.

RITUAL ACTIVITIES

Some of our connections are maintained through shared ritual activities rather than direct communication. Anderson and Foley[5] describe the Lotti family's ritual of calzone-making as an event that expresses the family's sense of connection, hierarchy, and boundaries. In this sample, two respondents described ritual activities that fill a void. In the first case, grief over a mother's mortality made it urgent for a daughter to learn her mother's recipe:

This summer in August I went over for a few days with a particular agenda—to learn from my mother how to make pickles. She seemed pleased to teach me and we had a wonderful Saturday. They came out well, I am happy to report. When my mother was very ill I was surprised to find myself aware that I did not know how to make her bread and butter pickles— yes, who can figure what comes into our minds at such time. Fortunately she recovered, but I have been angling to be there for pickle making. Now maybe we can do it again.

In the second case, grief persists over difficult intergenerational family relationships. The following respondent demonstrates the paradox of family life—a seeming contradiction between an unresolved disruption between parents and an adult child and the parent's felt need for continuity between the grandparents' and grandchild's generations. The paradox is lived through the legacy of rituals handed down.[6] No generation

may verbally recognize and affirm the way that the intergenerational rituals are handed down, yet behavior makes the legacy clear:

> (We keep in touch) mainly by perpetuating certain traditions or habits, be it
> how we buy or decorate the Christmas Tree, celebrate the church year, or what
> crafts I teach them that my mother taught me. I grew up climbing in the
> (mountains) from the time I could walk, every summer, and now find myself
> taking (our three year old daughter) out to hike whenever I can, teaching her
> not only stamina and fitness, but a deep love and understanding of the out of
> doors. . . . I also find myself perpetuating certain community-oriented habits
> my mother lived, such as now with (our three year old) visiting a few very
> elderly and very lonely neighbors, some of whom I was told about but never
> actually met, until I, a stranger . . . a foreigner, knocked on their doors. . . .

My mother visited us recently, and it really delighted her, in an unspo-
ken sort of way, to see her family's traditions and habits being handed on
to the next generation. Because conversation with my parents is difficult,
perpetuating traditions and habits becomes an important connecting
thing. I suppose at some unconscious level I have deliberately filled the
void of connection, but yet it continues to surprise me when I find myself
doing or saying something (like visiting elderly neighbors I don't know),
that I later realize my mother or father modeled for us.

CARE AND RESPONSIBILITY

When families live at geographical distance, can they continue to rely on
kin for direct physical care? In three vignettes respondents reflected on
the need to "go home" or "create home" for reliable, intergenerational
care. The first case demonstrates family interdependence in the midst of
the "functional loss" described by Anderson and Mitchell in *All Our
Losses, All Our Griefs: Resources for Pastoral Care*.[7] The care goes both ways:
a child experiencing functional loss can return home for care, and a child
can also provide support for a parent caring for another parent experiencing physical disability:

> We've been separated off and on for twenty years. . . .When I got an autoim-
> mune disorder I boomeranged and lived with them for a year—1995–1996. . . .
> now I drive (xx hours) once a month and spend the weekend with them. My
> dad has the beginning of senile dementia and mom is the primary caretaker.
> My visits are mostly to provide emotional support for her.

In a second case siblings and their spouses have transformed gender patterns of time for the men and time for the women in order to respond to

a mother's nonverbal expression of loss and to support a caretaking father's need for relief and companionship:

I have four sisters. We live in four states. My parents live in North Dakota. The closest to my parents is three hundred miles. Eight years ago my mother's diagnosis of dementia (Alzheimer's) was confirmed. One of her symptoms was always being cold. After checking to see that it was not physically based, her specialist told us that is was common among dementia patients. It was a way of somatizing the loss of relationships. So—the ritual—every year during the winter my three sisters and I take our mother to some place warm for four days—about as long as mom can be away from dad without becoming very frightened. Dad, who truly loves and is loved by his sons-in-law, goes somewhere else and golfs. We see it as a way of caring well for both parents but especially my father since it is the only time during the year my dad will be separated from my mother.

In a third case a parent of a young child reconnects intergenerationally to insure a "safe home"[8] for her child:

I use [my parents] for childcare occasionally, spending a few days to a couple of weeks with them while I get a lot of work done. Or they have come here while my husband is traveling to keep me company. Since we all seem to continue to adore each other, we have roughly developed the pattern in the back of our head as we make travel decisions. . . . it is a mutually acknowledged pattern. . . . they live six hours away . . . . I have been struggling with the question of childcare for young children since our nanny/babysitter quit suddenly, and we have since found out about some harsh punishment she used with [our daughter]. I am beginning to think the extended family is key to nurturing, trustworthy childcare. I realize many families are just as crazy and untrustworthy as our former babysitter, but as I scan for solutions to the problem of the two-career family with small children, I am wondering if geographical arrangements that allow extended families to be more involved in child care shouldn't be more of a priority.

OBLIGATION AND DELIGHT

Rituals sometimes express family obligations. According to family custom, there are prescribed times in which family members are expected to appear and reconnect.[9] But new rituals may be arising that replace obligation with an invitation to family participation and fun. Only two persons mentioned the sense of obligation that was for so long associated with intergenerational family contacts. One person suggests the way that the sense of obligation may have led to resistance and distance, until playing with technology invited the family to develop new communication patterns:

> For years it has been difficult to keep the kind of communication my parents "required" of me when in college, etc. In our experience, we moved away from letters—sad. And then came email. Suddenly, all members of the family are in touch with each other regularly in email.

Another respondent reports that over time vacations transformed his sense of obligation into genuine appreciation and delight. Common activities became the vehicle of transformation, rather than new communication patterns.

> One interesting pattern of connection we have kept with [my wife's] mother is to periodically have summer vacation with her. The first time we did it was about twenty years ago. She was part of a senior citizen's trip to Wildwood, New Jersey. [My wife, daughter and I] joined her on the trip to Wildwood with a busload of senior citizens. It was really a lot of fun. [She] has joined us on vacations in the Midwest. . . .I might add that in the beginning these trips back felt more like a duty or a chore. Now they are much more an important time of deepening roots and building a legacy. I look forward to these gatherings more and more.

In a third, the delight around common activities arises from a new, nonobligatory tradition, an example of enjoying each other through regular vacations and reunions that several respondents shared.

> Fifteen years ago our five kids and most of my wife's nephews and nieces started what they called the "Cousins' Campout" over Memorial Day weekend. About the third year, [my wife] and I "crashed" the party and have not missed one since. Other family and friends come from year to year. We usually have fifty-some people. We have camped at two different lakes, one in Missouri and one in Oklahoma, the current site. We also see our kids at other times of the year, but this is the highlight for most of us.

SEEING A DIFFERENT SIDE OF PARENTS

Vacations together create memories, but they also help to move the family through the "family life cycle" which Herbert Anderson discusses in *The Family and Pastoral Care*.[10] It speaks to a way of "reforming the family" in intergenerational relations that moves beyond the marital couple. A maturing family allows all of its members to share in transformation, including change and growth in the elderly. The first vignette shows a new relationship that emerges from a new way of being together.

In '97 my mother and I made our first trip together. Three days before the tendon tore in my ankle, but not knowing how serious it was, we went on and toured Nova Scotia. The crutches were a hindrance but we had a good time together. I enjoyed the time with mom and fully expect us to do more of these. Last summer she and I shared a cabin and hotel room on a ten day trip with my sister's family when we went to Greece and then a cruise. Again we had fun. It was very clear that I am gathering cherishable memories as Herbert Anderson puts it. I am seeing a side of my mother that I don't think I would have seen otherwise.

The second expresses the surprise of the child at an aging parent's intellectual and emotional growth:

Recently my father got active again as a ruling elder in the local Presbyterian church. Originally it was in protest for the awful minister neither of us could stand (a very conservative and schismatic guy) but it has provided Dad and me a good way to stay in touch as he calls with requests for info from the headquarters here or to tell me some agenda item on the Presbytery Council. . . . Recently he had the devotion to do and amazed me when he said he wanted to do it on religious pluralism and the importance of being open to difference (this from a conservative Republican!!).

OVERCOMING EXTREME
EMOTIONAL AND LOGISTICAL OBSTACLES

What are the obstacles inherent in geographical distance that families must overcome to maintain their relationships? The most painful obstacle, one that was reported in four stories, is the desire for contact on the part of a child or a parent that is not reciprocated. One correspondent, who had not seen her daughter in four years since her marriage, despite repeated efforts at contact, called this "the most heartbreaking subject." Another said of her parents, "I have no regular contact pattern . . . and have sometimes wondered how long they would go without contact if I didn't initiate." Two others spoke of the distance created when parents remained angry about their choice of marriage partner or place to live. The literature of pastoral care and counseling, however, is filled with such stories, with both unfulfilling and hopeful outcomes.

Parents and children who desire to communicate over geographical distance, however, also face logistical obstacles. Among the most formidable obstacles mentioned by respondents was negotiating time zones! In one case, a mother and daughter who are acquainted with each other's work patterns have developed a creative solution to the time zone problem.

Not surprisingly, our thirty-two year old [married daughter who lives in San Francisco and works in a stressful e-business start-up] and I use the "new technology"—cell phones!—to stay in touch. In spite of three hours difference, our work patterns allow us to be available to each other. Often in the evening she calls me. . .or I call her. . .for a chat on our commute home. She's driving with her headset, I'm talking in the back of a cab, and we each have thirty-minute commutes. I've learned to call saying, "are you in a meeting?" Or she calls and says, "feel like talking?" And we've both learned that it's okay to say "can't talk now." I used to put cell phones down. Now I'm grateful.

International families show particular creativity when faced with formidable logistics. For them, evolving technology has revolutionized family communications, even more dramatically than when parents and children live in the same country.

My husband and I are . . . missionaries, so our life has been full of travel and maintaining family relationships. The strategies have changed quite a bit since we began in 1973. . . . Back in the early years [my husband] and I were a young couple in Bolivia with parents in Texas and Illinois. International calls cost five dollars a minute so they were extremely rare. Instead we relied on letters, at least once a month, to each set of parents. . . .We also made arrangements to call at special moments (birthdays, mostly), using a phone patch through ham radio operators. In the 1980's direct dial long distance became available, and our parents called us on birthdays, anniversaries, and Christmas. . . . We have lived in San Jose, Costa Rica since 1986. . . .Our sons in college in Georgia and Illinois come home for Christmas and school breaks. . . . Even though our boys are quite used to traveling internationally, we have asked that they let us know when they arrive at their destination. Originally, this was a quick phone call or a fax, now either a call or an email. . . .As soon as we had a credit card and a phone card, we saw to it that both boys received a phone card that bills to our credit card. . . .For the most part, unless we just want to hear each other's voices, we rely on email for regular contact, even though messages are often just a few lines. Another way we take advantage of modern communication is the web page. . . . on our page, whenever I want our boys to see a picture, I post it to an unlisted address on the web site and send them a message with the address, so they can go have a look. I also scan and post a cartoon that appears weekly on the local newspaper's editorial page, as they are great fans of this cartoonist. . . . Technology has definitely improved both personal and professional communication.

Another missionary couple who have maintained three-generational relationships between parents and children spread out among the continents of Europe, Asia, Australia, Africa, and the United States conclude that close emotional relationships across geographical distance are quite possible.

Our experience is: as long as one takes the trouble to write letters and, if possible, for visits, the contact with far-away children can even be closer than with a child-around-the-corner. But letter writing, even when one sends the letter by email, takes trouble and time. That's the price one has to take to share thoughts, ideas, and feelings.

One father calls his correspondence with his son "more of an adventure than a ritual." He describes something of what we might expect as families become spread out not only around the country but also around the globe. There are particular difficulties when negotiating between Generation X postmodern communications and the rituals of family communication of the past.

> [Our son], now twenty three, is in the U.S. Peace Corps in Kazakhstan . . . in a remote village, Balbaluk, with no running water and no phones . . . eleven times zones east of us. On weekends he goes . . . to his cyber cafe where he keeps in touch with scores of friends in the U.S. and around the world by email, mostly "mass mailings." But he does send individual, personal email letters, and similarly keeps up with his grandparents and several girlfriends and others by personal email. . . . [He has also] developed an old fashioned, wide ranging handwritten correspondence with friends, family and neighbors . . . written at night in tiny cursive script crowded from paper edge to paper edge and written in ink on both sides of thin paper. It's a devil of a document to read and I usually resort to a magnifying glass under a strong light. . . . For some years he has also enjoyed drawing humorous cartoons for his own amusement and occasional gifts to friends, and recently has begin mailing a few to select correspondents. . . . Finally there is the telephone. . . . he calls from an open-air phone in downtown Almaty. . . .

This is only a short excerpt from the long email that I received from the father of the Gen-Xer, detailing the correspondence between this son and his family and friends. The regular forty-two-year letter-writing correspondence mentioned above, in my mind, wins the prize for continuity in the midst of significant family change. But the Gen-X son may be regarded in sheer quantity of correspondence, if not in longevity, Prince of Email and Airmail. But he's only taking after his father, who is known to be King of the Memo! True to form of a third-millenium correspondence, this duo took on a multinational corporation, which met its match:

> One further, somewhat amusing aspect of telephoning must be noted. . . . Before he left the Peace Corps I shopped around and came up with MCIWorldCom as the best deal for his phone from Kazakhstan, and indeed, when we had a number of calls from him the first summer (1999). Then MCI's security division called to be sure these calls were legit, and of course, we told them they were. But when their first bill arrived, it was about $900. Some desperate research revealed that they don't have touch-tone phones in Kazakhstan, so [our son] had been placing his calls through the operator which is what MCI had told him to do if he had difficulty using the automatic billing num-

ber. We hit the ceiling and immediately switched to ATT. We also protested to MCI that they had assured us that the cheap plan would work in Kazakhstan and had not explained that their alternative procedure would be billed at operator rate. Repeated phone calls and letters to MCI bearing this protest message brought no response except repeated bills and finally threatening form letters from a collection agency. My attempts to call MCI were especially frustrating. I was told, on one such call, that only "Iowa City" had the authority to adjust a bill; when I asked for Iowa City's phone number, I was told they couldn't give it out! It went round and round this way on several occasions in a Kafkaesque drama until I finally filed formal complaints with four state and federal agencies. That brought a quick response from MCI, which to my astonishment, simply wrote off the charges!

THE FAMILY AS A PLACE FOR THE MEANS OF GRACE

Human beings are made in the image of God. They reflect the nature of God—God's justice, compassion, and mercy. Just as God extends Godself toward humanity, making overtures toward humanity, seeking to establish, maintain, and grow God's relationship with humanity, human beings reflect God's image when they take the initiative to be in relationship with one another. The ways that God extends Godself to humanity may be anticipated. They may be as regular and dependable as Sunday morning worship. But God also extends Godself toward humanity in extraordinary ways, as we are told by the parables of the lost sheep or the lost coin. God and we become vulnerable when we take initiative to maintain relationship. God and we have great desires for mutuality and connection. We may be deeply disappointed: Those toward whom God and we extend ourselves may not be responsive. To extend ourselves in various degrees of vulnerability, over and over again, is part of what it means to enact God's means of grace as persons who are made in the image of God. In the family this enactment may be delightful, poignant, and heartbreaking, revealing to us ways that God is heartened, moved, or saddened when God extends Godself toward us.

Yet, especially when commenting on the family, pastoral theologians are tempted to focus on the way that the image of God is distorted in human beings, as evidenced by failures of the family, by painful alienation, or by the destruction family members wreak on one another. Pastoral theologians know much of that. But I leave that story to others. In the vignettes of these persons we find evidence that the nature of God is reflected and the means of grace *is* enacted within family relations. It is within the cradle of that faithfulness that all other disruptions must be interpreted.

In "ritual communications" the respondents make their connections across geographical distance with the regularity of a spiritual discipline.

The regular letter written, the regular phone call made (with coffee at the kitchen table!) reassure the participants of each other's presence in the way that regular prayer reaffirms in the prayer the belief in the possibility of God's presence. All contacts may not be equally satisfying, but the regularity of the contact is fulfilling, in and of itself. Some people respond to such rituals, however, as some believers respond to participation in regular prayer life as a spiritual discipline. For one person, regular letter writing, like prayer, is hard to maintain, even though it's seemingly desired and missed! For another person, the obligatory quality of weekly letter writing destroys its spirituality. For that person, writing weekly letters to a parent who expects to be written weekly is like denying Christian liberty and affirming irresistible grace! Freedom is a gift of God to humanity; humanity responds to God's overtures freely, or humanity cannot respond. If the form of the ritual were kept, the grace within it would be lost. The prevenience of God is exemplified in two ways in this exchange: by the faithfulness of the parents in their continued letter writing, and by the respondent's search for a genuine means of connection.

The "ritual activities" of the next respondents bear a resemblance to preparation and partaking of the eucharist. A mother's bread and butter pickles communicates for one daughter the very identity and remembrance of the mother. It echoes, "Do this in remembrance of me," especially when the mother's life is threatened. What if the mother should die without the daughter's knowing how to do this in remembrance of her mother? The process of making bread and butter pickles compresses the fullness of the life of the mother into an act that witnesses in a symbolic way to that life. It's an act that the daughter must carry on.

Eucharistic themes are revealed in a different way when the life and teachings of the grandmother are reenacted. This performance fills the void of absence. It too echoes eucharistic settings, such as the feeding of the five thousand, in which nature and compassion are central to the story. In Mark 6:30ff Jesus and the disciples have withdrawn to a place of rest, but the crowds followed. Jesus has compassion for the crowds who have nothing to eat, and instructs the disciples to feed the crowds with loaves and fishes. In so doing, the eucharistic meal is born from compassion and grows into a way that God and humanity can sustain and grow their relationship with one another. The means of grace is shown to be a thorough integration of mercy and piety. Similarly, a mother and daughter find that acts of rest and compassion grow and sustain their connection to an older generation and the family tradition they have established. The means of grace within the family is extended in concrete acts of "care and responsibility" for one another in the midst of physical disability. The early church understood *caritas*—acts of charity and mercy toward persons in need—to imitate the actions of Jesus and to fulfill the mandate that the needy be cared for, but the church sometimes forgot that the neediest persons might be within one's own home. The Lutheran Reformation reminded the church that *caritas* might first begin with the persons closest to us—persons in our own families and communities. The present era is challenged to retain the truth of each—that *caritas* can be extended *within and beyond* our immediate families. Care within the family, and care by the family for others, each may become means of grace.

In "obligation and delight" we turn from the means of grace through actions of compassion to the means of grace through activities that connect people through delighting in one another. By vacationing with a mother-in-law and by crashing the "Cousins' Campout" two respondents opened themselves to receive the grace of human beings delighting in one another. Their proactive participation reminds us that God's grace and human effort cooperate with one another. In *To Love as God Loves* Roberta Bondi cites Origen of Alexandria's metaphor for the cooperation of God's grace and human activity: God's grace is like the wind that fills the sails of the ship, and human participation directs the ship in a particular direction. She writes that the early church fathers and mothers believed that "what grace is, as they understood it, is simply God's help in seeing and knowing the world, ourselves, God and other people in such a way that love is made possible."[11] If vacationing with the elders or youngsters places us on the ship, God's grace may blow in the form of the energy, enjoyment and goodwill that comes from restful or enthusiastic times together!

Human cooperation in the means of grace deepens our knowledge of God. We know God, yet we never know all of God: God remains a mystery. We participate in the means of grace to deepen our knowledge of God, to enter into God's mystery. In so doing we get to know different sides of God, just as one respondent, vacationing with her mother and corresponding with her father, began "seeing different sides of the parents." In the human interaction she grows as she experiences their growth and their relationship finds a new footing. Similarly, our deepening experience of God through God's grace places us in a renewed and changed relationship with God.

Some family members are adept at "overcoming extreme emotional and logistical obstacles." They must be extremely proactive in maintaining and strengthening their family relationships. Often, when we think of that much human proactivity toward God we slide into thinking that human beings are saving themselves by their own effort. In each of these families, however, prevenient initiation on the part of God and various members of the family set the stage for proactivity. Human cooperation means responding to God's initiative, but it often is a highly active response! God's desire to extend God's grace may also take extreme forms. God's grace is mediated through relationships and through activities, through face-to-face presences, and maybe even through cyberspace. Might the contemporary parallel of the woman searching for the lost coin be the Peace Corps volunteer looking for the lost email address in a cyber cafe in Almaty or the father looking for "Iowa City's" telephone number? While I want to revolt and save my talk of the means of grace for those places where human beings are in direct, face-to-face contact with one another, the evidence of this study suggests that God may even use cyberspace in God's extraordinary efforts to reach us and to help us to connect with one another. The metaphor for God's grace, the wind in Origen's sails, might in a contemporary version be the electrical charge that humans can direct to send a message around the world.

CONCLUSION

Our colleagues demonstrate that leaving home and returning home is being facilitated by conversations and common activities, in face-to-face and technological communications. These modes of ritualizing family life have helped to maintain intergenerational connectedness even as the family and environment change.

Until a year ago I had not played Canasta since Grandma Louise died. My daughters had learned Canasta from their stepmother who learned it from her mother. When I spent a month with my daughter in Missouri a year ago, I relearned Canasta and played many rounds. Last summer when my brother, Jeff, from Minnesota and his wife took their eldest daughter to France to visit our exchange sister, his younger children spent two weeks with me in New York, and I taught them Canasta. When Jeff returned, he commented that he'd like to be able to remember how to play Canasta again. Then I learned that Katie, my eleven-year-old niece, had started playing Canasta online on "Yahoo Games." Now, Katie and I prearrange to meet at a Yahoo Canasta table during an evening. Occasionally, Jeff fills in. Once, in the "chat" line he wrote, "what do you think Grandma would say if she could see us doing this?" We expected to organize a Canasta game with my daughter Shannon, Katie, Jeff and me at Thanksgiving, but the cry from the middle generation was, "Play something everyone can play!" Canasta, for four, always gave way to a game that everyone could join. The most successful intergenerational generation games (spanning Willy at seven to Bob at seventy-seven) included Gestures and Balderdash. Our four-handed Canasta awaits the virtual table in cyberspace. Jeff and I have been more successful entering into family traditions at the game table, however, than recreating the dinner table. We use Grandma's recipe to reproduce the delights of stuffed cabbage, and those who knew Grandma still enjoy it. But the youngest generation to this point remains unconvinced. And since I usually fly to Minnesota and they pick me up at the airport, they have yet to realize they could charge me a toll to get in their driveway and be well within our family tradition.

NOTES

1. Herbert Anderson and Edward Foley, *Mighty Stories, Dangerous Rituals: Weaving Together the Human and the Divine* (San Francisco: Jossey-Bass, 1998), 22; see also Herbert Anderson, *The Family and Pastoral Care* (Philadelphia: Fortress Press, 1984), 98–105.

2. Herbert Anderson and Kenneth Mitchell, *All Our Losses, All Our Griefs: Resources for Pastoral Care* (Philadelphia: The Westminster Press, 1993), 22–25.

3. Anderson and Mitchell, *Leaving Home* (Louisville, KY: Westminster John Knox Press, 1993), 108.

4. Anderson and Mitchell, *Leaving Home*, 40.

5. Anderson and Foley, 23.

6. Anderson and Mitchell, *Leaving Home*, 15.

7. Anderson and Mitchell, *All our Losses*, 41.

8. Anderson and Mitchell, *All our Losses*, 34–47.

9. Anderson and Foley, 24.

10. Anderson, 37–39.

11. Roberta Bondi, *To Love as God Loves* (Minneapolis, MN: Fortress Press, 1987), 37.

11

✛

Honor Your Father and Your Mother: A New Look at "Family Values"

Dianne Bergant, CSA

I grew up in a household that witnessed a good deal of give-and-take between my parents, and between them and my sister and me. We constantly poked fun at each other, yet there was never any question about the authority that my parents exercised. We genuinely enjoyed each other—most of the time. I never thought that our family interplay was in any way unusual until my sister started to bring home the young man whom she would eventually marry. Although he came from a household in many ways quite similar to ours, the dynamic operative there seemed to be quite different. Actually, until he got to know us better, he thought that my sister and I were quite disrespectful of our parents. I didn't know to what I should attribute this difference, but I did realize that "honor your father and your mother" had very different meanings for different people. Today I would explain those differences in terms of the role that context or social location plays in interpretation and understanding.

If honoring parents and enjoying children can be understood so differently by two families that share the same religious tradition and approximately the same cultural and economic background, what can one expect from even greater cultural diversity? Put another way, what can a postmodern, Western, egalitarian, capitalistic, technological society learn about "family values" from an ancient Near Eastern, patriarchal, agrarian, prescientific society? That is the question that prompted this essay. The Book of Sirach was chosen for this examination for two major reasons. First, it contains longer instructional sections that provide a better insight into respective "family values" than do the simple proverbial sentences. Second, in the Preface, it specifically acknowledges the role that context plays in the process of interpretation. The interpretative method used here will be a form of canonical hermeneutics (to be explained below).

I became interested in canonical hermeneutics at the very time that I was involved in discussions about the principles of practical theology. I was immediately struck by the similarities of the two approaches. The clarity that I gained in one approach threw light on the elements of the other. I am indebted to Herbert Anderson for the role that he played in this learning experience and for the refinement that further discussion with him has afforded me.

CANONICAL HERMENEUTICS

In recent years, interpreters have acknowledged the difficulty in translating the formative theology of the biblical tradition for contemporary believers, since concerns and challenges differ from world to world, from culture to culture, and from generation to generation. The ancient world is not the same as the contemporary world, and so its theology cannot be easily transported across the ages. In a very real sense, such interpretation creates a kind of cross-cultural challenge. The limitations of historical approaches have led interpreters to employ new methods for analyzing the Bible. Some new critical approaches examine literary characteristics as ways of discovering meaning in the text. They maintain that once a piece of literature (or any form of art for that matter) is completed, its meaning is intrinsic to itself and does not need the artist to interpret it. Some insist on the "semantic autonomy" of the text[1] to the exclusion of any historical reference.[2]

Ricoeur maintained that a written text is removed from the immediacy of its composition in three ways: 1) Once it is written, it exists by itself, without the author to throw light on its meaning. 2) It is also removed from the original audience and is available to a limitless number of readers. 3) It can be carried beyond cultural and generational boundaries and convey its message in very diverse contexts. This distanciation or distancing makes interpretation necessary, for, while the text may still make sense, it has no specific reference and is open to a variety of referents. Ricoeur identifies this as the "surplus of meaning."[3] This "surplus" explains why a text can yield an array of meanings without compromising its literary integrity.

A new critical method lends itself to this kind of interpretive theory. Called canonical hermeneutics, it examines the actually recorded reinterpretations which various communities of faith formulated as they brought the religious tradition of the past to bear on their own unique experience. It employs both literary and historical methods to discover interpretive techniques used by ancient biblical communities. It does this believing that the same, or a similar, process can be used for interpreting the Bible in the present. It contends that in the formative process of the past, just as in the interpretive process of the present, a believing community resignifies (gives new meaning to) a religious message born of another time and of other circumstances. In other words, the community living in a new context understands a biblical message in a manner somewhat different from the way it was originally understood (Ricoeur's "surplus of meaning"). However, canonical critics are not satisfied merely with meaning as such. They are interested in discovering how the biblical message functioned, and can function, in the believing community. Does it console; does it challenge; does it instruct?

Evidence of recontextualization can be found throughout the Bible itself.[4] A careful literary comparison uncovers clues that suggest that the earlier material was resignified for the purpose of addressing new historical situations. This is precisely the interpretive method that canonical critics seek to develop for contemporary use.

Canonical critics recognize three components that make up this interpretive method: 1) the biblical text; 2) the new context within which the text is read; and 3) the process of resignification.[5] Each of these components plays an important role in enabling the biblical message to be understood in a new way. With regard to the first component, historical-critical, literary-critical, structuralist, linguistic or any number of analytical approaches can be used to discover whatever possible meanings the biblical passage might yield (Ricoeur's explanation). This task may appear to be quite technical, but most people today have some experience in, or at least knowledge of, interpretation of the biblical text. However, the yield of such biblical analysis is not yet an understanding in the hermeneutical sense; it is simply explanation. Furthermore, as already stated, canonical critics analyze the text not merely to determine what it says and what it meant, but to discover its rhetorical function within the communities that valued it and carried it through the traditioning process to the moment when it became canonical.

Regarding the second component of the method, canonical hermeneutics calls for insight into the new context that is receiving the tradition. This requires knowledge of the contemporary community and its local and global contexts. Such knowledge includes: some understanding of present-day social systems and the way they operate in our lives; an informed appreciation of the economic and political realities that shape our local, national and international societies; and insight into the respective community's *mythos* and *ethos*. Our contemporary North American society is a multiracial, multicultural, multilingual, multiclass, and multigenerational community of women and men. These dynamics constitute the social location of the reader and, consequently, shape the lens through which interpretation is done. Social location, with all of its particularity, can be neither ignored nor minimized.

Only after both the biblical text and the contemporary situation of the community have been analyzed, can the real reinterpretation or resignification take place. For this, various methods can be employed. The biblical material itself reveals that the ancient societies seemed to prefer some form of midrashic interpretation.[6] Allegory was another popular method,[7] as was typology.[8] Today scholars have developed numerous interpretive approaches that grow out of their critiquing of the biblical material and examining the findings of such critique through various liberationist lenses.

The approach of resignification employed here will be a form of critical praxis correlation in line with the one espoused by Matthew Lamb.[9] It will begin with a close reading of a passage from the Book of Sirach. The social character that underlies the message will then be critiqued from the perspective of contemporary social values. These values will then be brought into dialogue with the theological message. In this way the contemporary reality and the biblical message will interpret each other. The end of the entire interpretive endeavor will be a rhetorical move, in the sense of constituting a persuasion and not merely an explanation.[10] The Bible, if it is to be authentically the "word of God," must transform the minds and hearts of those who hear it. Such transformation is the final and true goal of interpretation.

SIRACH

Introduction

The book is known under several titles: Sirach, the Greek version of the author's name; The Wisdom of Ben Sira, from the Hebrew spelling; Ecclesiasticus or "church book" from the Latin Vulgate. The latter title dates back to St. Cyprian and may derive from the book's extensive use as a resource for early Christian catechesis.[11] Sirach's canonical status is disputed. Although it was originally written in Hebrew and in Jerusalem, the Pharisees who determined the list of sacred writings omitted it from their collection. They may have done so because Ben Sira challenged some of the theology that these Pharisees espoused, e.g., retribution in an afterlife. Despite this fact, many subsequent rabbis quoted passages from the book as Scripture. Protestants who adopted the Jewish listing consider it apocryphal, while Roman Catholics regard it as deuterocanonical.

Sirach is one of the few biblical books that is actually written by the ascribed author, "Jesus son of Eleazar son of Sirach of Jerusalem" (50:27). His panegyric on Simon (50:1–21), most likely Simeon II, the high priest from 219–196 BCE, helps to date the original Hebrew work around 180 BCE. The Greek version of the book, along with a Preface explaining the translation, was written by the Ben Sira's grandson around 115 BCE. It is clear that he is addressing diaspora Jews, for he insists that his readers should praise Israel for preserving and handing down its religious truths. He invites them to read his grandfather's instruction in this Greek translation, inadequate as this may be compared to the original Hebrew version. His concern for members of the diaspora community and his translation of the text into the Greek language highlight the inherent merit of a culture other than the original one as the matrix within which the revelation of the God of Israel can take root and flourish. This is a very clear example of recontextualization and possible resignification.

Sirach 3:1–16
[1]Listen to your father's right, children;
do so that you may live.
[2]For the Lord sets the respect of a father over his children;
and confirms the judgment of a mother over her sons.
[3]Those who honor their father atone for sins;
[4]and those who revere their mother store up riches.
[5]Those who honor their father will be gladdened by children,
and their prayer will be heard in the day of offering.
[6]Those who respect their father will live a long life;
and those who obey the Lord give comfort to their mother.
[7]Those who fear the Lord honor their father,
And serve their parents as those in authority.
[8]In work and word honor your father,
that his blessing may come upon you.
[9]For a father's blessing makes firm the house of the children
but the mother's curse uproots the foundation.
[10]Do not glory in the shame of your father,
for there is no glory for you in his shame.
[11]For a person's glory is one's father's glory,
and the children's disgrace is a mother's shame.
[12]Child, care for your father in his old age,
and do not cause him grief as long as he lives.
[13]Even if his mind fails him, be patient with him;
and do not dishonor him in the fulness of your strength.
[14]For compassion for a father will not be forgotten;
it will stand against your sins,
[15]In the day of our tribulation it will be recalled to your advantage,
like fair weather upon frost, it will melt away your sins.
[16]Like a blasphemer is one who neglects a father,
and like one who curses the Lord is one who provokes a mother.

(translations by the author)

Although several of the verses in this passage could stand alone as discrete proverbs, gathered together as they are in the book, they constitute extensive teaching on the responsibility of children to their parents. The instruction opens with a clear restatement of the commandment found in the decalogue: "Honor your father and your mother, that you may have a long life in the land which the LORD your God is giving you" (Exod 20:12). A later and somewhat expanded version reads: "Honor your father and your mother, as the LORD your God commanded you, that you may have a long life and prosperity in the land which the LORD your God is giving you" (Deut 5:16). As a restatement of a section of the decalogue, this introductory verse in Sirach gives theological significance to the entire instruction. By means of it we see that reverence for parents is not merely a matter of social custom; it enjoys divine legitimation. Furthermore, as a section of the decalogue, it constituted part of a covenant renewal ceremony.

This first verse, along with several following verses (vv. 5, 6, 9a, 14–15), includes an expression of the theory of retribution which states that righteous living will be rewarded while transgressions will be punished. This theory suggests that reality is rooted in the moral order and events generally conform to a cause-and-effect standard. The causal character of the theory probably functioned more as an incentive for virtuous living than as a description of the way events actually unfold. While the theory itself addresses both reward and punishment, this reading from Sirach is only concerned with righteous living and the blessings that it will bring. As it stands, it already constitutes a slight reshaping of the tradition. For pre-exilic Israelites, living freely and prosperously in the land of Israel was considered one of the greatest blessings that God could bestow. Several generations later, life in the land of promise was not as highly valued by the Jews of the diaspora to whom Ben Sira wrote.

The instruction is clearly father-centered, suggesting a patriarchal society. Some contend that each of the six instances in which mother is mentioned is merely as a component in gender-matched poetic parallelism.[12] However, since the main function of such parallelism is the presentation of as complete a picture as possible, one can argue for the importance of this inclusion. The passage contains three examples of proper congruent parallelism[13] in which the significant concepts follow the same sequence and express relatively similar ideas:

[2]sets respect	of the father	over his children
confirms judgment	of the mother	over her sons
[3]who honor	their father	atone for sins
who revere	their mother	store up riches
[16]like a blasphemer	one who neglects	father
like one who curses	one who provokes	mother

There are two examples of proper anticongruent parallelism in which the significant concepts follow the same sequence but express opposite ideas:

| [9]father's blessing | makes firm | house |
| mother's curse | uproots | foundation |

| [11]person's glory | father's glory |
| children's disgrace | mother's shame |

There is no parallel construction in the sixth mention of the mother (v. 6) nor in the verse that speaks of parents (v. 7). However, they both confirm the significance of the mother in the life and future of the children.

The question of gender preference also surfaces in the matter of the reference to children. Although there is general agreement among scholars that instructions such as this one were directed to the male members of the family, only once does this passage speak explicitly of sons υιος (v. 2). In all other instances the gender-neutral terms children τεκνα,vv. 1, 2, 5, 9,1 1) or child τεκνα, v. 12) are used. This allows the text to be interpreted in a more inclusive fashion than may have been originally intended.

The hierarchical structure of the family can be seen in verses 1, 2, and 7. The meaning of the first two verses does not raise any question. The first verse merely calls attention to the privilege or prerogative of the father. Although the Greek verb τεκνον in verse 2, translated here as "sets the honor," suggests that God glorifies the father over his children, the sense may simply be that parents enjoy a certain status that children do not. However, the situation sketched in verse 7 is quite different. There the Greek δεσττόταις δουλεύσει yields "serve their parents as masters," reflecting the absolute power that the head of a strict patriarchal household exercised. This passage becomes even more troublesome when we remember that biblical law and instruction were addressed to adults and not to children, as the final verses' directive to care for an aged father makes clear. All this indicates that the kind of control exercised by parents, particularly fathers, could be quite despotic. Such control would be deemed unacceptable in contemporary society.

It is obvious that the principles of honor and shame are important in the society depicted. Honor pertains to one's status in the community. In a patriarchal society it is the prerogative of the men. It seems to have been considered a commodity that can be possessed or lost. Honor can be inherited by being born into an honorable family or to a position of importance, such as the monarchy. It can also be achieved through distinguished service or by the performance of some extraordinary feat. It can be lost when one does not fulfill the obligations of one's state. This can happen to a king who does not govern well, to a soldier who is defeated in battle, or to a priest who is found to be unworthy of his office. Any man can experience shame if he cannot manage his business properly or keep the members of his household in line.

Although most of the references to honor in this passage pertain to the respect that parents have a right to expect from their children, honor in the sense mentioned above does enter the picture. The honor or shame of the household, which is rooted in but not limited to the honor or shame of the patriarchal head of that household, is the subject of verses 6 and 7. There we see that the honor of one member enhances the honor of all. Similarly, the shame of one member diminishes all other members.

Verses 12 through 15 direct the adult child to care for the father in his old age, when his strength has left him and he is no longer the powerful ruler that he once was. This injunction tells us that honor was not merely possessed through dint of brute force, but was retained through various other means. The primary reason one was honored was as the head of the household. In addition to this, traditional societies such as ancient Israel customarily accorded respect to those advanced in years, who had weathered the storms of life and had learned the lessons that it had to teach. Finally, respect for elderly parents reflects Israel's covenant responsibility to provide protection and comfort for the most vulnerable members of society.

This brief passage underscores several attitudes that characterize the ancient family, and which continue to be worthy of our consideration even today. The first is the respect that is due parents, simply because they are the ones who have brought the next generation to birth. They are also entitled to respect because they possess the wisdom that comes from living life and learning the lessons that it has to teach. Second, the passage reveals a certain level of gender sensitivity. The family unit described here may well be patriarchal in structure, but the instruction accords respect to the mother as well as the father, and it employs gender-neutral language when speaking of the children. Third, members identify with the family unit, even to the point where the honor or shame of one member reflects on other members as well. Finally, those members who are most vulnerable are cared for in a way that does not diminish their dignity.

A Broader View

This passage is not representative of the teaching of Ben Sira. In fact, it is really quite exceptional. Ben Sira generally depicts the authority of the father as autocratic, characterizes wives as untrustworthy, and exhorts an uncompromising approach to the rearing of children.

It is true that there are a few passages in which he praises the responsible wife (26:1–3, 13–16):

[1]Happy the husband of a good wife,
the number of his days are doubled.
[2]A worthy wife brings joy to her husband,

he will complete his years in peace.
³A good wife is a good portion;
A measure given to those who fear the Lord.

¹³A gracious wife delights her husband,
Her thoughtfulness will fatten his bones.
¹⁴A silent wife is a gift from God,
and her disciplined soul is unsurpassed.
¹⁵The grace of all graces is a modest wife;
and the value of her chaste soul cannot be weighed.
¹⁶Like the sun rising in the heavens of the Lord;
is the beauty of a good wife in her well-ordered house.

However, even such accolades judge the wife according to standards of male preference. She brings joy to her husband, because she attends to his needs; she is silent when such demeanor is deemed appropriate; and she manages a well-ordered household (cf. 26:13, 14, 16). This praise notwithstanding, Ben Sira's attitude toward wives is primarily pejorative, even contemptuous. He presents them as resembling shrews and he describes them as unreliable and promiscuous (25:22–23; 25–26; 26:7–12):

²² There is arrogance and great disgrace,
when a woman is the support of her husband.
²³Depressed mind and gloomy countenance
and wounded heart are caused by an evil wife.
Feeble hands and quaking knees
are caused by one who does not make her husband happy.

²⁵Do not allow an outlet for water,
or freedom of speech to an evil wife.
²⁶If she does not follow your lead,
cut her away from your flesh.

⁷A bad wife is a chafing yoke;
whoever takes hold of her grasps a scorpion with his hand.
⁸A drunken wife arouses great consternation;
she does not conceal her shame.
⁹An unchaste wife is recognized
in her haughty stare and by the manner of her glance.

Just as a wife was deemed virtuous if she conformed to the social criteria of patriarchal society, so a woman who deviated from those norms in any way was considered degenerate. Social independence and sexual autonomy, such as characterizes an increasing number of contemporary women, would most likely receive searing condemnation by the author of this book.

What is probably Ben Sira's most derogatory statement about women is found in his interpretation of the story of the sin in the primeval garden (25:22; cf Gen 3:1–6):

Sin originated from a woman;
and because of her, we all die.

It is because of the literary sequence in the mythological story, which depicts the woman inviting the man to sin, that women generally were considered temptresses of men, but men were not viewed as tempters of women. This explains why the author considers women so dangerous, and why rigid safeguards were established to safeguard her virtue and the honor of the men of the household.

Although Ben Sira prefers sons over daughters, he nonetheless advocates a very stern upbringing for them (30:1–13):

¹Whoever loves his son whips him continually;
in order that he may rejoice in him in later years.
²Whoever disciplines his son will benefit from him;
and in the midst of his intimates, he will boast.
³Whoever teaches his son provokes his enemies to jealousy;
and in the presence of friends delights in him.
⁴When the father dies, it is like he is not dead;
for he leaves behind one resembling himself,
⁵Who in life he looked upon and rejoiced.
And in death with no regrets.
⁶He leaves behind an avenger against his enemies,
and one to repay his friends with kindness.
⁷Whoever spoils his son will bind up his wounds,
and at every cry will tremble inwardly.
⁸An unbroken colt turns out stubborn,
and a son left to himself turns out headstrong.
⁹Pamper a child and he will shock you;
indulge him and he will grieve you.
¹⁰Do not be frivolous with him lest you share in sorrow;
and in the end you will gnash your teeth.
¹¹Do not give him freedom in his youth,
and do not overlook his errors.
¹²Bow down his neck in his youth, smite his ribs when he is a child,
lest he stubbornly disobey you, and be the grief of your soul.
¹³Discipline your son, take pains with him;
so that his shamelessness not offend you.

This passage offers several reasons for the disciplined upbringing of sons. While such rearing is certainly meant for the good of the son himself (vv. 7–8, 11), most of the passage seems to be concerned with the benefits that would accrue to the father. He would be gratified by a well-trained son (vv. 1–3, 7–10, 12–13), and he would be assured that his own interests would be carried on after his death (vv. 4–6). Motivation such as this corresponds to the father-oriented interests of a patriarchal society.

According to Ben Sira, even though daughters may be considered treasures (cf. 42:9), raising them is an even more precarious responsibility than raising sons. It is probably because he does not trust the virtue of women that he speaks so disparagingly about daughters (cf. 22:3–5):

³A father is shamed in being the parent of one who is ignorant;
the birth of a daughter is a misfortune.
⁴A discreet daughter is the treasured possession of her husband;
but a shameless one is a grief to her parent.
⁵A loose woman shames her father and her husband;
and she is despised by both.

Each of the verses addresses the shame that a daughter can bring upon her father, and later upon her husband. How she might shame them is not indicated. It could be through failure to conform to any one of the social customs of the group, social customs specific to a strict patriarchal society.

Just as Sirach 3:1–16 underscores a perspective that characterizes the ancient family, so these other passages highlight different family values. Chief among them is the prejudicial view of women that seems to have been held. Such a perspective will certainly determine the character of the most fundamental of family values, the relationship of husband and wife, which actually engenders the family. A second attitude is the conviction that children are meant to serve the designs of the autocratic head of the patriarchal household. To accomplish this end they are obliged to undergo a harsh program of discipline. This attitude defines the second fundamental family value, the relationship between parents and children. While these two relationships continue to be basic to family structure, neither of these ways of living out the respective relationship is espoused in an enlightened contemporary society.

Resignification

What then is one to make of the "family values" found in the Book of Sirach? From the historical point of view one will have to admit the male bias of both the society itself and the tradition that it produced and which reinforced its prejudice. To this feature one must add the ancient world's apparent lack of interest in the unique personality of the child. The present-day commitment to gender equality and to the specific nurturing of each individual leads some interpreters to question the revelatory value of all but the first of the passages examined here.

Canonical hermeneutics maintains that the biblical tradition continues to be revelatory in a new context, but probably not in the way that it originally was. It argues that recontextualization does not require an uncritical replication of the original message. Rather it calls for the contemporary reality and the biblical message to critique each other. We have seen that there is a relative acceptability of the values found in 3:1–16. Values such as respect for parents, gender sensitivity, family cohesiveness, and care for vulnerable family members continue to offer a challenge for families of today. However, the directives found in the other passages will not promote family values today. In fact, the opposite might be the case; they could undermine family unity. This is particularly true in respect to the role of women in society and the manner of child rearing. Here society challenges the biblical teaching.

If we pose the same rhetorical question to each of the passages— What will such behavior achieve?—we might be surprised to discover the same answer: A secure and well-functioning family unit! We can recognize acceptable values in the first passage, because what is described corresponds to a contemporary point of view. We may not be able to recognize the same values in the other passages, because the behavior dictated is not compatible with the behavior that we would prescribe to ensure these values. However, beneath the offensive directives we can detect genuine family values. There we find a call to spousal fidelity and unselfish service for wives, but our contemporary perspective would insist that the call is also for husbands. The instruction on raising sons reminds us of the social ramifications of rearing children. They do indeed carry our legacy into the next generation, and it behooves us, for their sakes and for the sake of society as a whole, to take their rearing very seriously. Finally, it is indeed imperative that we protect our daughters from whatever might violate them. However, a changed attitude toward women in general will alter the way we understand our concern for our daughters. If we look closely enough, we may find that the values are indeed there, though the means of achieving them have changed significantly.

Canonical hermeneutics insists that we must be faithful to our religious tradition, but not necessarily only in the way others have been faithful in the past. Our unique demonstration of fidelity requires that we take our own social location seriously and allow it to critique the cultural features of the received tradition. In this way, we continue the ongoing process that originally fashioned and continually refashions the tradition. In this way we open ourselves to the ever-present revelatory potential of the biblical tradition, even when aspects of its expression offend our cultural sensitivities.

NOTES

1. Paul Ricoeur, *Interpretation Theory: Discourse and the Surplus of Meaning* (Forth Worth: Texas Christian University Press, Eighth Printing, 1976), 25, 43–44.

2. Robert M. Polzin, *Biblical Structuralism: Method and Subjectivity in the Study of Ancient Texts* (Philadelphia: Fortress Press, 1977).

3. Ricoeur, *Interpretation*, 45–46.

4. E.g., Matt 1:23 uses Isa 7:14; Mark 1:2–3 uses Mal 3:1 and Isa 40:3.

5. James A. Sanders, *Canon and Community: A Guide to Canonical Criticism.* (Philadelphia: Fortress Press, 1984), 77–78.

6. 1 Chron 16:1–43 appears to be a midrashic expansion of 2 Sam 17–19.

7. Cf. Mark 4:1–20.

8. Cf. Rom 5:12–14.

9. Matthew L. Lamb, *Solidarity with Victims: Toward a Theology of Social Transformation* (New York: Crossroad, 1982), 68–73.

10. Wilhelm Wuellner, "Where is Rhetorical Criticism Taking Us?" *Catholic Biblical Quarterly* (1987): 448–63.

11. Roland E. Murphy, *The Tree of Life: An Exploration of Biblical Wisdom Literature*, Anchor Bible Reference Library (New York: Doubleday, 1990) 67.

12. Wilfred G. E. Watson, *Classical Hebrew Poetry: A Guide to its Technique* (Sheffield, UK: Sheffield Academic Press, 1995): 123–28.

13. Ibid., 114–22.

12

In Search of
Goodenough Families: Cultural
and Religious Perspectives

Anthony J. Gittins, CSSp

SHIFTING CONTOURS OF FAMILY

A class of schoolchildren was discussing *family* in the context of Christmas cards and gifts. One girl was asked whom she would be sending cards to, and quite innocently she said: "To my Mommy—and her boyfriend; to my Daddy—and his girlfriend; and to my Grandma—and her boyfriend."

When about half of American children are being raised outside the context of a stable nuclear family composed of both natural parents and all natural siblings, is it even possible to identify a "normal" family? This country has the highest divorce rate in the (Western) world,[1] perhaps globally; and though many divorced people remarry, the majority of babies are no longer reared in intact nuclear families. Most people[2] currently understand the Christian tradition to be heavily biased toward stable (nuclear) families,[3] and the marriages that produce to be the only normative form of marriage. In this view, (potential) parents should be legally married to each other, the marriage should be permanently monogamous, and the children should be the offspring of both parents and thus full siblings to each other. This is far from the typical domestic arrangement in the United States today, and many other—statistically normal—domestic arrangements occur cross-culturally. Can a single universal form of Christian family be defended?

Without shared norms or consensus it is virtually impossible to adopt consistent standards of social behavior and education. People without a moral compass become hopelessly lost. Yet magnetic north is not true north, and societies and individuals employ a variety of direction-finding techniques which offer results that are often good enough and sometimes excellent.[4] Discussions of ends and means are sometimes colored by explicitly religious principles, but in a pluralistic society purely pragmatic considerations are often given precedence: does something work, and if not, what can be done about it? Universally, most people struggle for stability, sociability, and responsibility; most are well-intentioned yet not the final arbiters of their destiny; and most operate out of convention or conviction rather than randomly. So, in an imperfect world, how might theologians and pastors respond to the trends and patterns that characterize the human family? Shall we simply reiterate ideals; shall we claim—counterfactually—that every household is a family and every family a household; or can we identify some components of a more or less adequate, or "Goodenough," family?[5]

MARRIAGE AND FAMILY

It is widely assumed—in the West and by Christians[6]—that marriage is the foundation on which a family is built: before a marriage there is no legitimate family, and even after a marriage there is no family as such until the spouses become parents. In this view then, the family has five characteristics: it requires at least three members; marriage is its necessary precursor; it will evolve as the status of the spouses changes from bridegroom to husband to father, and from bride to wife to mother; its evolution continues as more children are added to the basic family unit; and the fundamental building block of the family is the spouses.

Two observations are in order. First, increasingly in the United States, the traditional sequence of status-changes is often modified: parenthood often precedes marriage yet is not always followed by marriage; marriages (particularly second or subsequent marriages) do not always eventuate in parenthood; and the nexus between marriage and parenthood is by no means as obvious as it once was. Second, in every marriage the spouses themselves are already contextualized: they already relate to a previous network of relationships which might have some bearing on their own evolving marriage. Thus we make a conventional distinction between the *family of orientation* (the family into which we are born) and the *family of procreation* (the family created incipiently by marriage and extended by the inclusion of children). Yet as soon as we do so we can see both how different these respective families may be and how reductionistic and inadequate the distinction actually is. One response is to identify a third type of family: the *family of choice* (a social unit different from the other two family forms and identifiable by the freely undertaken commitment of its members).[7]

Universally, marriage is *a rearrangement of existing relationships* (of and between the spouses and between the spouses and their affines or in-laws). Until recently it has also been understood as *a rearrangement for the sake of subsequent relationships* (between the spouses and their offspring). But in the contemporary world, adults—unmarried people or even spouses—operate increasingly as independent individuals, while marriage itself has become optionally related to the production of families and indeed to the long-term ambitions of the consenting parties. The legal and sometimes the religious emphasis has subtly shifted from marriage as a public social institution requiring legal ratification and lifelong permanence, to marriage as an option to be chosen or declined, whether for unmarried or even for currently married persons.

Part of the reason for the perceived crisis in the institutions of marriage and family seems to be the increased emphasis on this isolation and individuation of the conjugal pair, and the privatization of marriage itself. This has largely replaced more traditional emphases both on the integration and socialization of the parties and on the social and moral sanctions intended to emphasize social responsibility rather than individual rights and choices.

Until recently, a huge majority of people around the world probably took for granted not only that families are created out of marriages, but that *marriage* refers to a union between a man and a woman.[8] One of the factors contributing to a reappraisal of these assumptions is the publicity given to gay unions and so-called gay *marriages*. Another is the rapid advances in genetics and biology that have produced *in vitro* fertilization or surrogate motherhood. Many people seem willing to reconsider the partners to a marriage, and even the relationship between biological and sociological paternity and maternity.

This essay goes beyond these developments to consider the most basic "building blocks" from which families are made. Having identified a variety of family forms and looked at some actual domestic arrangements, it assesses their strengths and weaknesses. Then it suggests the Church might reexamine some assumptions about what constitutes appropriate forms of Christian family.

MAKING FAMILIES

Politics, economics, kinship, and religion (or belief and thought) are the quartet of social institutions studied by cultural anthropologists and considered the core around which all human society is built. These institutions (conventionally defined as "standardized modes of coactivity"), may be perceived as analytically distinct, but they are often intertwined in complex ways and understood to be *embedded* in each other rather than isolated or *discrete*. Thus, even though one might want to focus on a single institution, one must carefully consider the others in order to understand the over-lapping of one with another.

We consider three building blocks of kinship (which includes marriage and deals with the basic social and biological facts of life). But we should note not only the religious implications that would strike a Christian reader, but the political or economic significance of building human societies from these raw materials. Since social institutions are often *embedded*, it follows that kinship systems will be related to other institutions, so that to undermine or proscribe one would be to affect others in critical ways: a point not always considered in Christianity's encounter with cultures.

Mother and child

It may seem perverse to claim that this is a basic building block, when clearly a woman must already have had an encounter with a man before she can become a mother. But we are addressing the *primary* relationships necessary for continuity, not merely physical contacts or temporary arrangements. A casual or one-time-only sexual encounter does not constitute a relationship.

The mother-child dyad is the most basic and symbiotic of human relationships.[9] Not only does the infant depend almost entirely on its mother for nurture and protection, but the period of gestation serves to bond mother and baby uniquely. The physical needs of a neonate can be provided by the mother and by her own bodily substance for several years, which would indicate that a dependent baby and its mother are, in principle, the best-adapted dyad for the baby's needs. After the first few years, and assuming mother and baby have continued to be together, the child's developing emotional needs can likewise be best provided, in principle, by the attendant mother. A girl baby can remain with the mother almost indefinitely as she grows to maturity, and even though a boy child needs to sever the maternal-child bond rather differently from his sister, nevertheless the former can grow to maturity in his mother's company, and in the course of so doing offer her the kind of physical protection that a girl may not be capable of. The mother-child bond then, irrespective of the sex of the child, is adapted to provide mutual support over a long period; it becomes a strong interpersonal link, so common in human groups as to be constitutive of them.

Sister and brother

A second social building block is the sibling group: specifically, the brother-sister unit. The "sibling bond" identifies mutual responsibility and interdependence, particularly for food and protection. 50,000 years ago *homo sapiens* operated not in discrete family units, but in small bands. Within a band, siblings would have had better reason than most to look out for each other.

Imagine that the sister becomes pregnant and produces a baby but that she is not in a long-term relationship with a man. Who will provide a modicum of protection, food, and shelter while she is vulnerably dependent on her vulnerable dependent? Human beings are social creatures, and a woman may—by choice as much as by accident—count a brother among her closest friends and relations. A brother, who has some biological interest in his sister's child, may take moral and legal responsibility for providing for them. This would make the sibling dyad quite strong and resilient, and the growing children would identify their mother's brother both as her supporter and as their own friend and mentor.

WIFE AND HUSBAND

Spouses are not related to each other when they marry, and they may have been strangers when they first met. The incest taboo is partly responsible for this: it extends beyond the core family members (mother, father, brother, sister, son, daughter) to include other persons. These are specified as unmarriageable, but by extension the proscription covers sexual relations, too. Thus the incest taboo is deemed to be broken not only when a woman becomes pregnant by a forbidden male, but whenever certain illicit, taboo-governed sexual relations occur. Universally, the choice of spouse is not entirely free: some close consanguines and even affines[10] are excluded. The husband-wife dyad is built, not on biological or natural ties, but on social or cultural foundations.

SUMMARY

Families can be created in various ways, by a combination of principles of bonding and recruitment. The mother-child dyad is the most basic human relationship and biological building block. However, since more than biology is involved in the creation and maintenance of human groups (such as the provision of sustenance, shelter, safety, and sex), and given the reality of sexual dimorphism, we can see what happens to the mother-child unit over time, by the addition of a permanent male. There are three possibilities: add a sibling, add a spouse, and add another (male) person. We have only addressed the first two, but the third possibility remains to be explored.[11] Let us look briefly at a cost analysis of our dyads.

THE MOTHER-CHILD DYAD

The strength of this unit lies in its potential for mutual well-being. The baby's well-being is almost totally dependent on the attendance, care, and nurture provided by the mother, but she in turn finds a unique measure of emotional and indeed physical satisfaction in her baby. A nursing child who is also a companion through the night becomes a kind of extension of its mother. The mother takes pride and satisfaction in her growing baby, which itself becomes a reward for her constant giving.

However, there is also a high maternal price to be paid. She is relatively incapacitated for months; she is physically depleted both by the baby's parasitic feeding habits and nocturnal demands on her rest; and she is slow-moving (and consequently in potential danger from aggressors) as she carries her child, and may also be sexually inactive and unavailable for months or years after giving birth. All these considerations are con-text-dependent, but still—and universally—if a mother-child dyad is the primary group, both are vulnerable.

THE SIBLING UNIT

The maintenance of the sibling unit is also costly. If the safety and rearing of her child is well-served by the mother's fraternal protector, the per-sonal needs of both siblings are only partially satisfied. Given the univer-sality of the incest taboo (particularly strong in proscribing brother-sister incest), the brother's sexual needs can only be met outside the immediate domestic sphere. Should he want a long-term sexual relationship, his presence in his sister's life will suffer. To serve his sister's best interests he will need to forgo such a relationship, leaving him to attend to his sister's children rather than those he might beget himself.[12]

As for the sister: if her brother is her significant adult male, she cannot seek sexual relations with him. But assuming she can become pregnant yet retain the child for her own group, the identity of the impregnator is relatively unimportant and his presence unnecessary; this may be a con-siderable evolutionary advantage. But it is unlikely that she will aspire to an active sex life: her priorities will be different. If she were to seek a per-manent sexual partner, her kinship structure would have to change.

If the mother-child dyad could be yoked to a sibling dyad the benefits would be substantial, though not without cost. But another arrangement might provide the best of all possible worlds.

THE CONJUGAL PAIR

Assuming (a critical assumption, this) that the purpose of marriage is the perpetuation of a social group, we can identify some strengths in the cre-ation of a spousal bond. The husband is the obvious person to mate with the wife and thus become father of her offspring, and clearly the wife is the obvious person to become pregnant by her husband, and subsequently a mother and the rearer of their children. The sexual needs of each party can be met by mutual agreement or convention. And while the wife is nursing, and dependent on her dependent child, her husband can be the best-placed person to assure her protection, shelter, and sustenance.

However, unless both parties honor their mutual obligations and responsibilities, the conjugal arrangement may be rather fragile, especially if the couple move to a new location, at some distance from one or both families of origin. Then, were the husband to abuse or neglect his wife or child, there may be little redress for these latter and little recourse to safety, protection, and nurture. The spousal bond can indeed be buttressed in a number of ways, the better to support the wife/mother and any dependent children. The most simple would be to have the new couple make their home with, or very near to, other members of their families, and to provide for mutual responsibility.

Modifications of the conjugal dyad

A woman who becomes a wife and mother may be expected to make her home within striking distance of her own brother. This combines the previously considered sibling dyad and the conjugal dyad. But that brother may also be someone's husband, so some choices must be made. If the sibling bond is given preference, the wife's own brother is within striking distance. But her husband is himself the sibling of a (married) woman, and if the sibling bond is given absolute preference, that husband must also live within striking distance of *his* sister. In practice this keeps sibling groups together by close residential ties and some form of mutual exchange marriage (two men exchange their sisters, who then become the wives of each); and it subtly erodes the conjugal relationship at the expense of the sibling relationship.

However, theoretically, this would only undermine the *nuclear* family, where emphasis needs to be placed on the marriage bond. It would not compromise other possible family forms, where emphasis is placed on the sibling relationship (and its lateral and vertical impact). Cross-culturally, whenever marriages and families are at stake, checks and balances maintain certain relationships but always at the expense of others. One can perceive constellations of expectations and responsibilities: where each element is strong, the greater good of the greater number is served. But where there is competition between persons or expectations, the whole structure may be compromised.

Thus, polygyny[13]—a collocation of overlapping conjugal dyads—may provide good care for many children, where high maternal mortality would leave many orphans. It also allows for a domestic workforce able to accommodate life-cycle changes (youthful strength, pregnancy-and-lactation, sickness, old age) of the women of a group. Furthermore, it can create stable units of population for farming, feeding, and shelter. But it cannot at the same time support individualism and self-interest.

Again, where land is scarce but critically important, polyandry—an alternative constellation of overlapping conjugal dyads—may create a widely extended family which is territorially compact, thus preventing the breakup of family land by apportioning it to many sons. Here, several sons are cohusbands to a single wife, cofathers to her children, and co-owners of a single piece of land. This may appear bizarre, but at its best it can produce and maintain good, strong, land-based families.

RECKONING FAMILY MEMBERSHIP

Every lasting form of human organization has adaptive potential and structural weaknesses; there are no perfect societies or even perfect families. But some appear to be "Goodenough," or at least better than others and relatively well-adapted. One social structure in serious crisis is undoubtedly the contemporary Western nuclear family. Can we, by examining the three building blocks we have identified, discover some potential ways of strengthening the family as we know it, helping it survive the often cataclysmic effect of divorce, or envisioning new forms of family which might be "Goodenough," even if regarded by orthodox Christianity as unconventional or worse?

Emphasizing the mother-child bond

"Does a woman forget her baby at the breast, or fail to cherish the son of her womb? Yet even if these forget, I will never forget you" (Isa 49:16). It is as if Yahweh is emphasizing God's faithfulness by identifying the very strongest and most fundamental of human bonds and then saying that God's steadfastness is stronger still. The scripture implies that it is virtually unthinkable for a woman to abandon her dependent child. The verse draws attention to the mother-child dyad.

Bolivia is the *locus classicus* of a recent and increasingly global phenomenon: women with memories of abusive men (their own fathers or the husbands of their peers) have been making choices, and what originated in individuals has now become a social fact, even "normal." Women are becoming pregnant intentionally, but without love and with absolutely no intention of entering a marriage. They want a child whom they would raise alone. They choose the mother-child bond over the husband-wife bond, for in their minds it is preferable to be a single mother than a bat-tered wife.[14] Frequently they seek women in similar circumstances, in or-der to find support and create a "Goodenough" family in intolerable cir-cumstances.[15] This arrangement may be neither conventional nor structurally sound—not to mention ecclesiastically approved[16]—but it represents the human struggle for dignity, peace, and social responsibility.

Emphasizing the sibling bond (i)

The Trobriand Islands lie off the southeast coast of Papua New Guinea. Like the women of Bolivia, most of the Trobrianders are Christian. Like the former they have their own understanding of marriage and family. The Trobrianders are matrilineal, which means, among other things, that the sibling bond is traditionally strong and the marriage bond corre-spondingly weak. An individual receives both name and lineage mem-bership through the mother, but a male cannot *transmit* membership: only females can. Thus a man reproduces for his wife's family rather than his own, and his wife's brothers have a significant relationship with their sis-ters' children. Similarly, a woman reproduces for her own family, and her children do not belong to her husband. Consequently, a man begets chil-dren that are not his own family. His sister's children are his family since they continue their mother's name, which is also his name.

The rule is this: a woman's brother, rather than her husband, has a fam-ily tie with the children she bears, since a man does not beget children for his own family but for his wife's. This may seem complicated, and the de-tails need not detain us. Sufficient to remark that in traditional Trobriand society, the most important woman in a man's life is his *sister* rather than his *wife*; and the most important man in a woman's life is her *brother* rather than her *husband* (the marriage bond is brittle). This society has built on the sibling bond as a structural foundation for the family, rather than on the marriage bond. It worked rather well, though with the advent of Christianity—and certainly with globalizing forces—the marriage bond has been increasingly emphasized. Currently, the society is in tran-sition, with people (mostly Christians) trying to hold on *both* to the sibling bond and to the marriage bond. But clearly, emphasis on the one is at the expense of the other, whichever way one proceeds.

Emphasizing the sibling bond (ii)

A recent learned article states: "The closest family tie in ancient Mediter-ranean society was experienced among siblings. Paul of Tarsus followed the historical Jesus in his attempts 1) to undermine the authority and so-cial cohesiveness of the blood kin [sic] group and patriarchal family, 2) to offer an alternative family structure made up of surrogate 'brothers and sisters,' and 3) to make viable a first-century Mediterranean person's choosing to live in such an alternative, trust-based form of social relations [...]. Paul's goal was ... a well-functioning family in the kinship sense, a family without fathers, in which the 'strong' would use their strength not for themselves but to empower the 'weak.'"[17]

The article is worth pursuing for those who seek alternative family models. The author quotes a recent dissertation that argues that "both the brother-sister rhetoric and sibling values continued to characterize a wide variety of Christian groups throughout the Roman Empire for more than 250 years!"[18] Clearly, the idea of the sibling group has some pedigree even among Christians.

Favoring the conjugal bond

"This is why a man leaves his father and mother and joins himself to his wife" (Gen 2:24). The classical Christian family pattern was built on the principle of "leaving and cleaving." It established a new family built with elements of two old families. Where the new family was buttressed and supported by the old, it could be formidably strong and resilient. If the conjugal relationship flagged, both families of orientation could undergird it, and the couple could be persuaded to do their social duty and find a way to live together for the good of both nuclear and extended family.

In an individualistic, egocentric, rights-based society, the conjugal bond is friable and the possibilities of fission in the domestic group are sometimes attractive alternatives to a loveless or career-inhibiting marriage. A relational, sociocentric, duty-based society will privilege the interests of the broader family above those of the individual spouses. If the conjugal bond is treated as a *datum* and divorce as pathological and abnormal, families will perdure in some form, despite spousal friction. In fact, conjugal dissent will not be allowed to destroy the family, because it is extended relationally and generationally, in such a way as to protect the best interests of its members, particularly children. But if the conjugal bond is treated more pragmatically and divorce seen as a reasonable option in the event of disharmony, families will be subject to fission and fusion, with attendant trauma to their members, particularly children. The conjugal bond is only as strong as the determination of the parties and the solidarity of the wider community.

DEFINING FAMILIES

In the "Western" world, where people marry freely and for love, the current malaise in the institution of marriage is palpable. Many couples happily cohabit before marriage, though this is no recipe for a stable marriage later.[19] Others have no intention of "tying the knot." Increasingly couples are making a life together without including children in the equation. Then there are lesbian and gay "marriages," many second or subsequent marriages, and a large number of *superadulta* marriages in which children are not possible. What has happened to "family"—at least, as we knew it?

It may be that a family is "the primary vital cell of society"[20] or that "the family exists at the heart of all societies." It is described as "the first and most basic community to which every human person belongs."[21] But if so, we may have to reexamine all three primary dyads rather than only the husband-wife dyad. Furthermore what is deemed "the most basic community" for middle-class white people in U.S. is very different from that in Ethiopia or Papua New Guinea. The U.S. Catholic bishops aver that "a committed, permanent, faithful relationship of husband and wife is the root of a family":[22] but clearly it is not the root of *every* family, and increasingly, not even most.

We are living through a redefinition of family, not only in a formal, literary sense, but existentially. We have at hand a number of building blocks; we have the experience of structures too weak to sustain the family, and of others untried and (as yet) without approval. But as human beings struggle to bond and to grow, to procreate and to recreate, we are constantly on the lookout for signs of families that manage to sustain each other and contribute to the broader community. There are several forms found in the Hebrew scripture and in cultures other than our own. There is a variety of evolving family forms and myriad existential families that are untypical or unique.[23] Is it possible that, though they are neither perfect nor complacent, but struggling and surviving, these "blended families" may be repositories of some critical "family values," and in fact be "Goodenough"?

EXTENSIVE AND INTENSIVE
DEFINITIONS: A TEST FOR FAMILIES?

Things can be identified in more than one way.[24] A definitional approach would complete the sentence: "a dog is ..." with the phrase "a domesticated canid": this is a connotative or *extensional* definition. Another kind of definition, called denotative or *intensional*, would allow a number of possible "fillers" to complete the phrase: ".... is a dog."[25] Thus, a doberman, a poodle, a chihuahua, or a German shepherd, though rather different in appearance, can equally well be included in an *intensional* definition.

What if, instead of insisting on an *extensive* definition of family (one that would attempt to say the final words of the sentence, "a family is ..."), we were to look at actual social arrangements and *intensive* definitions? Then perhaps we could first specify common characteristics such as adequate structure; the support, protection, dignity, and fulfillment of members; the intention of stability and endurance; and the relation to the wider world. And with these—and others, including some that are theologically generated—perhaps we could identify *this, that, these,* or *those* domestic arrangements, as different from each other, evidently not perfect, and perhaps not equally attractive as some, and yet all recognizable as "Goodenough families."

NOTES

1. USCC, "Putting Children and Familes First: A Challenge for Our Church, Nation and World," *Origins* (28 November 1991), 395.

2. But see reference to Bartchy, below (note 17).

3. The Vatican II document on the Laity, *Apostolicam Actuositatem*, states, without comment (n. 11), that "The Creator made the married state the beginning and foundation of human society;" and "the mission of being the primary vital cell of society has been given to the family by God." This begs a number of questions: what is "the married state" cross-culturally, or to what exactly does "the family" refer in this document? These are faith statements, but they hardly withstand academic anthropological scrutiny as they stand.

4. An example would be the Pacific mariners who can read the stars, skies, and seas so well as to be able to find a tiny landfall after a voyage of two months— and all without compass or sextant.

5. "Goodenough family" is used to identify an existential reality that may fall short of a cherished ideal, yet be more or less capable of sustaining its members and contributing to the broader society.

6. The U.S. bishops cite the Vatican document on the Laity, *Apostolicam Actuositatem,* to support their statement that "families are the 'first and vital cell of society,' the building block of community." *Putting Children and Families First*, 397.

7. See footnote 23 below.

8. *Woman marriage* and *ghost marriage* notwithstanding: by the former, a high-status woman (a sociological male) becomes a sociological *father* by "marrying" a woman whose children become filiated to the high-status woman; by the latter provision, a deceased and childless male is provided with an heir.

9. Pope John Paul II noted this, when he said: "While the responsibility for family development rests on both mother and father, still very much depends on the specific mother-child relationship," Address to Unemployed, Hobart, Tasmania, (1986), in *Origins*, 11 December 1986, 480. See also his encyclicals *Laborem Exercens* (n. 19) and *Familiaris Consortio* (n. 23).

10. For example, in a polygamous society a rule may specify that man may not have relations with any wife of his father, even though the woman in question is not his own mother.

11. This is a fascinating area, but outside our purview. A number of non-biologically related or sexually involved males might provide some of the needs of the mother-child dyad (food, shelter, and so on); but in the contemporary world, females (perhaps biologically or sexually related) might do likewise.

12. Here is another point that cannot be developed here. But about 17% of societies are matrilineal, and the bond between a mother's-brother and his sister's son may be as strong in those societies as a paternal bond in our own.

13. Polygyny (plural wives) is widespread in Africa and beyond. Polyandry (plural husbands) is less widespread, but a *locus classicus* is India, among the Nayar.

14. See note 16 below.

15. See note 9 above.

16. To quote out of context, the 1991 document, *Putting Children and Families First*, "Mothers and children make up an increasing proportion of the homeless in our land"; and "almost a fourth of our children are growing up in single-parent families, " (395–96). The Episcopal document "Follow the Way of Love" (in *Origins*, 2 December 1993), states: "we recognize the courage and determination of families with one parent raising the children" (437). Both statements still beg the question: what is a family? And in 1992 the U.S. Bishops' Pastoral Letter "When I Call for Help" called abusive husbands to account and affirmed the right of women to leave abusive situations. See Lisa Sowle Cahill, *National Catholic Reporter*, 8 March 1996, 10.

17. S. Scott Bartchy, "Undermining Ancient Patriarchy: The Apostle Paul's Vision of a Society of Siblings," *Biblical Theology Bulletin* 29:2 (Summer 1999): 78.

18. Joseph H. Hellerman, "The Church as Family: Early Christian Communities as Surrogate Kin Groups," Ph.D. dissertation (Los Angeles: University of California), as cited in Bartchy, 76.

19. Willard F. Jabusch, "The Myth of Cohabitation," *America* (7 October 2000): 14–16.

20. *Apostolicam Actuositatem* (n. 11).

21. "Follow the Way," 435.

22. Ibid., 437.

23. My own "family of choice" includes my adopted daughter, her three adopted children, and her one natural child; her common-law husband; and the adopted mother of my daughter, who is neither my wife nor my lover, but my friend. The common-law husband is the father of my daughter's natural child and also of one of her adopted children, who is the half brother of the two other adopted children. All three adopted children have different fathers but the same mother—who is not their adoptive mother. Evidently, this is not a family according to any conceivable sociological model. It is, however, an existential, permanent, real—and only—family for most of its members. It is not recognizable as what some would consider the "only form of family divinely mandated by God, . . . the patriarchal heterosexual family with working male breadwinner and dependent wife," Rosemary Ruether, *National Catholic Reporter*, 16 June 2000, 19. But it is a "Goodenough family" in the sense that it struggles, in an explicitly Christian fashion, to address the needs of each of its members and to act justly in the wider world.

24. The dictionary is instructively vague here, identifying 1. "parents and their children considered as a group, whether dwelling together or not"; 2. "the children of one person or one couple collectively"; 3. "the spouse and children of one person"; and 4. "any group of persons closely related by blood." This last, of course, fails to notice that the spouses themselves are not thus related.

25. John Lyons, *Introduction to Theoretical Linguistics* (Cambridge: Cambridge University Press, 1969), 449, 454.

IV

FOSTERING MUTUALITY THROUGH MINISTRY

13

The Black Churches' Response to Father Absence in the African American Family

Homer U. Ashby Jr.

The American family has become a major concern of the Church, government, scholars, social policy makers, and social service agencies throughout the United States for the past twenty years. The rapid increase in divorce rates, the growing number of children raised in single-parent homes, the increased number of children born out of wedlock, and the difficulty that American families have had in maintaining high-quality, stable family life have all contributed to what many have termed the "crisis" of the American family. Although the divorce rate has decreased recently and the number of teenage pregnancies has dropped, there still remains a deep concern about the future of the American family.

Critical perspectives on the nature of the American family crisis have changed frequently over these past twenty years. In the 1970s a number of socioeconomic developments contributed to changed viewpoints about American family "values." For example the rapidly increasing number of women entering into the workplace made women less dependent on a mate for financial support. This more independent state enabled women to consider divorce as a more viable option in the face of marital discord and conflict. In addition some research concluded that children growing up in a single-parent household did not suffer any more psychologically or developmentally than children raised in a two-parent household.[1] Later research, however, documented the detrimental effects for children when raised by a single parent.[2] They pointed to increased poverty for women and children in single-parent families and a variety of health and behavioral problems associated with children of disrupted families, including poor school performance, delinquency, teenage pregnancy, and

poorer performance on a variety of developmental indices.[3] Recognizing
that highlighting the negative dimensions of single parenthood and disrupted families either promoted guilt or blamed persons for situations
and circumstances over which they had no control, researchers and cultural critics began to focus on the benefits of intact families and marriage.[4]
These studies showed that children of intact families fare better than children from disrupted families on a number of indices. Concomitant research also touts the benefits of marriage.[5]

Some have argued that the simple thesis that it is better to be married
and raised in an intact family does not adequately address the complexities of modern life in America.[6] Such a simplified analysis of interpersonal
relationships fails to take into account issues such as marriageability,
agency, social environment, and safety. Marriageability has to do with
whether or not a person possesses the necessary capabilities to be a viable
marriage partner. Individuals who have grown up in chaotic and dysfunctional families with few models for effective interpersonal relating
are at a distinct disadvantage for getting married. Children have no say in
whether or not their parents divorce. Consequently, the production of research that indicates their less-than-ideal development and lack of potential for abundant life offers no assistance to them in coping with a situation not of their making. The social environment or ecology of society is a
crucial element in determining the success of a family's capacity to maintain a healthy and cohesive life together. When work that could provide a
livable wage leaves a neighborhood or community, then the financial
stress on the families in that community contributes to family disruption.
When the work that is available pays at a level that will not allow parents
to support their family financially, family stress and the potential for family disruption increases. Even for families with adequate income to support their lifestyle, society's emphasis on mobility and consumerism, its
failure to provide social supports for working parents, and its proclivity
to apply Band-Aid solutions to cancerous problems are serious threats to
the well-being of the American family.[7] No spouse (usually a woman) or
child should be made to feel guilty for "disrupting" a family where there
is abuse and/or a threat to personal safety.

A war of sorts has been raging in American society about how best to
address the crisis of the American family. Combatants have fallen into two
camps: those who advocate a cultural approach and those who advocate
a political approach. Sometimes the cultural approach is referred to as behavioral because it emphasizes changes in the behavior of individuals
and families. Often the cultural or behavioral approach is associated with
the political right or conservative viewpoints. The argument is that if society would reinforce its social and moral norms about fathering, while
individuals and families modified their behavior, then the difficulties

these families and the larger society encounter would begin to wane.[8] The political approach argues that environmental or ecological dynamics work against the efforts of individuals and families to maintain intact families. The necessary social supports and policies are not in place to assist families in their struggles to remain healthy and whole. Proponents of the political approach call upon government policy makers, the business sector, and community services to support and improve the societal context within which families seek to thrive.[9]

More balanced approaches to addressing the crisis in the American family have emerged recently. These more balanced approaches attempt not to champion one approach over the other. Rather they acknowledge the presence of both cultural and political factors in the cause of and solution to family disruption. One of the balanced approaches views cultural factors and political factors as cocontributors to the plight of Black families.[10] They recommend that solutions to the family crisis be both culturally and politically based. A second of the balanced approaches acknowledges that cultural and political determinants have placed the American family in crisis. However, when it comes to intervention a grass roots/small community strategy is proposed.[11] In this approach the emphasis is on the pathway through which cultural and political interventions are made. Working with mothers and fathers in small groups in local communities to share stories and resources, to lobby government officials, and to become involved in one another's lives is the approach they recommend.

One of the places where the cultural versus political debate has been raging recently has been in the Black community around the topic of father absence. Is father absence in the Black community primarily the result of decisions, actions, and options exercised by individual Black fathers or is father absence in the Black community the result of political forces that lie outside of the individual Black father's influence? The need to find a solution to the problem of father absence is motivated by some rather disturbing statistics about the degree of father absence in the Black community and its consequences. "Of all Black babies born in 1996, approximately 70 percent were born to unmarried mothers."[12] Black children suffer from the same consequences of single-parenthood as children in general:

> The evidence is quite clear: Children who grow up in a household with only one biological parent are worse off, on average, than children who grow up in a household with both of their biological parents, regardless of the parents' race or educational background, regardless of whether the parents are married when the child is born, and regardless of whether the resident parent remarries.[13]

In 1998 a group of prominent African American scholars and leading experts on the African American family came together to address the issue of father absence in the Black community. The Morehouse Conference on African American Fathers held at Morehouse College in Atlanta on 4–6 November 1998 examined the cultural and political factors associated with father absence and concluded that both play a mutually reinforcing role in father absence in Black America.

> Despite our differences, as a group we agree that it is difficult to disentangle cultural values from the effects of economics and policy. We agree that the forces driving father absence in the African American community are complex and mutually reinforcing, and that economics and cultural values, as well as public and private sector policies, play key roles in the crisis of father absence in the African American community.[14]
>
> We believe that we must address, with equal force, *all* the factors that would keep fathers from building caring and nurturing relationships with their children.[15]

This conference made significant contributions to the Black community's understanding of and strategies for addressing the issue of Black father absence. First and foremost the conference laid to rest the debate about the primacy of either culture or politics relative to Black father absence. As Carol and Don Browning reported:

> [T]he Morehouse statement gets us beyond the logic of either /or. Declining economic opportunities for inner city Black men have decreased their ability to marry and support their wives and children. Racial discrimination has been a significant factor behind economic disadvantage and has further damaged the self-esteem of Black men in their pursuit of jobs and marriage. Government programs have exacerbated the problem by linking welfare payments to the absence of a male provider.
>
> On the other hand, the institution of marriage has been weakened in the Black community—and in the rest of society—for reasons not always directly related to poverty.[16]

Second, the Conference highlighted the most salient issues that surround the father absence problem. In response to the question, "Do Black fathers matter?" the Conference attendees replied with a resounding "Yes!" The Conference report stressed that father absence in the Black community is in part fueled by larger national and global trends of increased out-of-wedlock births and divorce rates, and the diminished role of fathers as providers in families. The Conference did not ignore the impact of the legacy of slavery on current family disruption in the African American community, citing the cascading detrimental effects of slavery's assault on the Black family over the generations. While the Conference did not adopt a "marriage first" strategy to address the high rate of nonmarital births in the African American community, they did "strongly favor efforts to strengthen relationships between parents in ways that help fathers connect to their children."[17] The Conference also identified a spiritual dimension to the problem of father absence in the African American community. Because of the legacy of slavery and other injuries inflicted on Blacks by a racist society, the soul and spirit of African Americans has been sorely challenged in its attempt to respond to these external attacks. Care for the souls of Blacks is a necessary and essential ingredient in healing family life in the African American Community. The Conference challenged the Black church to redouble its efforts to heal and inspire fathers and mothers in their efforts to reverse the trend of father absence. Finally the report ended with ten recommendations that were equally balanced between cultural dynamics and economic/policy interventions.

While family disruption and father absence are problems that face all of America, there are specific realities that attend the African American experience that the Morehouse Conference identified. Those include the legacy of slavery, the "fractious and antagonistic"[18] relationship between Black men and Black women, and the spirituality of African Americans. Splitting out these three dimensions of African American experience is employed as a heuristic device so that they can be examined independently. However, there exists a great deal of overlap and mutual influence between these three aspects of African American life.

THE LEGACY OF SLAVERY

The legacy of slavery is tragically relevant to the issue of Black fatherhood, for the conditions of slavery in the United States provided exactly the opposite of what is required in order to preserve the fragile bond between father and child. By law, the male slave could fulfill none of the duties of husband and father. The institution of slavery created a sub-culture where all the societal norms, mores, expectations, and laws, instead of helping to connect men to their offspring, forcibly severed the bonds between fathers and their children.[19]

During slavery African American men were denied the opportunity to assume the roles of father and husband. As fathers they were not allowed to own their children. Their children belonged not to their natural fathers, but to the slaveholder who could sell the children and/or parents at any time. The slave fathers had no say in the ownership, treatment, or use of their children. By law the slave father had no legal rights in relationship to his children. His power and authority as a father were nonexistent. Slave fathers were reduced to a single role: progenitor. In addition Black male slaves were constantly undermined by the slave master in their role as a male figure in the lives of their children. Black children were denied the opportunity to witness their fathers as assertive and self-determining providers, protectors, and leaders alongside of their wives. No doubt, Black slave children witnessed their fathers being ridiculed, beaten, sold, and murdered. While slave fathers had difficulty assuming the role of father, Black children had just as difficult a time claiming a Black father. Under these circumstances fatherhood for Black males was a very tenuous proposition.

The limits placed upon Black male slaves as fathers also applied to their roles as husbands.

> Could he monopolize his partner's sexual services and guarantee that her progeny were in fact his own? Could he protect her from the sexual perdition of other men? Could he at least partly provide for her materially? Could he prevent her from being brutalized and physically punished by other men? Could he prevent her from being torn from the place where she was brought up, bundled like cargo, and sold away from him, her children, her kinsman, and her friends? If the answer to any of these questions is "No," the role of husband did not exist. If the slave could do none of these things, then the role of husband had been devastated.[20]

For over two-hundred years African American men were denied any opportunity to assume the roles of father and husband ordinarily associated with all human societies. This prolonged assault on the capacity and opportunity for Black men to assume the roles of father and husband has had a devastating impact on the cohesiveness of Black families in America.

Revisionist historians[21] have attempted to portray the African American slave family as more cohesive and less pathological in its patterns of relational commitment. They argue that there was less family disruption among slave families than was originally thought. Consequently the external factors of Jim Crow discrimination and public policy rather than internalized cultural/behavioral deficits are the cause of current family disruption in the Black community. Another argument against the influence of slavery on current African American family disruption is that family disruption is becoming increasingly widespread in America and across the globe for families that do not have a history of two-hundred years of enslavement. However, a comparative examination of the timetable of the growing incidence of family disruption in America supports the impact-of-slavery thesis.[22] In discussing the Black-White differential in fatherlessness David Popenoe suggests that Black family life appears to be a precursor of family life for the rest of American families.[23] He bases this observation on the fact that the characteristics of Black families in America foretell the characteristics of White families by a few decades. For example, in 1960 the amount of time spent by Black males living in households with children was 15.1 years, about the same amount of time for White males in 1980, 15.7 years. In 1965, 51 percent of Black teenage mothers were unmarried as compared to 12 percent of White teenage mothers. In 1990 the number of unmarried White teenage mothers had increased to 55 percent. In 1960, 22 percent of Black children and 7 percent of White children were living with only one parent. In 1990, 20 percent of White children were living with only one parent.[24] Popenoe does not answer the question of why African American family disruption antedates White family disruption, but we can begin to speculate that perhaps one of the reasons is the legacy of slavery. The devastating impact of slavery on family life for Blacks remains as a constant factor influencing all dimensions of Black family life. The prolonged assault on Black family life was of such a magnitude that its effects have carried through the generations. There may have been some abatement of its influence over the years, but there is still enough residual impact of slavery on the Black family that when it comes to the amount of time Black fathers spent in the households with their children, the number of unmarried teenage mothers, and the number of children living with only one parent, Black families have produced higher rates in these areas of family disruption earlier than their white counterparts. When addressing the issue of family disruption and father absence in the Black community, the legacy of slavery must be taken into account.

THE FRACTURED RELATIONSHIP
BETWEEN BLACK MEN AND BLACK WOMEN

"Afro-Americans are the most unpartnered and isolated group of people in America and quite possibly in the world."[25] Orlando Patterson draws this conclusion based upon two sets of data: 1) statistical evidence of anger between Black men and Black women, and 2) the fact that African Americans have the lowest rate of marriage in the nation and that those who get married have the highest rate of divorce of any major ethnic group.[26] In a 1996 General Social Survey conducted by the National Opinion Research Center at the University of Chicago, when researchers asked persons if they felt "really angry" at someone in their family, African American women as a subgroup had the highest percentage of affirmative responses (46.6%). African American men's response rate was 28.6%, Euro American women, 38%, and Euro American men, 18%. The survey results also indicate that African American men and women, more so than other groups, see the person who made them angry as responsible for their anger. 46% of African American men and women saw the other person as fully responsible. When asked what responsibility they had for the problem that caused the anger, 64% of African American women indicated that they were blameless, while 46% of African American men saw themselves as blameless. Not only are Black men and women angry at one another, they also see the other person as responsible for their relationship troubles. It is not surprising, then, that African American men and women have the highest rates of non-marriage and divorce.

In his analysis of the low marriage rates and high divorce rates among African Americans, Patterson challenges the three most frequently given reasons for these rates: 1) the male marriage pool argument, 2) the female independence argument, and 3) the school enrollment argument. The male marriage pool argument is that declining job prospects, and high rates of incarceration and homicide, create a severe shortage of marriageable African American men. However, "Educated and prosperous African American men are no more inclined to marry than their poorer counterparts."[27] The female independence theory suggests that the improved economic status of African American women over the past twenty years has made them more independent and thereby reduced their inclination to marry or remain in troubled marriages. Patterson cites data that indicate that the reluctance of African American men to marry and the emergence of diminished expectations of finding happiness in marriage at age thirty for African American women play more of a part in low marriage rates for African American men and women than women's financial independence. The school enrollment argument suggests that prolonged school enrollment by African American women, which delays entering into the workforce, accounts for the delay and increased disinclination to marry. Patterson points to the work of Mare and Winship that does not support the socioeconomic factor of increased school enrollment as a primary factor in the decline of marriage among Blacks.[28] Patterson convincingly argues that a complex set of factors interact to contribute to marriage rate decline and marital disruption increase in the African American community. These factors include the opportunity structure of marriage or the varying degrees of readiness for marriage between Black men and women depending upon age, class, sexual experience, and demography; expected benefits from marriage; premarital behavior including the presence of an out-of-wedlock child; family structure of the family of origin; religiosity; attitudes about infidelity; differing attitudes about gender roles and responsibilities; and sexual attitudes and practices. I will not describe in detail all the intricacies of these factors, but will provide one or two features of a few of these factors that are important to this discussion of father absence.

- Premarital behavior including the presence of an out-of-wedlock child: African American men are less inclined to marry the first person with whom they have a child because of the lack of financial incentive to do so (as was the case in sharecropping) and the lack of communal pressure to do so.
- Family structure of the family of origin: For African American boys and girls, being brought up in a female single-parent household has no effect on the odds of ever getting married. Similarly, being brought up in a stepfamily does not influence the odds. However, for

African American boys, being brought up by both natural parents increases the odds of ever marrying by 2.8 times.

• Religiosity: Going to church once a week doubles African American women's odds of ever getting married, whereas it has no effect for men.

• Sexual attitudes and practices: Of all of the factors listed above the greatest differences in viewpoint and perspective between African American men and women were in the areas of sexual attitudes and practices. This was especially true regarding extramarital affairs. These differences between men and women on sexual attitudes and practices are exponentially increased when religious guidance is introduced. For example, "Afro-American women are 260 percent more likely than others to say that religion guides their sexual conduct, while being an Afro-American man reduces the odds of such a response by 66 percent."[29]

All of these factors influence the marriageability and the marriage experience of African Americans. No easy, simple, or singular factor is sufficient to explain the crisis of marriage in the African American community, although Patterson believes that the legacy of slavery lay at the foundation of these various factors.

The pastoral theologian Lee Butler echoes Patterson's perspective. Butler argues that the Black experience in America can be described as a modified clinical condition of "protracted traumatic stress disorder."[30] Looking at the treatment of Blacks from the slave dungeons in Africa to the present Butler traces the negative impact of slavery and its influences on current relationships between African American men and women.

> If we look at the historical foundation of our relationships, it is not difficult to see why we treat each other in the ways that we do. When we look at our relationships through the lenses of the dungeons and Middle Passage, it is no surprise that African American women and men are searching for home. Women have made reclaiming sacred selfhood a high priority due to the violations of their bodies. Men continue to struggle with issues of control and respect because of their inability to function as patriarchs in a patriarchal world. This also makes it easier for us to understand why we have the sex and gender identities we do. The degree to which our gender identities have been constructed around the experience of our brutalization affects all of our relationships-brother/sister, covenantal, familial, communal, and social.[31]

Patterson is unequivocal and minces no words about what he sees as a dominant factor in why African Americans are the most internally isolated group in America: "This is so because the great majority of Afro-American mothers have been seduced, deceived, betrayed, and abandoned by the men to whom they gave their love and trust."[32] Patterson does not fall squarely into the cultural/behavioral argument camp, attributing all of the problems of marital and family disruption to the behavior of Black males. Rather, he forcefully argues that the ravages of slavery require that Blacks themselves, as well as the larger society that sanctioned and still benefits from slavery, together work at addressing the negative social consequences for African Americans.

SPIRITUALITY

The Morehouse Conference identified spirituality as an important ingredient in the survival of African Americans, especially in light of the legacy of slavery. The power of spirit has enabled African Americans to withstand the assaults upon their bodies and psyches during slavery and beyond. The Conference report also identified spirituality as an essential ingredient in turning the corner on father absence. A life of faith in which the spiritual disciplines of confession, forgiveness, reconciliation, remembrance, prayer, and fellowship are practiced produces hope and renewal, thereby resulting in commitment to live a righteous life. A few of the Conference's recommendations included the work of the Black church to help stem the tide of marital disruption and father absence. Just what that assistance could be has been referred to by some as "the faith factor."[33] Others have used various metaphors to describe the spiritual journey associated with healing disconnectedness in the African American community.[34] In all of these recommendations there is the realization that the well-being of the Black community and the Black family depends upon a spirituality that will strengthen and guide African Americans toward wholeness, internally and collectively.

Bernard Franklin attributes the difficulty that many African American fathers have had in fulfilling their parental role to the presence of a gaping wound in their souls.[35] This gaping wound, whose origins began in slavery, has grown over the course of the generations, resulting in a root of bitterness. The root of bitterness harbors anger, fear, anxiety, and other emotional demons that impede the African American male from establishing and maintaining the kind of loving and caring relationships of which he is capable. Consequently, there is a need for some soul healing for the African American male. The process of healing has two aspects: 1) expressing the anger and hurt associated with the root of bitterness, and 2) forgiving fathers and other males who did not model effective ways of dealing with the root of bitterness. Because the poor performance of some Black fathers is lodged in a damaged soul and because the Black church has the resources of a loving community that practices rituals of healing and renewal on a regular basis, the task of addressing father absence must include a spiritual component.

Returning to the data provided by Patterson it is clear that the faith factor influences Black male-female relationships. Church attendance by women doubles their chances of getting married, while it has no effect on men's chances. Conversely, regular church attendance by men reduces the prospect of marital disruption by 84%.[36] For women regular church attendance does not lessen their odds for getting a divorce. The figures suggest that for African American women the same ideals that influence their desire to marry and establish a family that are rooted in the values of their faith, may also make them less tolerant of their mates' nonadherence to those values of faithfulness and commitment. For African American men the reluctance to get married may have been replaced by a commitment to marriage that was instilled and reinforced by regular church attendance.

IMPLICATIONS FOR MINISTRY IN THE BLACK CHURCH

In light of the impact of slavery on contemporary Black marriages and families, the presence of deep contention between Black men and women, and the influence of spirituality in the life of African Americans, what should the Black Church be paying attention to and doing in order to address father absence in Black America? First of all the church should adopt a balanced approach to the problem of father absence. Father absence is not evidence of cultural and moral degeneracy within the African American community. Nor is father absence solely the result of socio/economic factors. Problems in the African American family, including father absence, are the result of a complex set of interdependent variables, all of which contribute in some measure. The Black Church, then, works to strengthen African American families as well as challenge public policies and practices that undermine the life of Black families. In this way the Black Church continues its historical legacy as an institution that engages in the dual dialectic of survival and liberation.[37] As the Black Church addresses the problem of father absence in Black America it must do so with a balance of programs that assist African American families to remain intact, while also advocating for public policy initiatives that make it possible for Black families to pursue their nascent desire to raise their children in stable households. To pursue only a cultural/behavioral approach may set Black families up for frustration and failure. If Black fathers are relegated to poor educational systems that do not prepare them adequately for work that will earn a livable wage; if the only jobs available for Black fathers are those that will not allow them to successfully fulfill the provider role; and if Black fathers are prevented from assuming their role as involved fathers by restrictive social policy and practice, then external factors are playing a key role in Black father absence. When the Black

Church fails to recognize these external factors or refuses to challenge them, then the Black Church joins others who unfairly blame the victims. On the other hand the Black Church must inspire and motivate Black couples to maintain their commitments to one another. In addition the Black Church must provide programs and resources that support Black families in their struggle to remain together and battle the racist forces in the larger society that contribute to Black family instability.

Motivating parents in Black families to remain involved in their children's lives can be pursued with either a shame-based approach or a pride-based approach. Shame-based approaches engender guilt, shame, and embarrassment and attack self-esteem. Pride-based approaches appeal to the best in persons and identify the assets they have inside of themselves. Some efforts to encourage Black fathers to take responsibility for their offspring do so with a shame-based approach. For example, in New Jersey a statewide initiative to curtail father absence displayed a poster on the side of buses with a picture of a baby and a caption that reads, "It's amazing how many guys disappear when one of these shows up." Another campaign poster picture with the picture of a rooster in gym shoes asks the question, "What do you call a guy who makes a baby and flies the coop?" This is the last thing that a Black father needs in order to motivate his greater involvement in his child's life. Over the past two-hundred-and-fifty years Black fathers have been engaged in a valiant battle to retain their self-respect in the face of brutal efforts to deny manhood to Black men. What Black men need is supportive encouragement to be the fathers they would like to be. Pride engendering strategies include taking every opportunity to praise fathers for their involvement in their children's lives. A pride-based approach counsels Black men that what they do as fathers has a tremendous impact on the development of their child's self-esteem and confidence. A poster that shows a picture of a father holding his baby with the caption, "God bless the child who's got his own," affirms the positive role fathers can have in the lives of their children. Black fathers should be helped to see that what they do with their children helps to ensure the availability of Black leadership for the future. In sermons, educational programs, small groups, and pastoral counseling Black pastors and Black churches can instill pride.

As was indicated above, the presence of fathers in the lives of their children is important. But beyond mere presence the nature and quality of that involvement are crucial. One set of experts defines competent parenting as: "the provision of a family environment conducive to children's cognitive, emotional, and social development; such an environment requires providing warmth and support, assisting with problems, providing encouragement, setting and explaining standards, monitoring, and enforcing discipline."[38] Fathers tend to spend time with their children joking, roughhousing, and other forms of play. The Black Church can provide written and experiential resources that delineate what quality involvement in a child's life entails. Short-term discussion groups on Sunday or midweek can review the various aspects of competent parenting and lead parents in discerning how they can be lived out in their own families. Nancy Boyd-Franklin and A. J. Franklin have recently written a book that assists Black parents in raising African American teenage sons. Discussion of this book would be an excellent opportunity to not only talk about competent parenting, but to also understand the special challenges that Black boys face in growing into Black men.[39] Many churches have prison ministries in which incarcerated fathers are encouraged to stay involved in their children's lives. Providing transportation to prisoners and the delivery of messages back and forth constitute a concrete way in which the father-child connection can be maintained. Given the mobility required by parents and families to stay afloat and given the number of incarcerated fathers, The National Institute for Building Long Distance Relationships has provided a helpful handbook for dads at a distance. Churches can pick, choose, and modify the activities in this handbook in their ministry with fathers who are separated from their children.[40]

Perhaps the most important intervention that the Black Church can make regarding father absence is to assist in healing the fractured relationships between Black men and Black women. The instruction has to begin early. Preteens should receive age-appropriate sex education that introduces them to the realities of their own physical development as sexual human beings as well as the realities of human reproduction. The Black Church must engage teens in conversations about decisions they have to make about sexual activity. Delay of sexual intercourse until marriage is the first line of defense against out-of-wedlock births. However, when young Black men and women engage in sexual intercourse without benefit of marriage, then the Black Church should not take the moralistic high ground and abandon its children at this crucial time in their lives. Instead the Black Church must address all of the health, responsibility, and safety issues that attend to premarital sex. Many Black churches include such discussions in their religious education classes. Other churches have partnered with health clinics to provide guidance about sexual reproduction, with parental permission in the case of minors, in order to protect their children from unwanted pregnancies and disease.

Once a Black couple has a child they need external support to keep the relationship intact. Certainly premarital classes[41] address issues of sexual fidelity, finances, role expectations, family of origin,[42] communication skills, and the practice of faith. Parenting classes before birth and supportive inquiries after the birth give support to couples making the adjustment to life with a child. If parishioners could offer these classes and field follow-up inquiries, then the whole church, rather than just the pastor, could be involved in the mentoring and support role.

Certainly pastors should offer pastoral counseling to couples in crisis. Providing them with a safe and supportive place to resolve their differences protects the couple from repetitive and destructive arguments that tear at the fabric of cohesiveness and mutual regard. Referral to a professional pastoral counselor or mental health practitioner may be necessary when the expertise of the local pastor has reached its limit in the counseling. In addition to crisis counseling, the church should offer opportunities for noncrisis care in the form of discussion groups and religious education classes that focus on the areas of conflict between Black men and Black women. The discussions could center on contemporary books or movies. The discussions might focus on a particular question or issue such as, "What are Black men (women) looking for from Black women (men)?" Needless to say the conversation will be lively, but hopefully, will also create better lines of communication between the sexes that are currently in disrepair.

If indeed church attendance significantly increases Black married males' commitment to the marriage, and thereby, to the family with children, then the Black Church needs to make itself a welcome and attractive place for Black males. The potential connection between decreased father absence and regular church participation moves the Black Church to consider the ways in which Black males are encouraged to attend *and* remain in church. Some churches offer a rites of passage program in which the adult males of the church actively participate in the mentoring and guidance of younger Black males. Other churches support housing programs in which Black males are recruited for help in building and construction. Religious education classes that focus on men's issues within the educational program are a way of offering programs that might encourage Black male participation in the church. Churches will have to be careful that in seeking to attract Black males they do not do so through patriarchal systems that diminish and denigrate women.

In addition to the efforts of the Black Church to strengthen the Black family and Black community in its fight against father absence through cultural/behavioral approaches, the Black Church needs to continue to address public policies that impede Black fathers in assuming their roles as providers, protectors, and nurturers. The Morehouse Conference named seven recommendations in the political/contextual arena:

- Reforming the Earned Income Tax Credit to eliminate its substantial marriage penalty;
- Allowing more fathers, including unmarried fathers paying child support and spending time with their children, to receive the Earned Income Tax Credit, structuring any reforms so that they do not weaken incentives to marriage;

- Reforming federal laws to allow states to extend child care and medical benefits for transitions off welfare through marriage as well as through work;
- Reforming housing policies to promote family formation, for example, by developing pilot projects within public housing to allow fathers of welfare families to live in public housing with their families without a rental surcharge for up to 18 months;
- Increased public and sector support to develop employment and entrepreneurship opportunities in urban areas;
- Increased public and private sector support for job training, job skills development, and transportation to jobs in suburban areas;
- Greater economic development opportunities in urban areas through private investment.

In addition to the above listed recommendations the Black Church should lobby for an increase in the minimum wage so that Black fathers can earn a livable wage with which to support their families financially. Churches can advocate for the reforms and alternatives that are listed above through letter writing campaigns, public forums, invited speakers, phone calls, visits to legislators' offices, rallies, protest marches, and voting.

On the spiritual front the Black Church has provided and needs to continue to provide encouragement, inspiration, and spiritual power to Black fathers as they struggle to be good fathers in spite of the legacy of slavery and the environmental constraints placed upon them. As Wallace Smith and J. Deotis Roberts[43] have written, the Black Church is a Black family, and in the family of the Church Black fathers can receive words of appreciation and encouragement for the positive roles they play in children's lives. The "faith factor" is often the crucial element in whether a Black man has the strength and commitment to follow through on the responsibilities of fatherhood. Helping Black fathers to make the link between their parenting and faithfulness to God not only reinforces their commitment to fathering, but also highlights the real and concrete ways that they can give witness to their faith through their parenting. The rituals of the church offer many Black fathers the opportunity to receive healing and guidance as they assume the role of father to their children. A number of recent books by African Americans describe how difficult it has been for them to grow up without a father.[44] Many of them feel thwarted in becoming the fathers they want to be because of the poor role models provided by their own fathers. Learning to forgive their fathers and confessing their mistakes in raising their own children heals past and present wounds, opening the way for better parenting in the future. The church's capacity to lead men and women in rituals of confession, forgiveness, and recommitment to a righteous life is essential to strengthening Black fathers for their role as spouse and parent. In the safe, supportive environment of the church

Black fathers can support one another through shared stories and prayer. Knowing that they are not alone in the struggle strengthens their capacity for continuing the struggle to remain present and involved in their families. No one local church can follow through on all of the ministries described above. However, depending upon the resources and programmatic strengths of the church a local congregation might chose which of the ministries fits best with its identity and mission. In addition, churches can form partnerships around the issue of Black fatherhood. In pooling their resources and augmenting one another's programs, a comprehensive program of support for Black fathers can be developed. When the Black church rallies around Black families through careful attention to father absence, then the Black community as a whole is served, and hope rather than despair will fashion that community's future.

NOTES

1. M. J. Bane, *Here to Stay: American Families in the Twentieth Century* (New York: Basic Books, 1976); Elizabeth Herzog and Cecelia E. Sudia, "Children in Fatherless Families," in B. Caldwell and H. Ricciuti, eds., *Review of Child Development Research 3* (Chicago: University of Chicago Press, 1973), 141–232; S. A. Levitan and R. S. Belous, *What's Happening to the American Family?* (Baltimore, MD: Johns Hopkins Press, 1981).

2. P. R. Amato and B. Keith, "Parental Divorce and the Well-Being of Children: A Meta-Analysis," *Psychological Bulletin* 110 (1991): 26–46; S. S. McLanahan and K. Booth, "Mother Only Families: Problems, Prospects, and Policies," *Journal of Marriage and the Family* 51 (1989): 557–580; S. S. McLanahan and G. Sandefuhr, *Growing Up with a Single Parent* (Cambridge, MA: Harvard University Press, 1994).

3. Focused more narrowly on the negative impact of fatherlessness, The National Fatherhood Initiative has produced a workbook that has compiled information on research related to father presence and father absence. *Father Facts*, 3rd ed. (Gaithersburg, MD: The National Fatherhood Initiative, 1998).

4. *Beyond Rhetoric: A New American Agenda for Children and Families* (Washington, DC: National Commission on Children, 1991); *Families First: Report of the National Commission on America's Urban Families* (Washington, DC: US Government Printing Office, 1993).

5. Linda Waite, "Does Marriage Matter?" *Demography* 32:4 (1995): 483–504; Kermit Daniel, "The Marriage Premium, " in M. Tommasi and K. Lerulli, eds., *The New Economics of Human Behavior* (Cambridge: Cambridge University Press, 1995), 113–125.

6. Don S. Browning, Bonnie J. Miller-McLemore, Pamela D. Couture, K. Brynolf, and Robert M. Franklin, *From Cultural Wars to Common Ground: Religion and the American Family Debate* (Louisville, KY: Westminster John Knox Press, 1997); James A. Levine with Edward W. Pitt, *New Expectations: Community Strategies for Responsible Fatherhood* (New York: Families and Work Institute, 1995);

Ronald L. Simons and Associates, *Understanding Differences between Divorced and Intact Families: Stress, Interaction, and Child Outcome* (Thousand Oaks, CA: Sage, 1996); William Julius Wilson, *When Work Disappears: The World of the New Urban Poor* (New York: Knopf, 1996).

7. Sylvia Ann Hewlett and Cornel West, *The War Against Parents: What We Can Do for America's Beleaguered Moms and Dads* (Boston: Houghton Mifflin, 1998).

8. See Don Eberly, *Confronting Father Absence: A Guide to Renewing Fatherhood in Your Community* (Gaithersburg, MD: The National Fatherhood Initiative, 1999).

9. Wilson, *When Work Disappears* and Elaine Sorenson, *The National Survey of America's Families* (Madison: University of Wisconsin Press, 1997).

10. *Turning the Corner on Father Absence in Black America: A Statement from the Morehouse Conference on African American Fathers* (Atlanta, GA: Morehouse Research Institute and the Institute for American Values, 1999).

11. Levine with Pitt, *New Expectations*.

12. *Turning the Corner on Father Absence in Black America*, 8.

13. McLanahan and Sandefuhr, 1.

14. *Turning the Corner on Father Absence in Black America*, 13.

15. *Turning the Corner on Father Absence in Black America*, 15.

16. Carol and Don Browning, *Chicago Tribune*, 26 September 1999, Section 1, 23.

17. *Turning the Corner on Father Absence in Black America*, 16.

18. William Julius Wilson, "Fatherhood and Welfare Reform," paper presented at a conference on "The Politics of Fatherhood," Howard University (23 March 1999), 3.

19. *Turning the Corner on Father Absence in Black America*, 10.

20. Orlando Patterson, *Rituals of Blood: Consequences of Slavery in Two American Centuries* (Washington, DC: Civitas/Counterpoint, 1998), 32.

21. Robert William Fogel and Stanley Engerman, *Time on the Cross: The Economics of American Negro Slavery* (Boston: Little, Brown, 1974); Eugene Genovese, *Roll, Jordan Roll* (New York: Pantheon Books, 1974); Herbert G. Gutman, *The Black Family in Slavery and Freedom, 1750–1925* (New York: Pantheon Books, 1976); and Paul Lammermeier, "The Urban Black Family in the Ohio Valley, 1850–1880," *Journal of Marriage and the Family* 35 (August 1973): 440–456.

22. Patterson, 55; David Popenoe, *Life Without Father: Compelling New Evidence that Fatherhood and Marriage are Indispensable for the Good of Children and Society* (New York: The Free Press, 1996), 26.

23. Popenoe, 26.

24. Popenoe arrived at these figures based on calculations from data provided by the Fertility Statistics Branch and the Marriage and Family Statistics Branch, U.S. Bureau of the Census, Washington, DC.

25. Patterson, 4.

26. Based upon Patterson's calculations of data from the U.S. Census Bureau, Washington, DC.

27. Patterson, 63.

28. Robert Mare and Christopher Winship, "Socioeconomic Change and the Decline of Marriage for Blacks and Whites," in Christopher Jencks and Paul Peterson, eds., *The Urban Underclass* (Washington, DC: Brookings, 1991).

29. Patterson, 118.

30. Lee H. Butler Jr., *A Loving Home: Caring for African American Marriage and Family* (Cleveland, OH: Pilgrim Press, 2000), 17.

31. Butler, 36.

32. Patterson, 4.

33. See Don S. Browning et al., *From Cultural Wars to Common Ground*; Don E. Eberly, ed., *The Faith Factor in Fatherhood: Renewing the Sacred Vocation of Fathering* (Lanham, MD: Lexington Books, 1999); Sheldon D. Nix, *Becoming Effective Fathers and Mentors: A Guide to Prepare Men for the Task of Mentoring African American Boys* (Colorado Springs, CO: Cook Communications Ministries and Woodbury, NJ: Renaissance Productions, 1996); James A. Levine with Edward W. Pitt, *New Expectations*.

34. Butler uses the metaphor of "Coming Home"; Archie Smith uses the metaphor of "Navigating the Deep River" (Archie Smith, *Navigating the Deep River: Spirituality in African American Families* [Cleveland, OH: United Church Press, 1997]); Edward P. Wimberly refers to the need in the Black community for mentoring "Relational Refugees" (Edward P. Wimberly, *Relational Refugees: Alienation and Reincorporation in African American Churches and Communities* [Nashville, TN: Abingdon Press, 2000]).

35. Bernard Franklin, "Fatherhood in the African American Church," in Don E. Eberly, ed., *The Faith Factor in Fatherhood*, 59–89.

36. Patterson, 80–92.

37. C. Eric Lincoln and Lawrence H. Mamiya, *The Black Church in the African American Experience* (Durham, NC: Duke University Press, 1990), 11—12.

38. Ronald L. Simons and Jay Beaman, "Father's Parenting, " in Simons and Associates, 100–101.

39. Nancy Boyd-Franklin and A. J. Franklin, *Boys into Men: Raising Our African American Teenage Sons* (New York: Dutton, 2000).

40. *Dads at a Distance: An Activities Handbook for Strengthening Long Distance Relationships* (Knoxville, TN: A & E Publishers); Dads at a Distance, P.O. Box 16659, Knoxville, TN 37996.

41. Herbert Anderson and Robert Cotton Fites, *Becoming Married* (Louisville, KY: Westminster John Knox Press, 1993) is a valuable resource for thinking about how to work with couples who plan to marry.

42. Ed Wimberly's, *Recalling Our Stories* (Nashville, TN: Abingdon, 1997) offers a helpful section on analyzing one's own family of origin.

43. Wallace Charles Smith, *The Church in the Life of the Black Family* (Valley Forge, PA: Judson Press, 1985); J. Deotis Roberts, *Roots of a Black Future: Family and Church* (Philadelphia: Westminster Press, 1980).

44. Jonetta Rose Barras, *Whatever Happened to Daddy's Little Girl?: The Impact of Fatherlessness on Black Women* (New York: Ballantine, 2000); Erma Jean Lawson and Aaron Thompson, *Black Men and Divorce* (Thousand Oaks, CA: Sage, 1999); Leonard Pitts Jr., *Becoming Dad: Black Men and the Journey to Fatherhood* (Atlanta, GA: Longstreet, 1999).

14

More than a Family Affair: Reflections on Baptizing Children and Mutuality

Gilbert Ostdiek, OFM

INTRODUCTION

Among its many purposes and meanings, baptizing children strengthens and expands the possibility of mutuality in life and faith. The practice of initiating children prepares a child for a life of mutuality because it fosters clear personal identity and autonomy within expanding communities of mutuality and care. In baptism, the child is not only particularized socially with a name. Baptism is also the beginning of a life of discipleship, which has priority over any and all other loyalties for Christians. It is therefore a sign to parents, Herbert Anderson has observed, "that their children are not their children, for they belong to God who has called them into existence and calls them into service of the world."[1] Baptism is a challenge to any parental inclination to possess a child or diminish in any other way the formation of a self well-defined enough to enter into relationships of mutuality and equal regard.

Baptism is more than a family affair. Several essays in this book have emphasized the reciprocity between justice in the world and a just family. Baptism is initiation into a community that calls every individual to seek for justice within the family and beyond the family in widening arenas of concern. "The family and the Church in turn are two contexts in which we may discover the faithfulness of God and so nurture our gifts for the world that we can also give them away."[2] Baptizing children enlarges the nurturing circle at the beginning of life to include the community of believers. It expands the horizon of mutuality beyond the family.

The brief reflections that follow examine the practice of baptizing children from the perspective of practical theology. The aim is to enhance the practice of infant baptism by understanding its implications for the growth of the self and the possibility of love as equal regard and mutuality.

ECUMENICAL CONVERGENCES IN BAPTISMAL PRACTICE

Baptism of infants and young children has been a regular practice of many churches throughout the long reach of Christian history. Paradoxically, the earliest and most developed theology for baptismal practice has been drawn from the Pauline letters, which were written in the early years of the Christian community when the baptism of adult converts would have been the normal practice. That understanding of the rite has been a mainstay for the infant practice as well.[3] One only need scan the rites of the first part of the last century to see what lasting impact the adult practice and theology have had on how the rite was celebrated for young children and infants. Two examples will suffice.

The Roman Catholic rite in effect before the Second Vatican Council[4] made it clear that the child is a passive recipient of the sacrament. The rite begins at the entrance to the Church with a series of questions and answers: "What is your name?" "N." "What do you ask of the Church?" "Faith." "What does faith offer you?" "Eternal life." These questions are addressed directly to the child, but the answers are given by the sponsors who speak for the child. The same holds true for the renunciation of sin and profession of faith, as well as the request for baptism. The only active participants named in the ritual are the priest and the sponsors. There is no mention of the parents or of a congregation. In fact, infant baptisms usually took place on a Sunday afternoon in a small, private ceremony at a font tucked away in a corner of the sanctuary or in a baptistry at the rear of the church. It was indeed a private family affair.

The rite of baptism authorized in 1928 for use in the Episcopal Church in the United States[5] shows similar features. The minister and godparents have active roles. The godparents are explicitly asked to respond in the name of the child: "Do thou, therefore, in the name of this Child, renounce the devil and all his works ...?" The congregation is mentioned, but it is assigned no active role. There is no mention of the child's parents in the rite.[6] Here, as in the Roman Catholic rite, the primary relationship proclaimed and enacted in the rite is that between God and the child. Little, if anything, is said ritually about mutual relations between the child and the parents, godparents, and community, although church practice assigned parents and godparents a role in raising the child in the faith.

In the last four decades, many churches have undertaken significant revisions of the rite of baptism. For Roman Catholics, the Constitution on the Sacred Liturgy (1964) directed: 1) that the rite of infant baptism should be revised in a way suited to the fact that the one being baptized is an infant, and 2) that the roles of parents and godparents should be brought out more clearly in the rite (n. 67). The revised rite for baptizing children (1969) carried out those directives in several ways.[7] Parents and godparents are drawn into the ritual dialogue with the minister and speak for themselves rather than in the name of the child. It is their faith and the faith of the Church into which the child is baptized. They are also invited to claim the child for Christ by signing its forehead, an invitation often extended in practice to others in the assembly as well. Children are to be baptized on Sunday in the presence of a gathered assembly, and the assembly is asked to give its assent to the faith professed by the parents and godparents. The baptism of children is thus a community affair.

Revisions of the rite in other Christian churches show similar traits. What is perhaps most striking is the role given to the congregation. In the Episcopal, Lutheran, Presbyterian, and United Methodist rites[8] the congregation has an active part. This typically includes welcoming the child, making prayers of intercession, professing the faith of the community, renewing their own baptismal promises, and consenting to support the one being baptized. The United Methodist rite expresses this last role in a particularly lovely way, joining the commitment of support with the renunciation and profession. First the parents and sponsors and then the entire congregation are explicitly asked if they will nurture the child and one another in the Christian life and faith. The child is to be drawn into the web of mutuality that binds all the members of the community together.

THEOLOGIES LATENT IN THE RITES

There is a remarkable ecumenical convergence in the revised baptismal rites just described, and particularly in the underlying theology. The revised rites still rely on both Pauline and Johannine images for their theology of baptism as an event of salvation by which the child dies and rises with Christ and is brought to new birth as God's child by adoption. Upon further reflection, however, these reformed rites can be seen to express and embody a different theological orientation. Several themes, latent in the rites themselves and in the pastoral introductions which accompany them, can be highlighted.

Who baptizes? In the older rites members of the community who might have been present were there simply as silent attendants at an action performed by the minister of the sacrament on behalf of God and the Church. The sacrament could be and often was celebrated just as easily without a congregation, except perhaps for a few family members and friends. Little was done ritually to enact mutually binding relationships and roles.

The revised rites convey something far different and invite a fresh look at the latent theology of sacrament. Though there is a presiding minister who performs the central ritual act of bathing the child in the name of God and the community, it is clear that the entire assembly has a part in the action. The assembled people are integral to the celebration. They, rather than the child, are called to renounce sin and profess the faith in their own name as the context for the sacrament. They accept the child into the community and pledge themselves to care for its growth in Christian living. In a larger sense, then, the community itself is being imaged as a baptizing community. This way of celebrating the rite calls for a broader understanding of sacrament, one which does not reduce it to the bare essentials required for validity in emergency situations (called matter and form in classical medieval theology). The celebration of baptism involves not only the minister, but also the community. Similarly, it has been suggested that the child is not the only one to receive God's gift of grace in this celebration; the gathered people, too, are its beneficiaries. "The community is called to be present at baptism not merely to act as stage props or to render the occasion more solemn, but because what happens in a baptism happens to everyone in the church."[9] In a paradoxical reversal, the child being plunged into the waters of the font now becomes a proxy for the community whose members are called to profess their faith anew and to renew their own baptismal promises to live as disciples of the Crucified One. It is a sacrament of faith and renewal for them as well; it invites them to renew their own commitment to the way of life they will share with the child.

Who is the child being baptized? The older rites, even though directed to the child, did acknowledge in their own way that an infant is not yet capable of personally renouncing sin or professing faith.[10] That is why the godparents acted as proxies for the child, while the child, as it were, spoke through them. Despite the use of birth imagery, the older rites seem to presume an adult model of faith and discipleship. This is particularly evident in the stress they place on the formation and growth that are to occur in the course of the child's life after it has attained the use of reason. This presumption matched an attitude prevalent until the seventeenth century, that children were the property of the family and were not yet persons before the age of reason.[11]

But in the case at hand the one being baptized is often an infant, literally a person "without speech." In the revised rites the child is not made to speak, even through the mouth of another. The rites accept the truth that children are not just adults-in-waiting, but persons in their own right. In so doing, the rites challenge the Church to develop an authentic theology of childhood needed to undergird the revisions. Some initial sketches for such a theology of childhood have been proposed, but major work remains to be done to flesh out this idea and to bring it to bear in pastoral practice surrounding baptism.[12] The question at issue is really a dual one: who is the child in human community and who is the child in the Church? What is at stake is the kind of solidarity and mutuality in faith and holiness of which Paul speaks in 1 Cor 7:14. Indeed, the baptized child is a full and equal member of the Church, endowed, as Paul would have it, with unique gifts for the building up of the Church. In a curious way, that calls parents and community to foster greater mutuality with their children, to temper the unequal parent-child relationship accordingly.

What does it mean for a community to baptize a child? We noted above that the community had little or no role in the older rites, other than perhaps attending the ceremony. The same was true of the child's parents. In the revised rites, both community and parents are present and involved in a way that embodies another kind of ecclesiology. The rites manifest the Church in two fundamental ways.

The first of these pertains to the community as a whole. In addition to renouncing sin and professing faith, the entire community promises to provide lifelong support for the child being baptized. The image of a life of discipleship lived out in community over a journey that spans the entire life of a Christian pervades the Rite of Christian Initiation of Adults (1973/1988). The ecclesiology underlying that rite sees the Church less an institution than as the People of God on pilgrimage. Initiation entails welcoming others to walk along with the community, which first accepts and tutors them as apprentices in the Christian way of life and then continues to companion them once their initiation has been completed. A similar ecclesiology is implied in the rite for children. Children are received into the community not simply as welcome additions to expand the parish rolls, but as fellow pilgrims for whom all in the community have a responsibility. They are called to exercise that responsibility very concretely, "to guide and nurture [the one being baptized] by word and deed, with love and prayer" as the Presbyterian rite puts it. What is at stake is the formative power which the example of others has for us. Baptizing and rearing children is the affair of the whole community of faith.

The second way in which the Church is manifested focuses specifically on the parents of the child. They, too, have an active role in the rite. They personally present their child for baptism, sign its forehead to claim it for Christ, renounce sin and profess faith, and commit themselves to rear their child in the gospel values of one who follows the way of Christ. Because the child will be entrusted to their daily care through its formative years into early adulthood, they in effect become not only the child's human family, but also the "Church on the ground" for the child. The ecclesiology at work here accepts the family as a "domestic Church," the "Church in miniature." This understanding, common in the early Church, has recently been reclaimed in several documents of the Roman Church and is slowly entering into contemporary thought about marriage and family.[13]

Several themes flow from this understanding of domestic Church. One is that the family is a place where parents and children together encounter God, where they contribute mutually to the sanctification of one another, and where the family replicates in miniature the way of life enjoined on the entire Church. This way of life is characterized by hospitality, love, forgiveness, justice, prayer, care for others, and witness. That brings us full circle. The baptism of children is indeed a family affair, but an affair where the family is more than just a human family. The family is a basic unit of the Church, ingrafted into the mystery of the Church and sharing its life and mission.[14] For the child the family is the gateway into the Church.

BAPTISMAL PRACTICE AND PASTORAL CARE

The revised rites for baptizing children thus invite us to draw out a theology of sacrament, childhood, and Church that takes relationships and mutual responsibility into greater account. The task does not stop with this reflection, however, for a practical theological approach recognizes that drawing out the latent theology is not meant simply to develop a theology for its own sake. The greater challenge for future practice lies in placing the rites and their theological underpinnings in the larger context of a pastoral care attentive to matters of mutuality. In the space remaining, several themes from the work of Herbert Anderson will be examined that contribute to integrating pastoral care and theology with the practice of baptizing children.[15]

The baptism of infants is not only an event, but also a process. "As a ritual of initiation, baptism is both an event and a process. It is a momentary and complete action that begins a lifelong struggle for human renewal that is punctuated by subsequent sacraments of the Church."[16] This immediately implies that the pastoral care must be exercised throughout the process, not just at the sacramental moment. Anderson spells out in detail the kinds of care needed before birth, at the time of birth and baptism, and thereafter.[17]

The parents are to be a central focus of that pastoral care from the outset. The birth of a child invites them to attend to their calling not only as married partners, but also as parents. Through such pastoral care, they will more easily come to understand and accept their parenting vocation and to appropriate what Anderson calls a "transforming vision for family living."[18] The typically brief prebaptismal preparation programs now in vogue may need to be rethought in light of the needed formation in parenting.[19]

A comprehensive pastoral approach is needed for the care of families. On this topic Anderson writes:

> In a broad sense the preparation for the addition of a child begins with the processes by which a man and woman leave father and mother in order to form a new family. If there is space in the togetherness of the marital pair, it is likely that there will be room for the child. How we help people get married, therefore, is a crucial beginning for the tasks of parenting.[20]

And it does not end there. In a five-volume series which Anderson planned and coauthored, he reflects on the pastoral care needed throughout the entire family life cycle.[21] That larger vision of caring for the family is badly needed in a society where family life is so vulnerable. Without it, the human and spiritual growth promised in baptism is at risk.

Family and Church are reciprocal contexts for growth and development. "The relationship between the family into which one is born and the Christian community into which one is baptized is a reciprocal one."[22] Human growth and growth as a believer are intertwined. Family and faith community each have their own unique contribution to make to the practice of mutuality. By its very nature, growth in the family circle is shaped by intimate, one-to-one and small-group relationships. The mutuality fostered within the larger circle of the church community has an alternate stress. It forms children to enter into relationships and accept responsibilities based primarily on the gifts they bring for the common good rather than on intimate relationships.[23]

Pastoral care will then help parents integrate compatible human and Christian values into their vision of family life. Anderson suggests five such values, all central to the practice of mutuality. The family is to be: 1) a welcoming, hospitable community; 2) a just community; 3) a forgiving community; 4) a compassionate community; and 5) a sending community.[24] These resonate well with and can be reinforced by the characteristics of the "domestic Church" noted at the end of the previous section.

Finally, children are a unique gift. This is one of Anderson's cardinal convictions. They are a gift given to the family by God, a pledge of God's faithfulness. Anderson loves to say that children given to a family are theirs but not theirs. They are destined to be members of society and Church at large. The family is a "holding environment" where that gift is nurtured and brought to maturity, so that it may be given over to others. The baptism of a child reminds parents that the child, entrusted for a time to their care, must in God's design be sent forth. During the time a child lives within the family circle, the uniqueness of that gift is to be fostered, but in a way that prepares the child to enter into fruitful adult relationships with others.

CONCLUSION

Baptizing a child is far more than a simple family affair. It reveals the family as the embodiment of the Church in the daily life of the child. It reveals the family as a place where God is encountered as the One who gives life and makes holy. It invites parents to serve, not as proxies for their child for this brief sacramental moment, but as lifelong proxies for the God who gives, who is faithful, who abides, who shelters, who loves. And then sends us into the world to establish communities of mutuality and just love.

NOTES

1. Herbert Anderson, "Pastoral Care in the Process of Initiation," in Bernard J. Lee, ed., *Alternative Futures for Worship*, volume 2: Baptism and Confirmation (Collegeville, Minn.: The Liturgical Press, 1987), 135.

2. Ibid.

3. The imagery of being born again and of being begotten from above found in John 3:1–8 and in the Johannine letters came into greater prominence in reflection on baptism in the fourth century and thereafter, but it never replaced the dominance of the Pauline theme of dying/rising with Christ.

4. "The Rite for the Baptism of a Child," in *Collectio Rituum* (New York: Benziger Brothers, 1964), 1–14.

5. "The Ministration of Holy Baptism," in *The Book of Common Prayer and Administration of the Sacraments and Other Rites and Ceremonies of the Church* (New York: Seabury, 1976), 273–282.

6. An introductory rubric allows that the child's parents may be admitted as sponsors, whose role is to arrange for the baptism. It is the godparents, not the sponsors, who serve as proxies for the child during the rite.

7. *Rite of Baptism for Children* (New York: Catholic Book Publishing Co., 1970).

8. Respectively: "Holy Baptism," *The Book of Common Prayer and Administration of the Sacraments and Other Rites and Ceremonies of the Church* (New York: The Church Hymnal Corporation, 1979), 297–314; "Holy Baptism," *Lutheran Book of Worship: Ministers Desk Edition* (Minneapolis, MN: Augsburg, 1978), 308–312; "The Sacrament of Baptism," *Book of Common Worship* (Louisville, Ky: Westminster John Knox Press, 1993), 403–418; "The Baptismal Covenant II," *The United Methodist Hymnal* (Nashville, TN: The United Methodist Publishing House, 1989), 39–43.

9. Nathan Mitchell, "The Once and Future Child: Towards a Theology of Childhood," *The Living Light* 12 (1975): 434. See also Tad Guzie, "Theological Challenges," in William J. Reedy, ed., *Becoming a Catholic Christian: A Symposium on Christian Initiation* (New York: Sadlier, 1979), 170: "Sacraments happen to the community, not just the individual. The individual person is not the starting point for understanding the effects of the sacraments."

10. Medieval theology addressed this anomaly of baptism being a sacrament of faith for an infant by distinguishing between the "habit" of faith, which an infant could receive, and actual "acts" of faith, which the child would be able to make later on after attaining the use of reason.

11. See the commentary of Mark Searle, "Infant Baptism Reconsidered," in Mark Searle, ed., *Alternative Futures for Worship*, volume 2: Baptism and Confirmation (Collegeville, MN: The Liturgical Press, 1987), 33–35, based on a study of the history of childhood by Philippe Ariès, *Centuries of Childhood* (New York: Knopf, 1962).

12. In addition to the work of Searle just cited, see Mitchell, "The Once and Future Child," 423–437; Karl Rahner, "Ideas for a Theology of Childhood," in his *Theological Investigations VIII* (New York: Herder and Herder, 1971), 33–50. The Johannine image of new birth will likely become more prominent in that theology.

13. See Vatican Council II, *Dogmatic Constitution on the Church* 11 and *Pastoral Constitution on the Church in the Modern World* 48 (in various editions); John Paul II, *On the Family* 49 (Washington, DC: USCC, 1981). For historical, theological, and pastoral commentary, see Joann Heaney-Hunter, "Domestic Church: Guiding Beliefs and Daily Practices," in Michael G. Lawler and William P. Roberts, eds., *Christian Marriage and Family: Contemporary Theological and Pastoral Perspectives* (Collegeville, MN: The Liturgical Press, 1996), 59–78; William P. Roberts, "The Family as Domestic Church: Contemporary Implications," in Michael G. Lawler and William P. Roberts, eds., *Christian Marriage and Family: Contemporary Theological and Pastoral Perspectives* (Collegeville, MN: The Liturgical Press, 1996), 79–90.

14. John Paul II, *On the Family* 49.

15. Anderson has been chosen as the "conversation partner" for these reflections because of his longstanding concern for the relationship between baptism and human growth. See, e.g., Herbert Anderson, "Christian Baptism and the Human Life Cycle" (Ph.D. diss., Drew University, 1970); Herbert Anderson, "Baptism and the Psychology of Growth: A Lifelong Task," *Liturgy* 4:1 (Winter 1983): 61–67; Herbert Anderson, "Pastoral Care in the Process of Initiation," in Mark Searle, ed., *Alternative Futures for Worship*, volume 2: Baptism and Confirmation (Collegeville, MN: The Liturgical Press, 1987), 103–136; Herbert Anderson, "What Does Baptism Have To Do with Christian Life?" in *Open Questions in Worship: What Is Changing in Baptismal Practice?* (Minneapolis, MN: Augsburg Fortress, 1995), 23–29; Herbert Anderson and Edward Foley, "The Birth of a Story: Infant Baptism in a Pastoral Perspective," *New Theology Review* 4 (November 1991): 46–62; Herbert Anderson and Edward Foley, "Welcoming the Child," in *Mighty Stories, Dangerous Rituals: Weaving Together the Human and the Divine* (San Francisco: Jossey-Bass, 1998), 57–74; Herbert Anderson and Susan B. W. Johnson, *Regarding Children: A New Perspective for Childhood and Families* (Louisville, KY: Westminster John Knox Press, 1994), passim.

16. Anderson, "Pastoral Care in the Process of Initiation," 104.

17. Anderson, "Pastoral Care in the Process of Initiation," passim; Anderson and Foley, *Mighty Stories, Dangerous Rituals*, 66–72.

18. Herbert Anderson, "Christian Themes for Family Living," *Dialog* 28 (1989): 169.

19. Though such preparation is not narrowly defined in "Infant Baptism: An Instruction of the Sacred Congregation for the Doctrine of the Faith," *The Pope Speaks*

26 (1981):15–19, canonical concerns remain prominent, especially in the case of nonpracticing parents.

20. Anderson, "Pastoral Care in the Process of Initiation," 132.

21. In addition to the previously cited work, *Regarding Children*, the series includes the following titles: *Leaving Home, Becoming Married, Promising Again,* and *Living Alone.* All are published by Westminster John Knox Press in Louisville, KY.

22. Anderson, "Pastoral Care in the Process of Initiation," 105.

23. The reciprocal, complimentary roles of family and Church might be compared with the "I-Thou" and "Essential We" relationships described by Martin Buber, *I and Thou* (Edinburgh: Clark, 1958); *Between Man and Man* (London: Fontana Library, 1961). In his *The Knowledge of Man* (New York: Harper & Row, 1965), 68, Martin Buber has described mutual empathy as fundamental for full humanity: "What is basic in human life is twofold, and it is one: the wish to be confirmed as what we are, even as what we might become, by others; and our innate capacity to confirm others in this same way." This vision of mutual empathy is not only essential for vital marriage and family living; it is a way of living out the call to discipleship from our baptism.

24. Anderson, "Christian Themes for Family Living," 168–174.

15

Conversion or Nurture:
When We Thought the
Debate Was Over

Thomas Groome

I wrote an essay on the topic of conversion or nurture twenty years ago, and felt lucky to get it published.[1] In the mainline churches at least, the fire had gone out of this old debate. The evangelistic revivals that had fueled the controversy had long lay dormant. So, I summed up what seemed like the consensus on a resolved controversy: that Christians will always need and, by God's grace, catechetical education should always promote *nurture in lifelong conversion*.

Though I did not presume to have had the last word, I certainly did not expect to write about it again in the new millennium. Yet, I find it fortuitous to be so invited at this time, but to now consider "nurture" within the context of family. Further, a recent Vatican document on catechesis is being overinterpreted—in my opinion—by enthusiasts for the catechumenate/conversion combination to the point of neglecting education in faith from womb to tomb. Evangelical Protestants will surely be surprised to find Catholic religious educators tipping the scales to favor a conversion-event over family nurture and education. With this essay I argue again for a balance of nurture and conversion, the former as including good religious education and the latter as always lifelong.

On 15 August 1997, the Congregation for the Clergy—the Vatican agency entrusted with oversight of catechetical education—issued a new *General Directory for Catechesis* (hereafter *GDC*).[2] The *GDC* replaces even as it builds upon the *General Catechetical Directory* of 1971. Like its predecessor, it is likely to set the tone and tenor of catechetical education for the coming era in the Catholic Church. It will be my conversation partner here as I reengage the "conversion or nurture" debate; this lens, in turn, will highlight other cautions to observe in interpreting the *GDC*.

Though the document is distinctly Catholic, I hope neighbors in the Body of Christ can listen in and hear resonant insights for their own ecclesial context. In that ecumenical spirit, I will begin by recalling the wisdom of Horace Bushnell (1802–1876), among the greatest religious educators of the past two centuries.

BUSHNELL'S CALL FOR FAMILY NURTURE

Like the "Great Awakening" heralded by Jonathan Edwards in the mid-1700s, the revival led by Charles Finney during the 1820s was an enthusiastic movement of evangelization, preaching God's word to convert to Christ or to revivify dormant faith. The intent was a cataclysmic moment of recognizing one's dire sinfulness and abandoning oneself to God's mercy. The revivalists took this conversion approach even to children. Their sentiment was that little could be done by way of children's faith until they were adult enough—around age twelve—for a conversion experience. Enter Horace Bushnell!

Around 1830, while a law student at Yale, Bushnell was touched by the revival movement, at least enough to abandon law and prepare for the ministry. However, he resisted its undue emphasis on evangelization for conversion, and particularly the neglect by revivalists of nurturing children in faith from the first days of life.

In 1847, Bushnell published the first edition of his classic work, *Christian Nurture*—still rewarding reading. He drew upon his own childhood memories of good family formation and found biblical inspiration in Ephesians 6:4: regarding children, "Bring them up in the nurture and admonition of the Lord" (King James translation). A work of extraordinary insight about the family as a source of grace, *Christian Nurture* reflects insights about identity formation that the social sciences of a hundred years later would verify.

Bushnell wanted the family to be more like a church and the church more like a family so that both would be capable of Christian nurture. Note that within nurture as formation he included education as well; "admonition" in the Ephesians text means "instruction." Bushnell summarized his central proposal: "What is the true idea of Christian education? *That the child is to grow up a Christian, and never know himself as being otherwise.*" And he went on, "In other words, the aim, effort, and expectation should be, not, as is commonly assumed, that the child is to grow up in sin, to be converted after he comes to a mature age; but that he is to open on the world as one that is spiritually renewed, not remembering the time when he went through a technical experience."[3]

Now, remember that Bushnell was swimming against a Puritan tide that viewed the human condition as essentially corrupt, and thus not capable of being nurtured into Christian identity. One could come to faith only by God's word working to effect a cataclysmic moment of conversion; grace could never "work" through the family. In fact, Bushnell's opposition to the conversion syndrome and his claim that the family could be a medium of grace earned him a heresy trial. He was spared suspension only when the church he was pastoring in Hartford withdrew from the Congregationalist Union.

Catholic Christians, however, do not look upon human nature as radically depraved. Further, they claim that God's grace "works" through both word and sacrament, including the sacramentality of life: for example, through the ethos and relationships of a family. And there is a strong Catholic tradition of conversion as lifelong. Catholics usually don't make claims of "being saved" as a *fait accompli*, believing that "it ain't over till it's over." Even people who *have* an intense conversion experience in Christian faith—the proverbial Damascus road—must continue to grow in holiness of life. Every Christian needs the support of faith communities and families to sustain their journey. Children should have the best of Christian nurture from infancy. So, the broad tradition of Catholicism does not neglect nurture or education in faith, or favor conversion as "a technical experience."

On the other hand, I've become apprehensive that the *General Directory for Catechesis* will be overinterpreted to favor conversion as an event and catechesis as catechumenate to the neglect of nurture and good religious education across the lifespan—from womb to tomb. My first reading of the *GDC* was overwhelmingly positive and that continues to be my sentiment.[4] However, other commentators have sent me back to reread it, alert for its potential to be overinterpreted. Though appropriate in missionary contexts of the church, its championing of evangelization, conversion, and the catechumenate must be read with caution, especially in contexts where vital Christian communities already exist. Though I have good friends aboard the conversion/catechumenate bandwagon as *the* paradigm for all catechetical education, I raise a yellow flag; that train is a "local" which won't travel as far as the whole church needs to go.

APPROACHING THE *GDC*: PROCEED WITH CAUTION

I will detail my caveat in five parts—two points of caution and then three negative consequences if not heeded. My positive intent, however, is to interpret the *GDC* in a way that values both conversion and nurture in faith identity, both socialization and education in Christian tradition, both effective initiation and lifelong growth into holiness of life. In summary: 1) we must move beyond old stereotypes and embrace the "new evangelization" that the *GDC* poses as the umbrella for catechesis, and 2) avoid totalizing the catechumenal paradigm, in order to avert the negative consequences of 3) downplaying the parental nurture of children in faith, 4) forgetting the lifelong character of Christian conversion, and 5) neglecting to provide catechetical education across the life cycle.

1. Evangelization as the Umbrella of Catechesis

The *GDC* describes evangelization from a variety of aspects, but a good summary would be "the process by which the Church, moved by the Holy Spirit, proclaims and spreads the Gospel throughout the entire world" (n. 48). Then it positions catechesis as the more formative function within the umbrella of evangelization. "Catechesis, distinct from the primary proclamation of the Gospel, promotes and matures initial conversion, educates the convert in the faith, and incorporates him [or her] into the Christian community" (n. 61, note the language of "conversion" and "convert"). As such, catechesis is to be "a school of faith, an initiation and apprenticeship in the entire Christian life" (n. 30). In sum, "catechesis [is] an essential moment in the process of evangelization" (n. 63).

My impression is that the first Christian communities recognized *evangelization* and *catechesis* as two distinct but symbiotic functions—a partnership. The job of the *evangelistes* was to preach the bare-bones *kerygma* to people who had not heard it already, to arouse interest and invite to initial Christian faith. Thereafter, the *didaskaloi* (teachers) moved in, as it were, to catechize the newcomers in the *didache* ("teaching") and to nurture their Christian identity. The two functions were sequential and complementary rather than hierarchically related.

As Avery Dulles notes, "The majority of Catholics are not strongly inclined toward evangelization. The very term has for them a Protestant ring."[5] In fact, the work of Karl Barth toward the middle of the twentieth century was a major influence in reviving the term in Christian consciousness. So, it was never mentioned at Vatican I (1869–1870), whereas the documents of Vatican II (1962–1965) uses the word "Gospel" (*evangelium*) 157 times, "evangelize" 18 times, and "evangelization" 31 times.[6]

After the Council, Pope Paul VI (d. 1978) continued to recenter evangelization in Catholic consciousness, not simply as what missionaries do in far-off lands but as the baptismal responsibility of all Christians. In his 1975 apostolic exhortation, *Evangelii Nuntiandi*, we read: "Evangelization is in fact the grace and vocation proper to the Church, her deepest identity. She exists in order to evangelize, that is to say in order to preach and teach, to be the channel of the gift of grace, to reconcile sinners with God, and to perpetuate Christ's sacrifice of the Mass, which is the memorial of his death and glorious Resurrection" (n. 14). Note how comprehensive was Paul VI's description of evangelization.

Under Pope John Paul II the term has continued to expand and gain currency; he has popularized the term "new evangelization" to signal some major developments. Now the *GDC* clearly designates evangelization as the umbrella description of the church's whole mission in the world, and situates catechesis as one function within it. I'm convinced, however, that this move will be pastorally wise and bear its best fruits only if we recognize how the church has redefined evangelization with a far broader understanding than its stereotypical meaning in Catholic consciousness. Essentially, *the new evangelization is about Christians developing real enthusiasm for their faith, renewing themselves to live it boldly and thus to share it in the world.* And this caveat is particularly urgent in pluralist societies and nonmissionary ecclesial contexts. I will cast my review to highlight the caution needed.

Evangelization is first and foremost about promoting personal encounter and relationship with Jesus Christ. This has been one of the richest aspects of the church's new evangelization: a reminder that the "heart" of Christian faith is not scriptures or traditions, not dogmas or doctrines, not churches or sacraments, not creeds or codes—integral as all of these are—but the person of Jesus. Evangelization and catechesis, then, should bring people into "communion and intimacy with Jesus Christ" (n. 80).

I love that the *GDC* uses "apprenticeship" interchangeably with "discipleship"; apparently the New Testament term *mathetes* can be translated either way. Christian faith will always be personal "following of Jesus" as apprentices to the Master (n. 41 and passim). This is not an individualized affair, of course, a "me and Jesus" syndrome. Christian faith is radically communal and yet should be a deeply personal relationship with Jesus—an intimacy of the heart and soul.

Evangelization is not so much "bringing them in" as "bringing Christians out." For so long, Catholics thought of evangelization exclusively as bringing "converts" into the church. Though this could be done "at home," it was eminently the work of missionaries who went to cultures that had not yet heard the Gospel. Thus, Vatican II understood it as the "mission *ad gentes*"—bringing people into the church who did not yet belong.[7]

By contrast, the Catholic Church now emphasizes evangelization as bringing Christians out into the world. It is not focused on making non-Catholics into Catholics, but about making Catholics into Christians who live their faith in every arena and on every level—personal, interpersonal, and social/political. This means "bringing the Good News into all the strata of humanity . . . transforming humanity from within and making it new," effecting God's "liberating salvation."[8]

So, the foremost evangelizing responsibility of every Christian person and community is to live their faith in the world. As the *GDC* insists, such evangelization is not a narrow spiritual exercise but intends "the integral

development of the whole person and of all peoples" (n. 18). Evangelization "includes a message of liberation" (n. 103), requiring catechists to
"arouse in catechumens and those receiving catechesis 'a preferential option for the poor'" (n. 104), to "stir Christian hearts to the cause of justice"
(n. 17). Essentially, evangelization is bringing about God's reign in the
world through lived Christian faith.

*Evangelization is not only toward "peoples where Christ and the Gospel are not
known" but also to mature the faith of those already Christian and, where necessary, to revivify the faith of old Christian cultures* (n. 58). The GDC recognizes
that evangelization and thus catechesis should always have "an accent on
missionary activity." Yet, the "new evangelization" emphasizes maturing
and renewing Christian faith. In other words, every Christian person and
community is always in need of evangelization. Particularly urgent is the
(re)evangelization of tired old cultural faith, enabling it to become a living
faith again, permeating its cultural setting rather than being an exterior
trapping (see n. 58). The whole church is both evangelizer and evangelizee.

*Evangelization is not only the ministry of the Word but includes all of the
church's ministries and realization of its whole mission* (see n. 46—48 and passim). Etymologically, evangelization implies a ministry of the word. Vatican II explicitly stated, "The chief means (of evangelization) is the preaching of the Gospel of Jesus Christ."[8] In Catholic tradition, however
"preaching the Gospel" always meant more than "*preaching* the Gospel."
It also includes celebrating the sacraments, the works of justice, peace,
and compassion, and building up Christian community. Now, however,
there is a deepened and explicit consciousness that besides its ministry of
kerygma—of the word—the church also "preaches" by being a Christian
community that gives living witness to Gospel values (its ministries of
koinonia and *marturia*), by its public work of worshipping God (its ministry of *leitourgia*), and by its works of compassion and justice (the ministry of *diakonia*). In sum, evangelization is every way that the church realizes its mission in the world.

*Evangelization must avoid all Christian hubris, being done with ecumenical
sensitivity and dialogue with other religious traditions.* A great gift of Vatican
II was its call to Christians to enter into real dialogue with people of other
religious traditions. The Council urged Christians to engage in "truly human conversation" with all peoples of good will and "to learn by sincere
and patient dialogue what treasures a bountiful God has distributed
among the nations of the earth."[10] And though the church "must ever proclaim Christ, as 'the way, the truth, and the life,'"[11] their very faith in Jesus should lead Christians into "dialogue and cooperation with the fol-
lowers of other religions."[12]

Interreligious dialogue should greatly nuance how Christians proceed
with evangelization; for sure, the dialogue cannot be a ruse to proselytize.

Even as they are committed to sharing and bearing witness to their own faith, Christians must respect the movements of God's grace and appreciate the many ways that God brings people home to Godself. The *GDC* echoes such sentiments; evangelization and catechesis should always have "an ecumenical dimension" (n. 197), must help to overcome all forms of religious prejudice (n. 198), and "in particular . . . every form of anti-Semitism" (n. 199).

Now, with these five developments beyond the old Catholic stereotype of evangelization—converting pagans or Protestants—the term may indeed be the best umbrella for catechetical education. It could set "fire in the belly" for the church to do it effectively in this postmodern age. We recognize that spirituality is now so much in vogue, but maybe evangelization can catch on too. It could enliven the faith of all Christians if they see themselves as full-time evangelists and ever in need of evangelization. It could help for parents to think of themselves as evangelists to their children.

But given the "effective history" that the term evangelization has had, the struggle to redefine it remains an uphill climb. This is not helped by the *GDC's* sequitur from evangelization to championing a catechumenal model for all catechesis, and speaking in the same breath of conversion and converts. Old Catholics are likely to continue thinking only of the mission *ad gentes*.

In making evangelization the church's overarching mission, there is also a danger of coopting all the functions of ministry and diminishing their proper intent. Indeed, the liturgy has great evangelizing possibilities, but one of its primary purposes is to worship God; it would be an abuse of liturgy to begin to "use" it to evangelize. Likewise, the church's ministry of *diakonia*—the works of mercy and compassion, of justice and peace—indeed evangelize by their witness, but Christians do them not to win people to Jesus but because Jesus gave us the mandate to do them, whether people ever become Christian or not. And it is difficult for people of other traditions not to fear Catholic proselytizing when Vatican documents make the insensitive claim that non-Catholics "are in a gravely deficient situation" by way of salvation. Add, too, that clarion calls to evangelization are particularly hazardous in the flash points of religious tension (from Belfast to Benares, Sarajevo to Sudan). So, while embracing the church's call to a "new evangelization," caution is in order.

2. The Catechumenal Paradigm: Inspiration Not Imitation

Vatican II mandated the restoration of the adult catechumenate, reviving the model of initiation practiced in many early Christian communities. A provisional text of the *Rite of Christian Initiation of Adults (RCIA)* was issued in 1972, and an official text mandated for the United States in 1988. Essentially it outlines a series of "stages" for initiation. It begins with evangelization and precatechumenate, moves to the catechumenate proper, then to an intensified "time of purification and illumination," and culminates with the sacraments of initiation or reception into full ecclesial communion—ideally at the Easter Vigil—followed by a postbaptismal catechesis traditionally known as *mystagogy*.

The *RCIA* offers a variety of liturgical rituals to celebrate each step of initiation. All should be enacted by the parish at worship, highlighting the essential role of the faith community in initiation. Though the Rite does not detail a pedagogy for catechumenal catechesis, the pastoral leaders of its implementation have forged a community-based faith sharing process[13] that nurtures "formation in the entire Christian life" until catechumens are "initiated into the mysteries of salvation and the practice of an evangelical way of life."[14] By any standard, this adult catechumenate has had phenomenal success; recent statistics indicate that as many as 200,000 adults yearly are initiated into the US Catholic community through the *RCIA*.

The *GDC* strongly recommends that "the model for all catechesis is the baptismal catechumenate"(n. 59). Though it often recognizes that it is "nonbaptized adults, to whom the catechumenate truly and properly corresponds" (n. 172), yet its "inherent richness . . . should serve to inspire other forms of catechesis" (n. 68). This is precisely where I urge caution, underlying the word *"inspire."* Before my caveat, however, let me summarize some of the ways that the catechumenal model can inspire all catechetical education.

As noted, the *Rite of Christian Initiation of Adults*, now considered "the ordinary catechumenate"[15] in the life of the church, does not recommend a particular pedagogy or approach to catechesis; it is literally a liturgical "Rite"—in fact, a series of rites. However, in the hands of some very creative leadership, the Rite has called forth a pastoral practice that reflects the best of catechetical education. As such, what is emerging as "the catechumenal model" can inspire all catechesis/religious education. It reminds:

- That Christian faith is for the whole person—head, heart, and hands—as communion with Jesus, to be realized as discipleship in every arena of life and on every level of existence;
- That catechesis should form and transform as well as inform people in Christian faith; it calls for "integral formation rather than mere information" (n. 29);
- That Christian community is the primary context of catechetical education, asking that all the ministries of the parish and the life of the family be shaped intentionally to educate in faith;

- That catechesis and liturgy are integrally related, each needing the other in that "ritual" and sacred symbol are essential to the pedagogy of Christian faith and, conversely, people must be educated for "full, conscious, and active participation"[16] in the liturgy;
- That the word of God through Scripture must be recentered in Catholic faith, as well as teaching Christian Tradition;
- That an inclusive and hospitable gathering of people, who reflect and share together on God's presence in their lives, and encounter Scripture and Tradition as a community in conversation, is an effective pedagogy for bringing Christian faith to life.

Inspiring, indeed! But these principles reflect the best of contemporary catechetical education; there is no reason to think of them exclusively as "catechumenal." For to speak of "catechumenal" is to think "stages" of initiation. To exclude the stages is to describe something other than the catechumenate. And to impose the catechumenate of initiation on all catechesis, especially within families and contexts that are already Christian, would be contrived and ill-fitting—the proverbial forcing square pegs into round holes.

Catechesis within the umbrella of the "new evangelization" and following the catechumenate might be well suited to a missionary context, but is less so to an already Christian family and community. In fact, if the document is overinterpreted without nuance in this regard, it could have at least three debilitating effects on catechetical practice in established Christian churches.

Rather than dwelling on the dangers, however, I will read the *GDC* "against the grain" of its favor for the catechumenal model, and draw from it instead three positive points that reflect its overall spirit: a) a renewed and deepened emphasis on family nurture; b) faith as a lifelong journey into Christian holiness; and c) the need of every Christian person and community for permanent education in faith.

A. Renew Family Nurture

All catechetical educators should feel confronted by the homeschool movement. With the numbers growing, well over two million children in the United States receive their formal education at home. Parents are discovering that with the help of curricula designed for homeschool, coupled with computers, Internet and CD-ROMs, local libraries and community resources, they can provide their children with a fine primary education at home. Now, I'm not an advocate of the homeschool movement. But it should challenge the overinvestment of modern society in the "schooling" paradigm. Certainly, it reminds of the power and potential of the home to be the primary educator. Without abandoning formal parish or school programs, catechist educators must surely embrace the wisdom of Bushnell that everyone should be "homeschooled" in Christian faith.

The nurturing Christian family does not need to be a model one; few of us have been blessed with as much. But I'm convinced that even the typical old "dysfunctional" family—whether two- or single-parent, whether extended, blended, or nuclear—if given a bit of support and resourcing, can be an effective agent of Christian nurture.

For sure, the *GDC* recognizes the centrality of the family. "Nothing replaces family catechesis" (n. 178) and the family is "the primary agent of an incarnate transmission of the faith" (n. 207). But why would Christian families find it helpful to think of their nurture as a catechumenal process? Why would it help to look upon children of a Christian home as being only at a precatechumenate stage? Indeed, I remember my mother addressing her brood of nine on occasion as "a bunch of pagans" (as when no one remembered to say grace), but we presumed—or hoped—that this was not her defining estimation of us. Surely it is more helpful to encourage parents in a "sharing faith" approach with their children, nurturing them in Christian identity from the beginning through the whole ethos of family life. To echo Bushnell, they deserve to grow up as Christians, not remembering a time when they were otherwise, or when they went through a "technical experience."

The Second Vatican Council revived the notion of the family as "the domestic church."[17] This implies that the family, within its own life and as appropriate to its context, should carry on the standard functions of Christian ministry. To the extent that the family is "domestic church," it will nurture effectively in faith. As a family, then, the members should have access together to God's word in scripture and tradition (*kerygma*); every family should have its sacred rituals and times of shared prayer (*leitourgia*); the ethos of every home should reflect a community of Christian faith, hope, and love (*koinonia*); every family must practice compassion toward those in need and justice toward all, both within itself and outward toward the world (*diakonia*).

Note, too, that the *GDC* makes a similar proposal (see n. 255). The parish should "nurture the nurturers," providing its families with the resources and training, encouragement and suggestions they need to function effectively as "domestic church." Beyond that, to impose the catechumenal stages on the nurture in a Christian family would seem contrived.

B. Favor Lifelong Conversion

Chapter 5 of Vatican II's *Dogmatic Constitution on the Church* restated with new vigor what had always been the better theology of baptism—that it calls every Christian to holiness of life. There is a strong old Catholic tradition, however, that becoming "an apprentice to Jesus" is a lifelong affair. Even the greatest of the saints were lamenting their sinfulness and lack of perfection until the end of their lives. And an ancient canon of the church directed wisely that a person should be at least three days dead before their cause for canonization could be entered.

If lifelong growth is inherent to Christian faith, in more recent times the developmental psychologists verify that the same is true of faith as a human universal. James Fowler and his colleagues assure that there are discernible "stages" throughout the faith-life journey, with the potential to live ever more deeply into realized faith. Though many may "settle" at an earlier stage, everyone has the horizon of limitless growth in response to God's love.

That God is never quite "finished" with any of us this side of eternity is to say that Christian conversion is a lifelong affair. And this is true, whether the faith emerges by gradual nurture or by an intense experience. Paul still had a "race to run" (see 2 Tim 4:7) after that Damascus road, and a "thorn in the flesh" (2 Cor 12:7) with which to contend. The *GDC* refers wisely to "the process of continuing conversion" (n. 69) "which lasts for the whole of life" (n. 56).

However, within the context of evangelization and the catechumenal model, the *GDC* speaks so often of conversion and of making converts that it could be overinterpreted as favoring a "one-time" event for neophytes, an arrival rather than the beginning of a journey. Oh, indeed, the catechumenate has a *mystagogy* that follows full initiation into the Christian community. But this intense period of reflection on the sacramental mysteries just experienced lasts only a short time—and rightly so. Some authors call for lifelong *mystagogy*, but why so redefine the word away from its traditional meaning? Why not recognize that after initiation, the catechumenate has done its job; now something more is needed to continue the journey. Why not lifelong catechetical *education*?

C. Provide Catechetical Education Across the Life Cycle

Over the past fifty years or so, Catholics have debated whether to use the language of catechesis or of religious education (Protestants have the same debate between Christian or religious education). Generally, catechesis has come to mean the socialization of people into Christian identity, whereas religious education is more the scholarly and reflective study of a faith tradition. I worry, however, about catechesis that shapes people's identity but without giving access to the whole rich tradition of Christian faith. On the other hand, Christian religious education that informs people's heads but neglects forming their identity is equally troublesome. In other words, a dichotomy between these two is false and debilitating; both values—socialization and education—must be realized. This is why I use the term "catechetical education," to emphasize the need for both.

Though the predominant language of the GDC is catechetical, it also reflects appreciation for good religious education. It calls for "permanent catechesis" and "continuous education in the faith," and seems to use the phrases interchangeably. It says that every Christian should have access "to the entire treasure of the Christian message" (n. 112). In other words, the baptized have a right to what I call "the whole Story" of Christian faith.

As for all education worthy of the name, good catechetical *education* encourages people to use all their gifts of mind—reason, memory, and imagination—to their fullest capacity, to contemplate and reflect, to perceive and analyze, to make judgments and decisions, to truly think for themselves. Encouraging such personal understanding reflects the ancient confidence of the church that faith and reason are partners, that truly "knowing" the faith fosters living it. The GDC says that personal probing and "searching" is needed for "a firm conviction" (n. 56). Later it adds that developing in people "the rational foundations of the faith . . . in conformity with the demands of reason and the Gospel . . . helps to overcome certain forms of fundamentalism as well as subjective and arbitrary interpretations" (n. 175; also see nn. 73–75 on "religious instruction in the schools"). In other words, getting people to really know and think for themselves about their faith is not only permissible but necessary in catechetical education.

However, the citations favoring good critically reflective education in faith are sparse compared to those favoring a socializing catechesis. At times, the GDC can even sound disparaging of education, urging catechists to go beyond "mere information" (n. 29), to "surpass mere instruction" (n. 68). Indeed, but well-grounded information and sound instruction in faith are never "mere." Further, good critical reflection is essential to faith education if it is to promote reform of church and society, justice and peace in the world. A socialization process alone tends to maintain the status quo—whatever it may be.

The lack of emphasis on good religious education in the GDC stems, in part, from its overembrace of the catechumenal paradigm. The latter's focus is more on the rites of initiation and on socializing people into conversion than on continuing catechetical *education*. In fact, the catechumenate's emphasis on initiation is not likely to encourage lifelong religious education. A more inspiring contribution in this regard is the recent statement from the US Catholic Bishops', *Our Hearts Were Burning Within Us*.[18] There the clear focus is "adult faith formation." American Catholics should read it alongside of the GDC to maintain commitment to "total catechetical education."

AS I WAS SAYING

The "catechumenal model," as it is coming to be called, is not comprehensive enough to be the defining mode for all catechetical education. The restored catechumenate is, undoubtedly, a gift to the life of the church; it has brought great pastoral renewal, not least through the enthusiasm of well-formed neophytes. After that, however, we should maintain it for its proper function—most eminently the initiation of nonbaptized adults.

Rather than totalizing the catechumenate, the GDC can be read as favoring an overarching approach that I understand as "total catechetical education." This calls for a coalition of parish, family, and school/program that engages the whole life of each agency to intentionally educate in Christian faith. Such a comprehensive model invites the active participation of every Christian person and community to engage in teaching and learning together—sharing faith. It would provide the mutuality of *nurture and education of lifelong conversion*—from womb to tomb.

NOTES

1. See my "Conversion, Nurture and Religious Education," *Religious Education* 71:5 (1981): 482–496.

2. Congregation for the Clergy, *General Directory for Catechesis* (Washington, DC: United States Catholic Conference, 1998).

3. Horace Bushnell, *Christian Nurture* (New Haven, CT: Yale University Press, 1947), 4.

4. See "Claiming and Breaking Ground: The General Directory for Catechesis," in *Empowering Catechetical Leaders*, eds. Thomas Groome and Michael Corso (Washington, DC: NCEA, 1999), 233–243.

5. Avery Dulles, "John Paul and the New Evangelization," *America*, 1 February 1992, 52.

6. Ibid., 53.

7. See the Vatican Document, *Decree on Church's Missionary Activity* n. 6, in ed. Walter Abbott, *The Documents of the Vatican II* (New York: America Press, 1966) 590–593.

8. Pope Paul VI, *On the Evangelization of Peoples*, (Washington, DC: USCC, 1975), nn. 18 and 9.

9. *Decree on the Missions*, n. 6, Abbott, *Documents of the Vatican II*.

10. *Decree on the Missions*, n. 11, Abbott, *Documents of the Vatican II*.

11. *Declaration on Non Christian Religions*, n. 2, Abbott, *Documents of the Vatican II*.

12. Ibid.

13. Some of the great pathfinders in implementing the *RCIA*, like Fr. James Dunning and Christiane Brusselmanns, footnoted my own work on a "shared

praxis approach" as influencing the pedagogy they proposed for catechumenal catechesis. See *Christian Religious Education: Sharing Our Story and Vision* (San Francisco: Jossey-Bass, 1999).

14. *Rite of Christian Initiation of Adults* (Washington, DC: USCC, 1988), nn. 76 and 38.

15. Ibid., nn. 18 and 365.

16. *Constitution on the Sacred Liturgy*, n. 14, Abbott, *Documents of the Vatican II*.

17. *Dogmatic Constitution on the Church*, n. 11, Abbott, *Documents of the Vatican II*.

18. *Our Hearts Were Burning Within US* (Washington, DC: USCC, 1999).

16

The Congregation
as a Healing Community

James N. Poling

In a seminary course with the title *The Congregation as a Healing Commu-nity*, I attempt to bring the insights of social systems theory into dia-logue with biblical and pastoral theology in order to improve the quality of pastoral care at a congregational level. In a healing congregation, God encourages us powerfully in intimate, face-to-face encounters. A healing congregation also supports mutuality in families by embodying the vision of a just *and* loving community. In their important book, *All Our Losses, All Our Griefs*, Herbert Anderson and Kenneth Mitchell reveal their vision of the congregation as a healing community:

> The Christian community is the primary context for [helping persons to re-spond to grieving individuals]. Neighborhoods, social organizations, and work associations also attend to grief in significant ways, but it is in the parish church that major losses are publicly spoken about and ritualized. Congregations are still places that can organize themselves to care for those who grieve.[1]

The congregation is an example of what we call a primary social sys-tem, that is, most of the interaction occurs through face-to-face conversa-tions and ritual behaviors.[2] Families, small work teams, and social groups are interpersonal systems that depend on regular face-to-face contact. There are other kinds of systems, such as cities, counties, states, nations, multinational corporations, and the media, etc., which depend on written communication and technology. Just think of your relationship with the Internal Revenue Service. Most of us hope we don't have any face-to-face interaction such as an audit.

Whenever people meet for face-to-face interaction on a regular basis, they construct a social system with its own history, rules, roles, leadership, rituals, symbols, meanings, values, and language. Being an effective congregational leader requires knowing how systems work. Systems theory explains how complex organizations like congregations function.[3]

Christian congregations are unique as primary systems because they understand themselves in relation to the Bible, particular historical traditions (such as denominations), and practices such as liturgy, education, and community activities. This means that theological and religious identity is important. While we can use systems theory to understand some of the generic characteristics of social groups, we also need to ask theological questions. For example, how does a congregation image God? Is God like a priest who comes out of the back room and feeds the people so they are healed? Is God like a storytelling preacher who encourages and chastises the people to have courage in the midst of suffering? Is God like a manager who helps the people get organized so they can become a community that cares about people? Is God like a social critic and prophet who helps the people understand the evils of society so they can act to change things? What kind of God-image guides a particular congregation and what difference does it make in their interaction with one another and with the world?

Walter Wink says that every congregation has a "spirit" that must be understood by its leaders.[5] In Revelation, St. John wrote to the angels at the seven churches and praised and criticized them for their faithfulness to Jesus Christ. He was writing to the corporate spirit of congregations, urging them to remain faithful under conditions of persecution. If we work in congregations, we also have to understand their spirits. This is not an easy job. It means understanding the history, the beliefs and values, the individuals and their families, and the shared practices of worship and service.

Healing is a popular word in US society. Many Christians have experienced psychotherapy, or have been in support groups such as Alcoholics Anonymous, Adult Children of Alcoholics, Adult Survivors of Child Sexual Abuse, or any of several dozen other self-help groups. Evangelical pastors on television and in congregations emphasize healing, and many liberal pastors have healing services, anointing with oil, prayers for the sick, and home and hospital visitation. In several cities, Roman Catholics, Protestants, and Jews join together in a service of healing for persons with HIV infection and AIDS.

I like the definition of healing by Larry Graham in the *Dictionary of Pastoral Care and Counseling*:

> Healing—the process of being restored to bodily wholeness, emotional well-being, mental functioning, and spiritual aliveness. Christian modes of healing have always distinguished themselves by achieving a spiritual advance in connection with the healing process. Healing may also refer to the process

of reconciling broken human relationships and to the development of a just social and political order among races and nations. In recent times, healing and wholeness have become metaphors for religious views of salvation.[6]

Graham has included physical, emotional, mental, and spiritual healing, plus reconciling human relationships and bringing a just social and political order. Later in the article he also mentions the need for ecological healing.

In this article, I use healing as a broad metaphor that includes several types of pastoral care: healing, guiding, sustaining, reconciling, nurturing, liberating, and empowering.[7] I sometimes teach a course on older adults and persons with disabling conditions, and I am convinced that holistic healing can occur for all people in spite of discriminatory norms imposed by society on certain groups of people.

This broad definition of healing is consistent with the Bible. Listen to a few examples. In 2 Chronicles 7:14 God promises healing for the land: "If my people who are called by my name humble themselves, pray, seek my face, and turn from their wicked ways, then I will hear from heaven, and will forgive their sin and heal their land."

The Psalmist remembers God's promises of healing and protection for the poor. Psalm 41:4, "The Lord protects the [poor] and keeps them alive; they are called happy in the land. You do not give them up to the will of their enemies. The Lord sustains them on their sickbed; in their illness you heal all their infirmities."

Again the Psalmist praises God for protecting the outcasts and healing from the pain of loss and grief. Psalm 147:3, "The Lord builds up Jerusalem; God gathers the outcasts of Israel. God heals the broken-hearted and binds up their wounds."

Jesus' ministry of healing was especially for those who were oppressed by society, the poor, the prisoners, and the blind. Luke 4:18–19, "The Spirit of the Lord is upon me, because God has anointed me to bring good news to the poor. God has sent me to proclaim release to the captives and recovery of sight to the blind, to let the oppressed go free, to proclaim the year of the Lord's favor."

Even demon possession, or mental illness, is a focus of Scripture. Luke 6:18, "They had come to hear him and to healed of their diseases; and those who were troubled with unclean spirits were cured."

The Bible is interested in the health of every part of our lives—our bodies, our minds, our emotions, our spirits, as well as our families, our congregations, our nation, and the natural environment. We live in a time of trauma at all these levels, and this leads to a desire for healing from these wounds.

The phrase, *Congregation as a Healing Community* implies that congregations are not always healing. In some ways our discussion could just as easily focus on the *Congregation as a Hurting Community*. It may sound strange to hear this, but we all know it is true. The church has caused the deepest wounds some of us carry. Why? Because we expect the church not to hurt people. We go to the church with high hopes that it will be healing. When we go to the police station to pay a traffic ticket, we hope they will be fair, but we don't expect someone to be extra nice and comfort us because a parent recently died. When we go to the shopping center, we hope to find what we are looking for, and hope that the clerks will be efficient, but we don't expect them to be concerned about how our life is going. But when we go to the church, we expect that the people will care.

Our expectations that the church will be a warm, nurturing, healing community make us vulnerable to being hurt much. If we attend an adult forum and someone expresses a nasty attitude, we are angry and think it shouldn't happen. If we send our children to Sunday school and the teacher frightens them with stories of hellfire and damnation, we might be upset. If we go to a pastor for spiritual direction, and he makes a rude sexual comment, we are startled. And if we have been active in a congregation for a long time, and that congregation has a serious conflict, divides into two groups, and eventually separates into two congregations, we feel betrayed and cynical. So we must talk both about our experiences of healing in the church, and our experiences of hurt and trauma caused by the church. It is important for congregation leaders to understand when a congregation is healing and when it is hurting, and we must focus on both positive and negative experiences.

The root word for community is the Latin word *communis*, which means common, such as in Acts 2:44–45, "All who believed were together and had all things *in common.*" The Latin *communis* is also the root word for communion, which means to share the bread and wine in common, in togetherness, as one body.[8]

When we use the word community, we are talking about more than a group of people who happen to be together in one place at the same time. We mean something more—a group of people who have something important in common, who share important values and beliefs in common, who care about one another enough to spend time together, who eat together. A church community is not just a collection of people, but people who have a communion of spirits. The church is a primary social system that defines itself in relation to Jesus Christ. What does it mean for a congregation to be a healing community?

PRINCIPLES OF PASTORAL CARE IN THE CONGREGATION

From my experience in the church, and through the study of systems theory, I have developed seven principles for understanding congregations so we can help them to be healing communities.

Principle # 1: Suffering and healing are embedded in *narrative histories* with plots, unfinished stories, and an open future; that is, human wounds and strengths develop over time, often intergenerationally, and can be observed through the use of genograms and storytelling.

Principle # 2: Suffering and healing are embedded in *social and cultural contexts* of institutions, ideologies, and economic forces that determine the available power and values for human life. Congregational leaders need to be sensitive to the power of society and culture to influence the normative ideas that affect human behavior in families and groups.

Principle # 3: Suffering and healing are shaped by *religious beliefs and practices* that determine the ways for nurturing life and creativity and redeeming sin and evil. Congregational leaders must be attentive to explicit religious behaviors as well as implicit religious ideas that have significance in the lives of persons and groups.

Principle # 4: Suffering and healing occur within socially constructed *developmental passages* such as age, gender, race, class, ability, and disability, each with particular psychological tasks. Congregational leaders need to understand human development and the social expectations that accompany the passages of individuals, families, and groups.

Principle # 5: Suffering and healing occur in congregations with particular *structures of organization and leadership* that determine power relationships through temporary hierarchies, subsystems, triangles, and the various coalitions and alliances that become patterns as people construct their shared life.

Principle # 6: Suffering and healing involve attention to congregational *dynamics*, the range of creativity about boundaries, roles, rules, and the development and resolution of conflict.

Principle # 7: An effective congregational leader identifies suffering and facilitates healing for persons and communities through the *use of self*. Through self-awareness and self-correction within a context of ongoing supervision, and education, a congregational leader may engage in empathy and empowerment for the transformation of self and others.

Principle 1, History: Remembering our history is one of the first tasks of the congregation. Where did we come from? Who were our ancestors? What have we been through together? What have we suffered? How has God brought healing and hope through our interaction with one another and the community?

Murray Bowen, one of the founders of family systems theory, believed that it took three generations to create a dysfunctional family. He taught us to do family genograms that go back at least three generations.[9] Anyone who does this is surprised at how persistent certain family problems are: alcohol, incest, physical illness, resilient women, high achievers, musicians, etc. It is impossible to understand our own lives apart from our family of origin, whether biological or adopted.

The same thing is true for congregations. Whenever there is a crisis, the leaders should review the history of the congregation. It is inevitable that similar patterns have occurred before, sometimes before any of the present leaders were born. Systems theory can help us recover the truth of the biblical mandate to remember our past without glossing it over. Parenthetically, this is also true in our personal histories, and we need all the self-awareness we can get, which is principle 7.

Memory is one of the most important functions of faith. The Bible encourages us to remember everything that has happened to our people, both the good and the bad, the suffering and the salvation:

> Deut 5:6, 15.: I am the Lord your God who brought you out of the house of Egypt out of the house of slavery, you shall have no other gods before me. . . . Remember that you were slaves in Egypt, and the Lord your God brought you out from there with a mighty arm; therefore the Lord your God commanded you to keep the Sabbath day.

The commandments against idolatry and for the Sabbath helped the Hebrews remember what they had been through and how Yahweh has saved them. Joshua 4:6-7, "And when your children ask. . . tell them [the story]."

We remember the suffering and victory of Jesus every time we take communion. 1 Corinthians 11:26, "Whenever you eat this bread and drink this cup you remember the Lord's death until he comes again." We are called to remember that Christ was unjustly arrested, tortured, and killed for his faithfulness to God, and that he was taken up in glory and sits at the right hand of God.

Over the years students have written personal case studies about their experiences in congregations. One theme that has appeared is the tendency of congregations to remain silent about important events in the past. In one story, a white congregation had three dysfunctional pastors in a row: a sex abuser, an alcoholic, and an activist who provided no care for the families. Each time a pastor left, the congregation vowed to make a clean start, but the people did not understand the importance of healing from what had happened in the past. Many people in the local community used to belong to this congregation, but were hurt by one or another of the pastors. Only when a pastor was called who understood healing did some of the issues get resolved, and a new beginning could occur.

Principle 2, Social Context: Congregations exist in every kind of social situation, from the elite wealthy on Wall Street to the poorest villages in

Latin American, Africa, and Asia. The Scriptures emphasize the inclusive unity of the church as the body of Christ. There must be no distinctions by class, race, gender, and other social categories.

> Deuteronomy 16:11–12. Rejoice before the Lord your God—you and your sons and daughters, your male and female slaves, the Levites resident in your towns, as well as the strangers, the orphans, and the widows who are among you—at the place that the Lord your God will choose as a dwelling for his name. Remember that you were slaves in Egypt and diligently observe these statutes.
>
> 1 Corinthians 12:12–13. For just as the body is one and has many members, and all the members of the body, though many, are one body, so it is with Christ. For in the one Spirit we were all baptized into one body—Jews and Greeks, slaves or free—and we were all made to drink of one Spirit.

The Bible teaches that the church should be intercultural and inclusive of the diversity of experiences of all people in its community. Jesus ate in the homes of the wealthy and the poor; he had no regard for social station as long as a person was open to the spirit of God and willing to be transformed through discipleship. When the rich, young ruler could not give up his attachments to his property, Jesus was sad.

Yet the church is one of the social systems most rigidly organized by class and race in the world, and most churches discriminate against women as leaders. Educated, wealthy persons of European ancestry write most of the theology about the church, but the majority of Christians are poor and non-European. Social context largely determines the distribution of power and values within and between congregations. Too often the church is a reflection of the injustice of society rather than a prophetic presence for change.

I remember one student who came from a poor family and went to the local white church regularly. Everyone had seats that were assigned by traditions long forgotten, but organized largely by class. The wealthy sat in the front middle pews on the aisle, and the poor sat in the back and ends of the pews. The image of this unfair system made an indelible mark on the student. In contrast, another congregation had a strong ministry with about fifty persons with mental disabilities who lived in a public housing project nearby. During worship, they sat front and center and gave an inclusive image of the church. This diversity required sensitive leadership to make the congregation work for everyone.

Principle 3, Religious Beliefs and Practices: Within systems thinking, God is "that than which no greater can be thought" (Anselm), that is, the largest system that can be imagined. In Larry Graham's important work on systems thinking and pastoral care, God is the system beyond all systems including individuals, families, local communities, societies, and global and universal systems.[10] Those who emphasize God as transcendent could say that God is the foundation for the very existence of social systems.[11] Those who emphasize God as immanent could say that God is present within the spirit of every system.[12] The Scriptures teach God as creator and redeemer of the world:

> Genesis 1:1. In the beginning, God created the heavens and the earth.
> John 3:16. For God so loved the world that he gave his only Son, so that everyone who believes in him may not perish but may have eternal life.

Within congregations, there are different ways of conceiving God and of practicing the worship that God inspires. For example, we are aware of the different theologies of the world religions, especially Judaism, Christianity, and Islam. Each celebrates different sacred holidays, different Sabbath rituals, and different daily prayers and piety. Within Christianity there are different ways of being religious between Orthodox, Catholic, Protestant, and Pentecostal, and between and within various denominations. Systems pastoral care is especially interested in how religious beliefs and practices shape everyday values and identity.

Students have learned that they must be aware of the religious beliefs and practices of congregations. In one white congregation, Lutheran Social Services had been a strong influence for many generations, and the congregation had responded to these beliefs by developing a strong prison ministry. The pastor's life was changed when he joined in with the parishioners and worked with prisoners from a distant metropolitan area and learned what their lives were like. Later the same pastor moved to another congregation where individual Lutheran piety was stronger than the interest in the social problems of the community. For a while the pastor was lost because he missed the service orientation of the previous congregation. But then he discovered a deep spirituality that influenced young people to dedicate their lives to the church. The religious beliefs and practices must be respected for what they have to contribute to the larger mission of Christ's church.

Principle 4, Developmental Passages: Every congregation is in some stage of group development and includes members who are in various stages of development. The Scriptures call us to nurture the receptivity to the Holy Spirit like a child, while acting grown-up and mature when we make decisions and exercise power.

> Matthew 18:4–5. Unless you change and become like children, you will never enter the kingdom of heaven. Whoever becomes humble like this child is the greatest in the kingdom of heaven. Whoever welcomes one such child in my name welcomes me.

1 Corinthians 13:11. When I was a child, I spoke like a child, I thought like a child, I reasoned like a child; when I became an adult, I put an end to childish ways.

Ephesians 4:11–15. The gifts he gave were that some would be apostles, some prophets, some evangelists, some pastors and teachers, to equip the saints for the work of ministry, for building up the body of Christ, until all of us come to maturity, to the measure of the full stature of Christ. We must no longer be children, tossed to and fro and blown about by every wind of doctrine, by people's trickery, by their craftiness in deceitful scheming. But speaking the truth in love, we must grow up in every way into him who is the head, into Christ.

But how do we know when to be childlike and when to be mature? This is one of the great challenges of congregational leadership. In order to make these decisions, we must know something about human and group development. For example, elementary-age children and many adults are concrete thinkers according to Piaget.[13] This means that they learn best through stories and concrete examples. None of us loses our ability to learn in these ways. The power of music and poetry with young people, especially within the Pentecostal traditions, illustrates this point. The Eucharist, with its simple appeal to eating and drinking in community, shows the intergenerational appeal of narrative and ritual.

Productive congregational leadership is aware of the developmental needs of members. Many students over the years have chosen ministry with children—how children are often caught in dysfunctional family dynamics and how congregations misperceive their needs. In one class discussion, a student presented a nine-year-old African American boy who was having a severe reaction to the death of his dog. Neither the pastor nor the Sunday school teacher could understand why he did not want to attend church and seemed so sad. The seminary intern eventually connected his depression to the death of his grandmother several years previously. His grandmother had been his caregiver and served as his primary parent during his preschool years. The family had done everything they knew at the time of her death, and did not realize the importance of his dog as a transitional object after her death. After several sessions of pastoral counseling, the boy asked if he could have a funeral service for his dog. Further family counseling was required before everyone could understand the wisdom of his request. Eventually, the pastor, seminary intern, and immediate family gathered for a religious ritual for the beloved dog. It seemed to be the right thing to help the boy reconnect with his family and his religious community.

Congregations themselves have a developmental life cycle. Common in social work training are the terms: *form, storm, norm, perform*. A congregation is formed when it is first founded, and when it has a major critical event that reshapes its identity. A congregation *storms* when it experiences disagreement or conflict over its direction and values. A congregation *norms* when it comes together and makes choices about how it will develop and use its resources. A congregation *performs* when its identity is secure and its members are productive with a clear mission. This cycle can repeat itself many times over the history of many generations. A Korean American congregation was formed when a strong lay leader broke from a large congregation to start a new church. About seventy people joined in the new project, excited by the new possibilities. They built a new building and parsonage and, even though they had disagreements, they were happy for the new opportunities of leadership in a smaller church. Everyone was generous with his or her money and time and the new church seemed to have a good future. About seven years after its founding, a conflict developed over leadership. The strong layperson who had the original vision and gave much of the money at the beginning also exercised strong control over everything that happened. In a confrontation, his leadership was challenged and he resigned from the board in anger. However, other lay leaders picked up the responsibilities and broadened the opportunities for all members. A new era developed with new norms and new vision.

Principle 5, Structures of Organization and Leadership: Leadership, authority, and organization determine the structures of power in social systems. Systems theory has developed its own unique vocabulary to talk about how power structures work: subsystems, hierarchies, triangles, coalitions, and alliances.[14] Social systems, even when small as in a family, are always divided into subsystems: parents and children, male and female gender roles, older and younger, big and little, employed and unemployed. How these subsystems function determine hierarchies: who makes what kinds of decisions for the group, and what decisions are permitted for individuals. Triangles, coalitions, and alliances are ways that individuals can increase their influence within a system through joining with other persons, sometimes for the good of the system, sometimes in competition with others.

The Scriptures tell many stories of intrigue about how people get along in families and how the leaders of nations compete for dominance. Israel grew tired of the informal leadership of the judges and demanded a monarchy:

> 1 Samuel 8:4. Then all the elders of Israel gathered together and came to Samuel at Ramah and said to him, "You are old and your sons do not follow in your ways; appoint us, then, a king to govern us, like other nations."

Jesus experimented with various images of leadership to help the disciples understand the nature of God's love: teacher, Lord, servant, friend.

Each of these images has its own contribution to make to congregational life:

> John 13:12–15. After he had washed their feet, had put on his robe, and had returned to the table, he said to them, "Do you know what I have done to you? You call me teacher and Lord—and you are right, for that is what I am. So if I, your Lord and Teacher, have washed your feet, you also ought to wash one another's feet. For I have set you an example that you also should do as I have done to you.
>
> John 15:15. I do not call you servants any longer, because the servant does not know what the master is doing; but I have called you friends, because I have made known to you everything that I have heard from my Father.

How should congregational leaders understand themselves within a congregation that is dedicated to following Jesus Christ? How should they exercise authority and what is the role of democratic decision making within a God-centered society? This depends on the image of God. Many images of God are available to the Christian faithful: creator, father, mother, king, lord, omnipotent, son, daughter, servant, rock, eagle, mountain, spirit, lover, etc. How congregational leaders imagine and practice their leadership determines much of what the character of a congregation will be.

Two congregations come to mind. In the first, a white congregation had a history of benevolent patriarchy that seemed to work well in the past. In the golden period, the church was large and flourishing even while very few leaders made the important decisions. However, subsequent generations had followed the same leadership pattern without the same success and the congregation experienced a gradual but dangerous decline. Finally the leadership was reduced to one couple that controlled a small group through secret coalitions and scapegoating. Five pastors had come and gone in seven years. It took many consultations to unravel the complex history of this congregation and outside authority had to intervene to change the leadership pattern. It was a long time before this congregation made a positive contribution to the community.

In a second Hispanic congregation, the leadership had been strong and encouraged participation at many levels. Unfortunately, the pastor was invited to take a new position and a key lay leader died at the same time. The congregation was such a complex system that no new leader with enough skill emerged to fill the need. The new pastor was not up to the job, and simple mistakes eventually compounded to create a crisis. Fortunately, consultants were invited in time to resolve the problems and help the congregation make new decisions about leadership and future directions. This congregation remained a vital force in the community for many years.

Principle 6, Dynamics: A system that is fulfilling its task is characterized by creativity and conflict, and these dynamics determine the flexibility of a system to follow its calling and resolve differences between subsystems. Scriptures tell many stories about conflict that had edges of violence and destructiveness:

> Genesis 32:11. Deliver me, please, from the hand of my brother, from the hand of Esau, for I am afraid of him; he may come and kill us all, the mothers with the children.
>
> 1 Corinthians 1:10–11. Now I appeal to you, brothers and sisters, by the name of our Lord Jesus Christ, that all of you be in agreement and that there be no divisions among you, but that you be united in the same mind and the same purpose. For it has been reported to me by Chloe's people that there are quarrels among you, my brothers and sisters.

Jacob feared for his safety after the betrayals of years ago. This story reminds us that intergenerational issues can have profound effects on the members of our congregation. Paul complained to the Corinthians about the conflict that kept them from their evangelistic mission, and urged the factions to make peace with one another.

> 1 Corinthians 12:26. If one member suffers, all suffer together with it; if one member is honored, all rejoice together with it.

In Paul's ideal congregation, everyone would get along because they would understand one another's feelings so deeply that they could cry and laugh together, whatever was required. However, we know that such an ideal does not always exist in the reality of daily life.

The Presbyterian Church recommends a "conflict intensity chart" to evaluate the kind of trouble a congregation is in.[15] The five levels go from 1) problem to solve; 2) disagreement; 3) contest; 4) fight-flight; 5) intractable conflict—with suggestions for what should be done at each level of conflict. The value of such a chart is that it is a quick way for practitioners to evaluate what is happening in a congregation. One principle of systems theory is that conflict is a fact of life in communities, and that conflict can be creative or destructive depending on the leadership and maturity of the group. When people are encouraged to honestly express themselves, conflict not infrequently erupts and the foundational beliefs and values of persons become evident. However, great leadership skill is required to make conflict be creative; otherwise, it can be destructive to persons, especially those who are vulnerable by age, maturity, or circumstance.

Carrie Doehring, in her excellent book, *Taking Care*, uses fiction to discuss the importance of power and boundaries in families and congregations.[16] One of her chapters is about Tom Marshfield, the white pastor from John Updike's *A Month of Sundays*. By sexualizing his relationships with women, and acting out his fantasies with several women of the congregation, Marshfield caused enormous harm to persons and families and eventually precipitated enough conflict that he had to resign his position and enter an inpatient treatment program for professional offenders.[17] This story is a reminder of the widespread conflict and destruction caused by pastors who abuse their professional trust and power through exploitation of those who are vulnerable. Often congregational conflict escalates to levels 3 or 4 as people choose who to believe and how to cope with their feelings of loss and betrayal. Several students in my classes have reported that they were teenagers in congregations where clergy sexual abuse occurred. They carried the wounds for decades afterward, even though they were not directly involved with the pastor themselves. Destructive conflict is potentially harmful to many people in ever-widening circles, while creative conflict that brings enlarged mission and vision can transform the lives of parishioners.

Principle 7, Use of Self: Systems theory often focuses on the role of leaders as change agents. A leader is only as good as her or his self-awareness. This leads to the seventh, and perhaps the most important principle: use of self.

> Psalm 139:23–24. Search me, O God, and know my heart; test me and know my thoughts. See if there is any wicked way in me, and lead in the way everlasting.
> Mark 12:28–31. Which commandment is the best of all? Jesus answered, "The first is, 'Hear, O Israel: the Lord our God, the Lord is one; you shall love the Lord your God with all your heart, and with all your soul, and with all your mind, and with all your strength.' The second is this, 'You shall love your neighbor as yourself.' There is no greater commandment greater than these."
> Matthew 7:12. In everything do to others as you would have them do to you; for this is the law and the prophets.

Clergy sexual abuse is an extreme but not uncommon example of congregational leadership that becomes destructive of persons, families, and congregations themselves. Such painful examples illustrate the importance of self-awareness and self-correction within a context of ongoing supervision and education. Systems theory can help congregational leaders understand the need for adequate support systems as they try to deal with the powerful structures and dynamics of power. I sometimes tell students that they need a system of support that is equal in strength to the congregational system they are trying to lead. This means individual supervision, peer supervision and support, judicatory support, continuing education, and a personal life that is separate from the congregation. Unfortunately, many congregational leaders do not have adequate support, and they become dependent on the congregation as their primary community. It is impossible to provide leadership for a congregation and to be dependent on the same community to meet all one's emotional and spiritual needs. I have heard many sad stories of pastors who got themselves in trouble in a congregation, then turned to the judicatory for help and received nothing that was helpful. Of course, district superintendents and area ministers are often in the same difficulty and do not have the skills or strength to help others.

It is important for congregational leaders to recognize the symptoms of stress that tell when leading the congregation is becoming too much. The following list are the big five that indicate the leader is in trouble and needs help from an outside support system. Whenever a congregation leader engages in the following behaviors, it is time to get some help: sexualizing, demonizing, injuring, guilting, controlling.[19] Sexualizing means obsessing about the sexual dimension of human life to the exclusion of the many other aspects. Examples include obsessive fantasizing about others, masturbation, use of pornography, sexual activity with multiple or unsafe partners, etc. Demonizing means obsessing about the negative motives of others and turning them into demons, thinking aggressive thoughts, showing excessive anger or rage, acting destructively toward those perceived to be "enemies." Injuring means being overly self-centered in one's evaluation of self and others and deliberate behaviors designed to hurt the reputations of others. Guilting is usually directed against the self, and includes inner conflict with one's values (guilt) or one's identity (shame). Controlling is the overmanagement of oneself and others, sometimes micromanagement of details, at other times a need to control all decisions.

Whenever a leader observes or suspects these five symptoms, it is time to get help from outside sources. Pastoral counseling or spiritual direction are often the place to begin a self-evaluation. Sometimes a congregational leader will discover that something more foundational is needed, such as sabbatical or study leave, a new educational program, or a break from one's ministry for a season. Such decisions are most difficult to make, especially for congregational leaders who are dedicated to their calling. But paying attention to symptoms and getting help are likely to prolong one's ministry. The alternative is having a crisis that forces others to make decisions for you.

CONCLUSION

Congregational ministry is a trust that we hold in the name of Jesus Christ. We who are leaders have been entrusted with responsibility for the healing ministries of local communities of faith. The seven principles in this article are designed to support congregational leaders as they attempt to help the church be the body of Christ. By attending to history, social context, theology, development, structure, dynamics, and use of self, we will be better equipped to understand and lead congregations as they follow Christ.

NOTES

1. Ken Mitchell and Herbert Anderson, *All Our Losses, All Our Griefs: Resources for Pastoral Care* (Philadelphia: Westminster Press, 1983), 107.

2. George Mead and Charles Morris, *Mind, Self, and Society from the Standpoint of a Social Behaviorist* (Chicago: University Of Chicago Press, 1967).

3. Lynn Hoffman, *Foundations of Family Therapy : A Conceptual Framework for Systems Change* (New York: Basic Books, 1981).

4. Ludwig von Bartalanffy, *General Systems Theory: Foundations, Development, Application* (New York: Braziller, 1968).

5. Walter Wink, *Naming the Powers: The Language of Power in the New Testament* (Philadelphia: Fortress Press, 1984).

6. Rodney Hunter, ed., *Dictionary of Pastoral Care and Counseling* (Nashville, TN: Abingdon Press, 1990), 497.

7. Emmanuel Lartey, *In Living Colour: An Intercultural Approach to Pastoral Care and Counselling* (London: Herndon, VA: Cassell, 1997), 37–42.

8. James Poling and Donald Miller, *Foundations for a Practical Theology of Ministry* (Nashville, TN: Abingdon Press, 1985).

9. Murray Bowen, *Family Therapy in Clinical Practice* (New York: J. Aronson, 1978).

10. Larry Graham, *Care of Persons, Care of Worlds: A Psychosystems Approach to Pastoral Care and Counseling* (Nashville, TN: Abingdon Press, 1992).

11. Paul Tillich, *Systematic Theology* (Chicago: University of Chicago Press, 1951).

12. Alfred North Whitehead, *Process and Reality: An Essay in Cosmology*, corrected edition, eds. David Ray Griffin and Donald Sherburn (New York: Free Press, 1978).

13. Erik Erikson, *Childhood and Society* (New York: Norton, 1950).

14. Salvador Minuchin, *Families and Family Therapy* (Cambridge, MA: Harvard University Press, 1974).

15. Office of Professional Development, General Assembly Mission Board, *Conflict Intensity Chart, A Resource for Committees on Ministry of the PCUSA* (Louisville, KY: PCUSA, n.d.).

16. Carrie Doehring, *Taking Care: Monitoring Power Dynamics and Relational Boundaries in Pastoral Care and Counseling* (Nashville, TN: Abingdon Press, 1995).

17. Marie Fortune, *Is Nothing Sacred?: When Sex Invades the Pastoral Relationship* (San Francisco: Harper & Row, 1989).

18. Marie Fortune and The Center for the Prevention of Sexual and Domestic Violence, *Clergy Misconduct: Sexual Abuse in the Ministerial Relationship* (Seattle, WA: Center for the Prevention of Sexual and Domestic Violence, 1992).

19. James Poling, *The Abuse of Power: A Theological Problem* (Nashville, TN: Abingdon Press, 1991).

Bibliography of Herbert Anderson

ARTICLES AND CHAPTERS IN BOOKS

"Alfred Adler's Individual Psychology and Pastoral Care." *Pastoral Psychology*, Vol. 21, No. 207, October, 1970.

"Individual Psychology and Pastoral Psychology." *Journal of Individual Psychology*, Vol. 27, No. 1, May, 1971.

"Youth and the Abuse of Drugs." *Pastoral Psychology*, Vol. 22, No. 217, October, 1971.

"Recent Books in Pastoral Care." *The Princeton Seminary Bulletin*, December, 1970; July, 1972; Spring, 1974.

"Review Essay of Literature on Death." *Theology Today*, Spring, 1974.

"The Sex Education of Ministers." In *The New Sex Education*. Ed. Herbert Otto. Chicago: Association Press, 1978.

"The Use of Family Systems in Preparation for Ministry." With C. George Fitzgerald. *Pastoral Psychology*, Vol. 27, No. 1, Fall, 1978.

"The Death of a Parent: Its Impact on Middle-Aged Sons and Daughters." *Pastoral Psychology*, Vol. 28, No. 3, Spring, 1980.

"What Seminaries Expect of CPE." *Journal of Pastoral Care*, Spring, 1980.

"You Must Leave Before You Can Cleave: A Family Systems Approach to Pre-marital Work." With Kenneth Mitchell. *Pastoral Psychology*, Vol. 30, No. 2, Winter, 1981.

"Simulated Families in a Training Session." With Kenneth Mitchell. *Journal of Supervision and Training in Ministry*, Vol. 4, Summer, 1981.

"The Spirituality of Learning to Care." *Journal of Supervison and Training in Ministry*, Vol. 4, Summer, 1981.

"The Purpose of Families." *Television and Children*, Vol. 5, No. 2, Spring, 1982.

"The Family under Stress: A Crisis of Purpose." *Moral Issues and Christian Response*. 3rd Edition. Ed. Paul T. Jersild and Dale A. Johnson. New York: Holt, Rinehart and Winston, 1983.

"Baptism and the Psychology of Growth." *Liturgy*, Winter, 1984.

"Incarnation and Pastoral Care." *Pastoral Psychology*, Vol. 32, No. 4, Summer, 1984. Reprinted in *The Church and Pastoral Care*. Ed. LeRoy Aden and J. Harold Ellens. Grand Rapids, Michigan: Baker Book House, 1988.

"The Recovery of Habitus." *Trinity Seminary Review*, Vol. 6, 1984.

"The Family as a Context for Change and a Changing Context." *The Journal of Psychology and Christianity*, Winter, 1984. Reprinted in *The Church and Pastoral Care*. Ed. LeRoy Aden and J. Harold Ellens. Grand Rapids, Michigan: the Baker Book House, 1988.

"Toward a Constructive Anthropology: Hiltner's Paradoxical View of Persons." *Journal of Psychology and Christianity*, Winter, 1985. Reprinted as "A Paradoxical Understanding of Persons" in *Turning Points in Pastoral Care*. Ed. LeRoy Adens and J. Harold Ellens. Grand Rapids, Michigan: Baker Book House, 1990.

"Pastoral Care in the Process of Initiation." In *Alternative Futures in Worship: Baptism and Confirmation*. Ed. Mark Searle. Collegeville, Minnesota: The Liturgical Press, 1987.

"Human Forgiveness is Possible." *The Journal of Pastoral Care*, Vol. 40, No. 2, June, 1986.

"Supervision of Ministry in a Parish Context." Ed. with Homer Ashby and David Lindberg. *Journal of Supervision and Training in Ministry*, Vol. l0, 1988.

"Facing Family Change." *The Lutheran*, Vol. 10, No. 8, May 11, 1988.

"A Home with a Room of One's Own." *The Lutheran*, Vol. 10, No. 9, June 1, 1988.

"Making Families Good Enough." *The Lutheran*, Vol. 10, No. 10, June 22, 1988.

"The Family: Making Christian Disciples." *The Lutheran*, Vol. 10, No. 11, July 13, 1988.

"Liturgy and Pastoral Care." With Edward Foley. *New Theology Review*, Vol. l, No. 4, December, 1988.

"The Congregation: Health Center or Healing Community." *Word and World*, Vol. 9, No. 2, Spring, 1989.

"After the Diagnosis: An Operational Theology for the Seriously Ill." *Journal of Pastoral Care*, Vol. 43, No. 2, Summer, 1989.

"Christian Themes for Family Living." *Dialog*, Vol. 28, No. 3, Summer, 1989.

Four "Liturgical Homilies." In *Homilies for the Christian People*. Ed. Gail Ramshaw. New York: Pueblo Publishing Company, 1989.

"Baptism and Confirmation," "Pastoral Care and Counseling of Family," "Foster Children and Foster Parents" and "The Pastor's Husband." In *Dictionary of Pastoral Care and Counseling*. Ed. Rodney J. Hunter. Nashville, Tennessee: Abingdon Press, 1990.

"The High Adventure of Leaving Home." *Entrée*, September, 1989.

"A Wedding of Stories." With Edward Foley. *New Theology Review*, Vol. 3, No. 2, May, 1990.

"The Congregation as a Healing Resource." In *Religious and Ethical Factors in Psychiatric Practice*. Ed. Don S. Browning, Thomas Jobe, and Ian Evasin. Chicago: Nelson Hall Publishing Company, 1990.

"Modern Maladies of the Soul: Waiting in the Darkness." *The Lutheran*, May 1, 1991.

"The Paradox of Being Bodies and Having Bodies." *The Bible Today*, Vol. 29, No. 3, May, 1991.

"The Birth of a Story: Infant Baptism in a Pastoral Perspective." With Edward Foley. *New Theology Review*, Vol. 4, No. 4, November, 1991.

"Preaching as Validation: The Christmas Story and Family Birth Stories." *New Theology Review*, Vol. 4, No. 4, November, 1991.

"To Be a Man: Maleness as a Gift of God." In *Interact 1*. Minneapolis, Minnesota: Augsburg/Fortress, 1991.

"Hope for the Future Family Through Pastoral Care." *Care Cassettes*. Vol. 19, No. 4. The College of Chaplains, 1992.

"Preaching and Pastoral Care in the Meantime." *Resource Tapes*. Minneapolis, Minnesota: Augsburg/Fortress, Series 19, No. 11, 1992.

"What Consoles?" *Sewanee Theological Review*, Vol. 36, No. 3, 1993.

"Do We Value Our Children?" *The Lutheran*, Vol. 6, No. 8, August 1993. Reprinted in *The Covenant Companion*, Vol. 83, No. 6, June, 1994.

"Suicide: A Protestant Perspective." In *Clergy Response to Suicidal Persons and Their Family Members*. Ed. David C. Clark. Chicago: Exploration Press, 1993.

"Complicated Obligations: Caring for an Aging Parent." *New Theology Review*, Vol. 7, No. 1, February, 1994.

"Waiting in the Darkness: A Good Friday Reflection." *Currents*, Vol. 21, No. 2, April, 1994.

"Pastoral Epilogue." *Developmental Disabilities and Sacramental Access*. Ed. Edward Foley. Collegeville, Minnesota: Liturgical Press, 1994.

"The Recovery of Soul." In *The Treasure of Earthen Vessels: Explorations in Theological Anthropology*. Eds. Brian H. Childs and David W. Waanders. Louisville, Kentucky: Westminster John Knox Press, 1994.

"A Tapestry with Many Threads." *The Journal of Supervision and Training in Ministry*, Vol. 15, 1994.

"Gender and Pastoral Care." With Bonnie Miller-McLemore. In *Pastoral Care and Social Conflict*. Eds. Pamela D. Couture and Rodney J. Hunter. Nashville, Tennessee: Abingdon Press, 1995.

"A Sanctuary for Childhood in a Culture of Indifference." With Susan B. W. Johnson. *Word and World*, Vol. 15, No. 1, Winter, 1995.

"The Gift of Grieving." *The Lutheran*, Vol. 8, No. 2, February, 1995.

"Belated Grief for a Miscarriage." *New Theology Review*, Vol. 8, No. 2, May, 1995.

"Pre-wedding Work: A New Approach." *Dialog*, Vol. 34, No. 2, Spring, 1995.

"When You Come to a Fork in the Road, Take It." *Journal of Pastoral Theology*, Vol. 5, Summer, 1995.

"What Does Baptism Have To Do with the Christian Life?" In *Open Questions in Worship: What Is Changing in Baptismal Practice?* Minneapolis, Minnesota: Augsburg/Fortress, 1995.

"Open House: The Gift of Hospitality." *The Lutheran*, Vol. 8, No. 12, December, 1995.

"In-Corporated Souls: Human Wholeness in Community and in the Presence of God; The Theological Anthropology of James Ashbrook." *Journal of Supervision and Training in Ministry*, Vol. 16, 1995.

"Men and Grief." In *The Care of Men*. Eds. Christie Cozad Neuger and James Newton Poling. Nashville, Tennessee: Abingdon Press, 1997.

"Between Rhetoric and Reality: Women and Men as Equal Partners in Home, Church, and the Marketplace." *Word and World*, Vol. 17, No. 4, Fall, 1997.

Reprinted in *Family Ministry: Empowering through Faith*, Vol. 13, No. 2, Summer, 1999.

"Seeing the Other Whole: A Habitus for Globalization." *Mission Studies*, Vol. 16, Nos. 27 & 28, Fall, 1997.

"Experiences in Need of Ritual." With Edward Foley. *Christian Century*, November 5, 1997.

"Moment and Process: Rethinking Pastoral Theology." In *Finding Voice to Give God Praise*. Ed. Kathleen Hughes. Collegeville, Minnesota: The Liturgical Press, 1998.

"Spirituality and Supervision: A Complex and Necessary Connection." *Journal of Supervision and Training in Ministry*, Vol. 18, 1997.

"Pastoral Theology after Christendom." *Journal of Pastoral Theology*, Vol. 8, 1998.

"Premarital Education: A Protestant Perspective." *Threshold: A Magazine about Marriage Education* (Australia), 58th Edition.

"Ritual and Narrative, Worship and Pastoral Care, and the Work of Pastoral Supervision." With Edward Foley. *Journal of Supervison and Training in Ministry*, Vol. 19, 1998–99.

"The Lonely Male." *The Lutheran*, Vol. 12, No. 2, February, 1999.

"A Burdensome Gift: Birth by *in Vitro* Fertilization." With Thomas A. Nairn. *New Theology Review*, Vol. 12, No. 2, May, 1999.

"The Agreed Statement of Justification: A Lutheran Perspective." *Ecumenical Trends*, Vol. 28, No. 5, May, 1999.

"Reconciliation as Widening the Circle." *New Theology Review*, Vol. 12, No. 3, August, 1999.

"Feet Planted Firmly in Midair: A Spirituality for Family Living." *In Spiritual Resources in Family Therapy*. Ed. Froma Walsh. New York: The Guilford Press, 1999.

"Fitting Time." With Thomas A. Nairn. *New Theology Review*, Vol. 12, No. 4, November, 1999.

"Pastoral Supervision at the Crossroads." *Journal of Supervision and Training in Ministry*, Vol. 20, No. 1, 2000.

20th Anniversary Issue of the *Journal of Supervision and Training in Ministry*, Editor. 2000.

"Whatever Happened to Seelsorge?" *Word and World*, Vol. 31, No.1, Winter, 2001.

"Redundancy as a Way of Life: Thoughts on Time and Popular Culture." *Journal of Pastoral Theology*, Vol. 16, 2001.

"Sense and Nonsense in the Wisdom of Dr. Seuss." *New Theology Review*, Vol. 14, No. 3, August, 2001.

"Spiritual Care: The Difference an Adjective Makes." *The Journal of Pastoral Care*, Vol. 55, No. 3, Fall, 2001.

AUDIOCASSETTES

Herbert Anderson and Phyllis Anderson. "Two Ministries, One Marriage." *Resource*. Series 6, No. 9. May 1979. Augsburg Publishing House.

Herbert Anderson, James Qualben, and Richard Jensen. "Conversation on Cults." *Resource*. Series 7, No. 8. April 1980. Augsburg Publishing House.

Herbert Anderson. "A Life-Cycle Approach to the Pastoral Care of Families" and "The Pastor's Family of Origin—Implications for Ministry." Care Cassettes. Vol. 12, No. 5. May 1986. The College of Chaplains.
Herbert Anderson. "Premarital Counseling: Families of Origin." *Resource*. Series 15, No. 8. April 1988. Augsburg Publishing House.
Herbert Anderson. "Hope for the Future Family through Pastoral Care." Care Cassettes. Vol. 19, No. 4. May 1992. The College of Chaplains.
Herbert Anderson. "Preaching and Pastoral Care in the Mean Time." *Resource*. Series 19, No. 11. November 1992. Augsburg Publishing House.

BOOKS AND PAMPHLETS

All Our Losses, All Our Griefs. With Kenneth R. Mitchell. Philadelphia: Westminster Press, 1983. Translated into Dutch as *Omgaam met verlies en rouw*, 1985.
The Family and Pastoral Care. Philadelphia: Fortress Press, 1984.
Leaving Home: Helps for Parents and College Students. Produced by Campus Ministry Communications, ELCA, 1990.
Outpatient Pastoral Care. With Ron Sunderland and Larry Holst. Minneapolis, Minnesota: Augsburg/Fortress Press, 1991.
Leaving Home. Family Living in Pastoral Perspective. With Kenneth R. Mitchell. Louisville, Kentucky: Westminster John Knox Press, 1993.
Becoming Married. Family Living in Pastoral Perspective. With Robert Cotton Fite. Louisville, Kentucky: Westminster John Knox Press, 1993. Translated into Korean.
Regarding Children: A New Respect for Childhood and Families. With Susan B. W. Johnson. Louisville, Kentucky: Westminister John Knox Press, 1994.
Promising Again. With David Hogue and Marie McCarthy. Louisville, Kentucky: Westminster John Knox Press, 1995.
Living Alone. With Freda Gardner. Louisville, Kentucky: Westminster John Knox Press, 1997.
Mighty Stories, Dangerous Rituals: Weaving the Human and the Divine. With Edward Foley. San Francisco: Jossey-Bass, 1998.
The Family Handbook. Ed. with Don S. Browning, Ian Evison, and Mary Stuart van Leeuwen. Louisville, Kentucky: Westminister John Knox Press, 1998.
Jacob's Shadow: Christian Perspectives on Masculinity. Louisville, Kentucky: Bridge Resources, 2002.

Index

About the Contributors

Joel Anderson is a Senior Lecturer in Philosophy and the Associate Director of Social Thought & Analysis at Washington University in St. Louis. He works in the areas of ethical theory, applied ethics, and social theory. He has edited, with John Christman, *Autonomy and the Challenges to Liberalism: New Essays*.

Herbert Anderson is an ordained Lutheran minister, Professor Emeritus of Pastoral Theology at Catholic Theological Union, and Director of Pastoral care at St. Mark's Episcopal Cathedral in Seattle, Washington. He is the author of numerous books and articles, many of which are cited throughout this volume written in his honor.

Homer U. Ashby Jr. is the W. Clement and Jessie V. Stone Professor of Pastoral Care at McCormick Theological Seminary in Chicago. A United Methodist pastor, Professor Ashby is a fellow in the American Association of Pastoral Counselors and a member of The Society for Pastoral Theology.

Dianne Bergant, CSA, is Professor of Biblical Studies at Catholic Theological Union in Chicago. She is the author of several books, including a three-volume work on *Preaching the New Lectionary* (1999–2001). She is currently working in the areas of biblical interpretation and biblical theology, particularly issues of peace, ecology, and feminism.

Don Browning is Alexander Campbell Professor Emeritus of Religious Ethics and the Social Sciences at the Divinity School of the University of

Chicago. He is author of a *Fundamental Practical Theology* (1991) and coauthor of *From Culture Wars to Common Ground: Religion and the American Debate over the Family* (1997, 2000). He is director of the Religion, Culture, and Family Project, funded by the Lilly Endowment, Inc.

Pamela D. Couture is Professor of Pastoral Care and Practical Theology at Colgate Rochester Crozer Divinity School. She is the author of *Blessed Are the Poor? Women's Poverty, Family Policy and Practical Theology* (1991) and *Seeing Children, Seeing God: A Practical Theology of Children and Poverty* (2000), and coauthor of *From Culture Wars to Common Ground: Religion and the American Family Debate* (1997, 2000).

Edward Foley is Professor of Liturgy and Music at Catholic Theological Union and the Founding Director of the Ecumenical D.Min. Program. Among his many publications is *Mighty Stories, Dangerous Rituals* (1998), which he coauthored with Herbert Anderson.

Anthony J. Gittins, CSSp, is the Bishop F. X. Ford, M.M. Professor of Missiology at the Catholic Theological Union, Chicago. A cultural anthropologist, he has written numerous books and articles, including *Life and Death Matters: The Practice of Inculturation in Africa* (2000), *Reading the Clouds: Mission Spirituality for New Times* (1999), and *Bread for the Journey: The Mission of Transformation and the Transformation of Mission* (1993).

Thomas Groome is Professor of Theology and Religious Education at Boston College and a senior faculty at its Institute of Religious Education and Pastoral Ministry. The paperback edition of his *Educating for Life* was published in 1998, and his most recent book, *What Makes Us Catholic*, was published in 2002.

Pauline Kleingeld is Associate Professor of Philosophy at Washington University in St. Louis. Her academic interests are in 18th-century philosophy (especially Kant), and in political philosophy and feminist theory.

K. Samuel Lee is Visiting Professor of Pastoral Care and Counseling at Yale University Divinity School. A counseling psychologist and an ordained minister, he is the author of numerous essays and book chapters on the topics of multicultural pastoral care and practice and Korean-American churches.

Bonnie J. Miller-McLemore is Professor of Pastoral Theology and Counseling at Vanderbilt University Divinity School. Her publications include *Let the Children Come: Reimaging Childhood from the Christian Perspective* (2003), *Also a Mother: Work and Family as Theological Dilemma* (1994),

Feminist and Womanist Pastoral Theology (1999), and the coauthored *From Culture Wars to Common Ground: Religion and the American Family Debate* (1997, 2000).

Christie Neuger is Professor of Pastoral Care and Pastoral Theology at United Theological Seminary of the Twin Cities. An ordained United Methodist elder, she is a Diplomate in the American Association of Pastoral Counselors and is the current Chair of the Society for Pastoral Theology. Her publications include *The Arts of Ministry A Feminist-Womanist Approach* (1996), *The Care of Men* (1997), coedited with James Poling, and *Counseling Women: A Narrative Pastoral Approach* (2001). She is married to Win Neuger and they have two adult children.

Carolyn Osiek, RSCJ, is Professor of New Testament and Early Church History at Catholic Theological Union. She is author of many books and articles on New Testament themes, including the commentary on *The Shepherd of Hermas* in the Hermeneia series (1999). She also coauthored, with David Balch, *The Family in the New Testament: Households and House Churches* (1997) as part of the Religion, Family, and Culture project of the University of Chicago.

Gilbert Ostdiek, OFM, is Professor of Liturgy at Catholic Theological Union and directs the Institute for Liturgical Consultants. His interests include reweaving liturgy and other forms of pastoral ministry. The author of *Catechesis for Liturgy* (1986), he and Herbert Anderson have been longtime colleagues and collaborators at Catholic Theological Union.

James N. Poling is an ordained minister in the Presbyterian Church (USA), a pastoral psychotherapist, and Professor of Pastoral Theology, Care, and Counseling at Garrett-Evangelical Theological Seminary. He is the author of many articles and books including *The Abuse of Power: A Theological Problem* (1991) and *Deliver Us From Evil: Resisting Racial and Gender Oppression* (1996).

Robert Schreiter is the Vatican II Professor of Theology at Catholic Theological Union and conjointly the Professor of Theology and Culture at the University of Nijmegen. Among his many publications are *Constructing Local Theologies* (1985) and *The Ministry of Reconciliation* (1998).

Paul J. Wadell is Associate Professor of Religious Studies at St. Norbert College in De Pere, Wisconsin. He is the author of *Friendship and the Moral Life* (1989) and has written in the areas of virtue ethics, ecological ethics, and liturgy and ethics. His most recent work explores the relationship between worship, friendship, and the virtues.